During ten years as film correspondent of the *Scotsman*, Brian Pendreigh helped persuade Franco Zefirelli to shoot *Hamlet* in Scotland, wrote about *Braveheart* when it was still at the script stage and was there on its night of triumph at the Oscars three years later. He became a full-time freelance film journalist in 1997 and now writes regularly for the *Sunday Times*, *Guardian* and the Scottish press.

Previously he was a feature writer and reporter on the *Scotsman*, during which time he accompanied the Royal Marines to Central America, swam with sharks, took part in experiments in the paranormal, regressed to 'past lives' under hypnosis, and filed copy from Edinburgh District Council meetings. He overcame his fear of heights by crewing on a sailing ship and had one of his pieces selected for a school exam paper by the Scottish Examination Board. It was about what seagulls think about people in outdoor swimming pools and was written on a day when its author was stuck for inspiration.

His books include *On Location: The Film Fan's Guide to Britain and Ireland*, *Mel Gibson and His Movies*, *Ewan McGregor* and *The Scot Pack*. Awards include Ainsworth Film Journalist of the Year, in 1995 and 1999. His favourite film is *The Magnificent Seven*.

He lives in Edinburgh with his wife Jenny, children Ewen and Catherine, and almost half a million other people, most of whom he does not know.

# PLANET OF THE APES

## OR HOW HOLLYWOOD TURNED DARWIN UPSIDE DOWN

## BY BRIAN PENDREIGH

BOXTREE

*This book is dedicated to the memory of Ham*

First published 2001 by Boxtree
an imprint of Pan Macmillan Ltd
Pan Macmillan, 20 New Wharf Road, London N1 9RR
Basingstoke and Oxford
Associated companies throughout the world
www.panmacmillan.com

ISBN 0 7522 6168 1

1 3 5 7 9 8 6 4 2

A CIP catalogue record for this book is available
from the British Library.

Typeset by seagulls
Printed and bound in Great Britain by
Mackays of Chatham PLC, Chatham, Kent

# CONTENTS

# ACKNOWLEDGEMENTS

When I started out on this book, I was like Taylor in the film – I did not know what I would find out there. I knew enough to believe *Planet of the Apes* merited a book; I was intrigued by the concept of the film, its continuing popularity and its influence; I knew Edward G. Robinson had been involved at one stage, but I had no idea just what else I might find. That I managed to uncover so much new material so long after the event reflects the degree of cooperation I received from (almost) everyone involved. Even Richard Zanuck, head of Twentieth Century Fox at the time of the original, managed to take time off on the set of the new *Planet of the Apes* film, which he was producing.

First and foremost, however, I would like to thank Mort Abrahams, associate producer of the original film, for a series of interviews over the phone and face to face in Los Angeles. He gave freely of his time to talk me through the film from writing and casting through production to the sequel. He also provided priceless insights into the character of his colleague, the late Arthur P. Jacobs, whose vision and commitment kept the project alive when every studio in Hollywood turned it down.

Secondly, a huge debt of gratitude is due to Cynthia Becht and her helpful staff and volunteers in Archives and Special Collections at the Charles Von der Ahe Library, Loyola Marymount University, Los Angeles, in which Arthur P. Jacobs's papers, photographs and illustrations have been deposited – including sixty-five feet of boxed records from his production company, Apjac. After more than thirty years, memories of individuals proved fallible, to say the least, and the contemporary letters, memos and other papers in the collection were a gold mine. Together, personal recollections and contemporary records shed light on each other and formed the basis of a fascinating story, full of ambition and intrigue, with a cast of characters as rich as many a novel.

Thanks are due not just to Mort Abrahams and Richard Zanuck, but to several others who played key roles on the original film and its sequels – actresses Kim Hunter and Linda Harrison and actors Lou Wagner and James Gregory, who spoke to me despite having being debilitated by a stroke; to John Chambers, who won an Oscar for his make-up design and who saw me in hospital in California; to art director William Creber, who played such an important role in the look of the film. Ted Post, who directed *Beneath the Planet of the Apes,* welcomed me into his home in Brentwood and entertained me with the memories of a lifetime in film, television and theatre. Frank Capra Jr took time off from running Screen Gem Studios in North Carolina, where *Dawson's Creek* is filmed, to talk about the other three sequels, on which he was associate producer.

Director Franklin J. Schaffner and writers Rod Serling, Michael Wilson and John T. Kelley are all dead now, but a special thanks is due to those who worked on the film in the first half of the sixties, before it arrived at Twentieth Century Fox, who shared none of the glory of the film's triumphant release and legacy but who helped me understand the tortuous process of trying to knock the project into shape and find backers. They are directors Blake Edwards and J. Lee Thompson (who later directed *Conquest of the Planet of the Apes* and *Battle for the Planet of the Apes*), writer Charles Eastman and artist Don Peters. Thanks to Lisa DeMatteo, Charlton Heston's publicist; Kimberly Wire and Hilary Clark in the Los Angeles press office of Twentieth Century Fox and Stephanie Wenborn and Milly Swain in the London office; to Eileen Peterson, unit publicist on the new *Apes* film; and to Terry Martin, who runs Time Machine Collectibles (www.timem.com) and the official websites of several *Apes* stars, including Linda Harrison (www.lindaharrison.com/indexn.html) and Lou Wagner (www.louwagner.com/).

I am especially indebted to Terry Hoknes, organizer of the International Planet of the Apes Fan Club, who provided me with copies of the television programmes, his *Ape Chronicles* fanzine and his memorabilia database. And to Luiz Saulo Adami, organizer of the Brazilian fan club, who generously sent me a copy of his book *O Unico Humano Bom é Aquele que Está Morto!* (The Only Good Human is a Dead Human!), a second unpublished book, *Man Has No Understanding!*, and photographs from his personal collection. Thanks also to Brian Penikas, the distinguished Hollywood make-up artist, *Apes* fan and organizer of the Apemania re-enactment troupe. And to all the other fans who provided an insight into their passions – John Roche, editor of *Simian Scrolls* fanzine, 'Andrew', Dave Ballard, Christopher S. Brown, Jack Krueger, 'LordTZer0', Alan Maxwell, Dean Preston,

Alexander Ruiz, Robert Thorpe, 'Tim' and 'Urkorules'. You know who you are ... I think.

Thank-you Rod Serling expert Gordon Webb, assistant professor of television and radio at Park School of Communications, Ithaca College, New York; Mark Kratzner and Diane Steele, who helped track down Don Peters; staff at the Arts Library Special Collections of the Young Research Library, UCLA, where I was able to inspect Twentieth Century Fox's original production files; the Margaret Herrick Library of the Academy of Motion Picture Arts and Sciences, Los Angeles; and the National Library of Scotland.

Thanks to Dr Christopher Welch, principal lecturer in astronautics at Kingston University, Surrey, for his patient explanation of time dilation, special relativity and other scientific matters; to Professor Nick Barton, Edinburgh University; Professor Richard Byrne, professor of evolutionary psychology at St Andrews University; Professor Peter W.H. Holland, professor of zoology, at Reading University; Dr Jamie Stevens, Wellcome Biodiversity Research Fellow at the Department of Biological Sciences, Hatherly Laboratories, Exeter University; and Dr D.W. Yalden, senior lecturer in zoology at Manchester University; for their expert views on whether apes really could turn the tables on mankind; and to the Media Resource Service and AlphaGalileo, the Internet press network of experts on science, medicine and technology.

I am also indebted to AOL; to my agent Giles Gordon at Curtis Brown and his former assistant Susie Brumfitt; to Ewen McDonald, who once more brought his indexing skills into play; and, last but not least, to Jenny Pendreigh, who transcribed interviews, assisted in research and was ever present with help and advice, and to our two children, Ewen and Catherine, who sat with me while I watched every single *Planet of the Apes* film and television programme. Over and over again.

# CHAPTER ONE
# THE END

*What will he find out there?*
*His destiny...*

And so Charlton Heston leaves the apes behind and rides off in search of his destiny, accompanied by the primitive, mute beauty Nova. Their dark-brown mount walks and occasionally canters, across beach after empty beach, until they come upon a huge structure, half-buried in the sand, a building, or perhaps a statue. Heston, naked but for a loincloth, dismounts and looks in horror at the edifice that towers above him. A tiny figure, with waves breaking on his bare legs, Heston is framed between huge, dark, shadowy spikes. 'Oh my God,' he gasps. 'I'm back.' And then he hangs his head, as if he can bear to look no more. 'I'm home ... all the time,' he concludes, slowly and painfully. 'We finally really did it.' His voice wells up with a terrible anger. 'You maniacs.' He drops to the ground and pounds the wet sand with his fist in a futile gesture of despair. 'You blew it up. God damn you. God damn you all to hell!' And the surf sweeps in around him, wiping away the violent disturbance he has made in the sand.

Finally the camera pulls back from Heston, square-jawed hero of *The Ten Commandments* and *Ben-Hur*, standing, virtually alone on a beach, on a distant planet, where apes rule and humans are hunted for sport. The camera retreats along the beach to reveal the top half of a statue poking through the sand, a familiar crowned head and an arm holding aloft the torch of freedom and welcome. The Statue of Liberty is instantly recognizable, in its symbolic glory, and now its ultimate shame. What its appearance in the sands means is that spaceman Charlton Heston has travelled hundreds of years into the future, but has gone ... nowhere. The Planet of the Apes is Earth in the year 3978. Man has come full circle from those ancient days when Heston collected the Tablets on the Mount, led the species out of the wilderness and smashed the chains of slavery and oppression.

1

This is the planet that spawned Ben-Hur, El Cid and Moses … now ruled by apes.

That final scene was one of the most effectively shocking in the history of cinema. *Planet of the Apes* was filmed in 1967, during the Cold War, when the world lived in the shadow of nuclear apocalypse. Despite the subsequent collapse of the Soviet Union, that scene of Heston on the beach remains one of cinema's most dramatic and chilling, and one of the most surprising for any viewer unfamiliar with the story. In its day the appearance of the Statue of Liberty played like the revelation that Norman Bates's mum was really just Norman in a frock or that Bruce Willis in *The Sixth Sense* was dead all along. It was to become one of the most famous scenes in cinema, so much so that when Twentieth Century Fox Home Entertainment issued the *Planet of the Apes* films in a boxed set they had Heston and the Statue of Liberty on the cover; Greenpeace used the monument on a poster, declaring: 'Do nothing, and nuclear testing will eventually come to an end'; and in an episode of *The Simpsons* cartoon series, when Homer is chosen to become an astronaut, he tells a press conference: 'the only danger is if they send us to that terrible Planet of the Apes.' Then he recalls the full impact of that scene on the beach. 'Wait a minute … Statue of Liberty. That was our planet. You maniacs. You blew it up. Damn you. Damn you all to hell!' That was not the first, nor the last reference to *Planet of the Apes* on *The Simpsons,* one of the most cineliterate shows on TV, and a barometer of American popular culture.

In that famous ending lay the beginnings of a phenomenon, and a legend. There were to be four sequels; two TV series – one live-action, one cartoon; comics; novelizations; and a huge range of merchandising tie-ins, from bubblegum cards and mugs to waste-paper baskets and ape masks – long before George Lucas accepted merchandising rights as part of his deal to make *Star Wars.* In another *Simpsons* episode Troy McClure stars in a *Planet of the Apes* musical, whose lyrics include the wonderful line 'I hate every ape I see, from chimpan-A to chimpan-Z.' In the popular TV series *Buffy the Vampire Slayer,* Xander reprises Heston's cry of 'It's a madhouse, a madhouse,' but Willow interrupts to identify the source of the quote before Xander can finish. There are references to *Planet of the Apes* in the seminal 'Generation X' movie

*Reality Bites*; the Robin Williams comedy *Mrs Doubtfire*, in which a puppet orang-utan complains that humans got the best roles; and *The Spy Who Shagged Me*, when Austin Powers travels back to the sixties and claims that in the future the world will be run by 'damn dirty apes'. These films and programmes were all made in the nineties, twenty years after the last of the sequels and the television programmes. Those final efforts were hampered by restricted budgets, which showed in the make-up and shortage of extras. The writers were beginning to run out of ideas and the symbolism of Heston and the Statue of Liberty seemed to have been replaced by the cutesy appeal of the Halloween mask and the dollar sign. Nevertheless, *Planet of the Apes* would not go away. Quite the reverse, with the phenomenon gathering pace again throughout the nineties.

In the original film Heston and his colleagues hibernated in capsules while they travelled through space at close to the speed of light for eighteen months – which, due to the vagaries of 'Dr Hasslein's theory of time' (an apparent variation on Einstein's thoughts on relativity), was the equivalent of 2,000 years on Earth. They woke up to find a planet ruled by apes. The 1993–4 season of the American TV show *Saturday Night Live* featured Heston falling asleep in his dressing room and waking up centuries later to find the TV studio run by apes, with simian versions of regular characters. And in 1998 *Planet of the Apes* became the subject of an elaborate Internet joke when veteran astronaut John Glenn went back into space on a ten-day mission. While he was away some bright Earthling thought up the idea that everyone should put on ape suits for his return and he would think *Planet of the Apes* had come true. 'It swept across the vast expanse of cyberspace like an electronic firestorm, jumping from private mailbox to joke forum to Usenet newsgroup until it seemed to engulf the entire World Wide Web,' reported CNN. 'By most accounts, it ranks as the most popular joke in Internet history.' One Californian web designer received the joke from fifteen different people and the message itself quickly began to evolve. Danyel Fisher, a graduate student of computer science and folklore at the University of California, began researching the origins and spread of the joke. 'Where other folklorists talk about hundreds of years of diffusion, I talk about hours of spreading,' he said. He found several musical versions, some of which fitted the tune of the New Seekers' song *I'd Like to Teach the World to Sing*:

'I'd like to see the world dressed up
In ape suits black and grey,
So when John Glenn comes back from space
He thinks he's far away.'

Not everyone embraced the idea, however. 'I have recently received several messages from some "very amusing people" suggesting that when John Glenn comes back to planet Earth the entire human race dress up in ape suits,' wrote one Mark Bakalor, in a communication that wound up in Fisher's e-mailbox. 'It's all fun and games when it comes to fooling John Glenn but no one seems to be thinking about the consequences of your "silly joke". What happens when the apes see that they've taken over the Earth? You think they'll be happy to go back to their little forest enclaves and sit around with homely scientists picking bugs out of their fur? I don't think so. If I were them I'd be mad and I'd start to figure a way to get even. Believe you me, you don't want to be on the business end of a gorilla wedgee [whatever that is]. Also what happens the next time the Earth is actually taken over by apes? Then the astronauts come home and laugh at all the monkeys and say, "great gag". But within minutes they're ambushed, captured, neutered, and sent to work on a banana farm. Then who's left to save the Earth? Not you Mr Funny Pants. You'll be busy building tree cities and ape mobiles at spear point. But I guess it's all just a goof to you. I just wish people would think before they decide to contact everyone they know with idiotic e-mail.'

And they said Americans had no sense of irony.

During the nineties devotees launched fanzines and set up sites on the Internet entirely devoted to the *Planet of the Apes* films and spin-offs. Brazilian fan Luiz Saulo Adami spent more than ten years researching and writing his book *O Unico Humano Bom é Aquele que Está Morto!* (The Only Good Human is a Dead Human!), which was finally brought out by a local Brazilian publisher in 1996. It was followed two years later by an American guide to the value of *Planet of the Apes* collectibles. Meanwhile, at the other end of the spectrum of intellectual respectability,

4

American academics carried out heavyweight studies into various aspects of the series. Wesleyan University Press published Eric Greene's well-researched and thought-provoking, if occasionally overbaked, *Planet of the Apes as American Myth: Race, Politics, and Popular Culture*, which argued that *Planet of the Apes* was 'perhaps the most sophisticated treatment of racial conflict Hollywood has ever produced', and the film merited a chapter in James F. Iaccino's *Jungian Reflections Within the Cinema: A Psychological Analysis of Sci-Fi and Fantasy Archetypes*. The chapter was entitled *Planet of the Apes: The Evolution of an Archetypal Shadow Species*, prompting the question, in the words of that immortal inquisitor Griff Rhys Jones, 'Wot's that then?' 'The Jungian shadow can best be described as the person's 'dark, inferior side' which is more animalistic than human, more bestial than civilized,' writes Iaccino. 'At times the shadow can assume an outward identity so that it can display its primitive, demonic urges for all the world to see. The trickster figure is one such shadow projection. This character delights in playing malicious jokes on people and shows no remorse in whatever dangers he has inflicted upon humanity. One of the more common representations of the shadow trickster is that he is simia dei, or "the ape of God", to highlight his negative subhuman nature. The science-fiction series *The Planet of the Apes* is an excellent extension of the shadow trickster. Here the apes of God are actual simians …' Indeed.

While the film developed a dedicated fan base and a certain academic kudos, the wider truth was that it had become an inescapable part of popular culture, even for those who had never seen it. And some were pleasantly surprised when they did. Reviewing the film on the Internet Movie Database in 1999, one ordinary, non-Jungian viewer, 'Pates' from Boise, Idaho, wrote: 'No one I know under 40 had seen this film, though we all joked about it as being a stereotypical "bad" film, based on rumours, the title, and clips seen here and there. Finally one weekend, when I was working until 2.00 am, I went home and there was a sequel on late-night TV, during the 30-year *Planet of the Apes* marathon. It made me curious about the original and I tracked it down. I have to say it blew me away! The film is philosophical, creative, absorbing and scary. Excellent commentary on religion and just about everything else. I strongly recommend it to anyone who has not seen it. So far

I haven't even been able to convince my friends to see it because there seems to be such a strong prejudice against it and some sort of entrenched belief it must be bad; in fact it is one of the finest films I've seen and I can see why it is a classic. If you enjoy films that make you think, you simply can't dislike *Planet of the Apes*.'

There is no doubt that 'Pates' represents many younger viewers who regard the whole notion of *Planet of the Apes* as camp, a notion based on Halloween masks, cartoons and comics, rather than the original film, which was a major commercial – and critical – success at the time of its release in 1968. By the turn of the millennium *Planet of the Apes* had established itself as a mainstream classic, a cult hit and a joke – all at the same time. After years of rumours and speculation about a new film, involving the likes of Oliver Stone, James Cameron and Arnold Schwarzenegger, Twentieth Century Fox began shooting a big budget 'reimagination' of *Planet of the Apes* at the end of 2000. It would be directed by Tim Burton, who previously brought a dark, offbeat sensibility to *Batman* and *Edward Scissorhands*. Mark Wahlberg, the star of *The Perfect Storm*, was taking over from Heston as principal *Homo sapiens* and the simian cast included Tim Roth and Helena Bonham Carter.

*Planet of the Apes* is a brilliant concept that truly does – to exploit an old cliché – work on various levels. On the one hand it is a straightforward and colourful action-adventure film, in the style of *Star Wars, Raiders of the Lost Ark* and a slew of traditional westerns, with goodies and baddies, and apes instead of Indians, their costume and make-up readily lending themselves to childish imitation. There are some who would claim it is no more than that. Richard Zanuck, former head of Twentieth Century Fox and producer of the new film, insists the twist ending in the original was chosen purely on dramatic grounds and was not intended to deliver any sort of message. And Charlton Heston wrote in his autobiography, *In the Arena*, in 1995: 'I'd volunteered for my own war as we were supposed to do … I'd also given God heartfelt thanks that two atom bombs had cancelled my scheduled inclusion in the invasion of the main islands of Japan, with a projected cost of a million American lives and twice as many Japanese.' Not exactly an endorsement of nuclear disarmament. 'The object of the picture was entertainment,' says Zanuck. 'We weren't trying to send any

profound messages, most of which have been concocted and interpreted as time has passed … and were never really particularly
intended. I mean, we wanted to show an upside-down world where
apes were in charge and humans were the slaves, so to speak, but
we were going for that idea on an entertainment level. We weren't
trying to send a message or preach any social statement.'

It is certainly possible to read too much into the film, poring
over the videos and finding deep and multiple symbolism in every
scene. Eric Greene, in his book, notes that 'Nova finally speaks in
*Beneath* [the first sequel]… She is shot and killed by a gorilla.
Message? Beautiful women should just be beautiful – and keep
their mouths shut.' But everyone is killed in *Beneath the Planet of
the Apes*. So how does that mass slaughter fit in with the silent
women theory? It doesn't. Elsewhere Greene writes: 'The threat
of castration by apes, who were traditionally associated with darkness, sexuality and, by extension, femaleness, suggests that there
was also a crisis of masculinity built into *Planet* … Indeed, the final
shot of the film shows him [Heston] fallen in front of a giant
woman who is both darker and stronger than he.'

Far from debating the social, political and racial implications
of the film, prospective backers were worried audiences would
simply laugh at the idea of apes running the world, any world.
It is one thing to carry off such an idea on the printed page, but
quite another to manage it in the more literal medium of the
cinema. Producer Arthur P. Jacobs trooped round every
Hollywood studio without success. Even the personal involvement
of Charlton Heston, one of Hollywood's biggest names, was not
enough to convince studio bosses that viewers would take it
seriously. It was while Jacobs was producing another film for
Twentieth Century Fox that he persuaded Zanuck to at least put
up the money for a screen test to see if the ape make-up might
work. By this time another major Hollywood name was expressing
an interest and he was prepared to have himself coated in fur to
play an ape. Edward G. Robinson, star of many gangster classics,
was ready for what could be the most challenging role of his
career, as an orang-utan. Like many of the principal players in this
drama, Robinson is dead. But the screen test he recorded with
Heston survives and Robinson is remarkable in it. 'We wrote a
long dialogue scene, you know, so you could see their faces

moving,' Jacobs later recalled. 'Well, Dick liked it and said he wanted to show it to Darryl [his father, the legendary Darryl F. Zanuck, who ran the studio from its inception in the thirties till the fifties and was once again part of the Fox hierarchy]. So we brought it to New York. Jesus, there were nine guys in that screening room, watching the test. If any one of them laughed, we were dead.' No one laughed.

Robinson's health was failing and he never did appear in *Planet of the Apes* (though ill-health is just part of the reason why he never made the film, as we shall discover in the course of the story). But his screen test helped persuade Twentieth Century Fox to go ahead with an expensive project that might still make them the laughing stock of a Hollywood that was already in fast decline. Ironically, Jacobs's other film was another big movie about talking animals. But whereas *Doctor Dolittle* flopped, *Planet of the Apes* was a hit, grossing more than $25 million from its initial US release against a cost of less than $6 million. Its success led to demand for a follow-up, despite the opposition of Heston, who thought a sequel would reduce *Planet of the Apes* to the level of the Hardy family, the subject of a series of popular and inoffensive comedies in the thirties and forties. The success of the sequels rewrote the Hollywood rulebook and, for better or worse, set the fashion for action 'franchises' for three decades. *Planet of the Apes* spawned a fashion not just for sequels, but for science-fiction films set in a post-apocalyptic future, including *The Omega Man*, with Heston, and, of course, *Mad Max*; and for sci-fi that was more than a parade of people in weird costumes (a phenomenon that reached its self-deprecating nadir with a homicidal human carrot in *Lost in Space*) – sci-fi that also raised social, political and religious questions.

To suggest *Planet of the Apes* is no more than a clever and imaginative action-adventure film is to ignore its origins in the 1963 novel *La Planète des Singes* by Pierre Boulle, the French writer whose other work includes *Le Pont de la Rivière Kwaï*. He won an Oscar for the script of *The Bridge on the River Kwai*, without writing a single word of it, which must surely have amused an author noted for his sense of the absurd. *La Planète des Singes* was intended as satire and widely compared with Voltaire and Swift, specifically the section of the latter's *Gulliver's Travels* in which the hero visits a land ruled by horses. Most of the characters and many dramatic incidents in *Planet of the Apes,* as well as the central premise, came from Boulle's novel, though not the final scene. *La Planète des Singes* was adapted as a screenplay by Rod Serling, a former paratrooper who created *The Twilight Zone,* the pioneering early sixties science-fiction TV series that mixed high drama and flights of imaginative fantasy with serious philosophical questions about the nature of man and his place in the universe. It specialized in time warps, and the appearance of the Statue of Liberty in *Planet of the Apes* is characteristic of the twist endings in the series. As a Jew, Serling had first-hand experience of racial bigotry in the land of the free. The second credited writer was Michael Wilson, who won an Oscar for *A Place in the Sun,* an indictment of American morality. He adapted *Le Pont de la Rivière Kwaï,* but had to forego his screen credit, and a second Oscar, after being blacklisted during the McCarthy witch-hunts for his left-wing politics, an experience that coloured his views of his fellow man.

In *Planet of the Apes* Heston's character's status is debated in a lengthy 'courtroom' sequence that recalls both the Scopes Monkey Trial – the case of the Tennessee schoolteacher who was arrested in the 1920s for teaching Darwin's theory of evolution, filmed as *Inherit the Wind* with Spencer Tracy – and also the infamous Dred Scott judgement of 1857, when the US Supreme Court ruled that slaves, and the descendants of slaves, had no constitutional rights. Darwin's theory that man evolved from the apes remained controversial in schools, in America and elsewhere. The controversy was further fuelled in 1967, the year in which *Planet of the Apes* was shot, when Desmond Morris published *The Naked Ape,* arguing that man may have evolved from the apes … but he had not evolved very far. Man, according to Morris, was still an intrinsic part of the order of primates, particularly in his sexual and social habits. Boulle made the point in his novel that chimpanzees, gorillas and orang-utans were all supposedly equal, though on page and screen the practice seemed at times to depart from the ideal, reflecting the reality of human life on twentieth-century Earth. The United States was riven by racial conflict, and the assassination of Martin Luther King in April 1968 sparked race riots. Racists have long been accustomed to bracketing Africans with apes, with football thugs treating black players to monkey chants and showers of bananas. And in Spike Lee's *Do the*

*Right Thing*, John Turturro's character, an Italian-American, complains that his Brooklyn neighbourhood is turning into Planet of the Apes. The changing social status of apes in the *Apes* series made for an obvious, if dangerous, parallel with African-Americans, particularly as the storyline developed and created a speculative future history for the world. White supremacists saw the films as a warning and carried banners at rallies urging the public to 'remember' *Planet of the Apes*, ignoring the central, liberal message of peaceful co-existence.

To dismiss *Planet of the Apes* simply as entertainment is to ignore the times in which it was made and the contemporary concerns that coloured the perceptions of the writers, filmmakers and actors. This was a period of enormous social turmoil and revolution. The United States was being sucked into a war against a peasant army in Vietnam, a war which it would ultimately lose and which threatened to tear American society apart, with the young fleeing the country to avoid military service and protesters burning the Stars and Stripes, an act akin to the desecration of the Statue of Liberty. At the same time Charlton Heston visited the troops in Vietnam and when they thanked him for coming he said: 'Thank *you* for coming.' America was a nation divided and confused. Elsewhere, in May 1968, within months of the film's US premiere, French students fought street battles with riot police and took control of parts of Paris. Boulle's homeland seemed to be on the threshold of a new revolution. Established values were being questioned, undermined and rejected, not just on the Planet of the Apes, but in London, Paris, New York and even in the likes of Boise, Idaho. Other genres, particularly westerns, began to use their storylines to comment on contemporary social issues and on the war in Vietnam, an issue which would be addressed, rather unsubtly, in *Beneath the Planet of the Apes*. But the first film also attempted to tap into youth rebellion, with its own young chimpanzee rebel Lucius – the Spirit of '68 – declaring: 'You can't trust the older generation,' just before Heston rides off like a traditional cowboy hero, towards his unconventional sunset.

Heston's roles had made him a symbol of Western civilization from its earliest times, while the Statue of Liberty was a universally recognized symbol of the United States, and its own variation on that civilization, a modern, multicultural variation, encompassing

10

democracy, technological progress and a scale that rivalled the empires of Ancient Rome and Victorian Britain and extended by the late sixties to the moon. But how solid were the foundations of this civilization? That is the question. The combination of Heston, the biblical hero, and the Statue of Liberty, the symbol of modern America – one half-naked on his knees, the other neglected and half-buried in sand – was simply devastating. And the film-makers knew it. They knew exactly what they were doing with the politics of the film and with the image of Charlton Heston ... even if he did not.

The late Franklin J. Schaffner, who directed *Planet of the Apes*, once said: 'More or less it was a political film, with a certain amount of Swiftian satire, and perhaps science fiction last.' So how come Zanuck maintains there was no message? And what about Heston, the darling of the American Right, who offered heartfelt thanks to God for dropping atom bombs on Japan? Clearly Heston's politics were the exact opposite of those of the film. 'Clearly,' says Mort Abrahams, the film's associate producer, Jacobs's right-hand man and the most senior member of the film's production team still alive. Although his title was associate producer, he hired writers and actors and in today's parlance he would simply have shared the producer credit with Jacobs, who might even have been labelled executive producer. And did Abrahams see it as 'a message film'? 'Yes.' So how come the studio and Heston did not seem to know that? The answer is simple – there was a conspiracy not to tell them. 'We never discussed the political aspects with the studio or the actors,' says Abrahams, 'because that would have raised an issue. If there were an issue for these people, the studio, financial people, whatever, let them raise it. I wasn't about to. Frank and I had a pact: we would not discuss it with the actors; we would not discuss it with the studio. If they picked it up, we would handle it, but unless they did we weren't about to.'

*Planet of the Apes* is much more than an action-adventure film, but it is still a first-rate action-adventure film too. Its action sequences, including the early scenes in which gorillas hunt men with guns and nets, compare with anything in *Ben-Hur, Raiders of the Lost Ark* or *Gladiator*. It is superb storytelling and entertainment, and folklore. And like the best folklore, it can survive the passage of time. It can even survive satirical rhyme, and exposure to the music of the New Seekers:

'I'd like to take the astronaut
And lead him by the hand,
And show to him old Liberty,
A-buried in the sand.'

The final word goes to an anonymous Internet poet, for no other reason than that it is a fine example of postmodern irony, and *Planet of the Apes* went a long way to introducing America to the concept of irony:

'I'd like to ride to meet John Glenn,
A-dressed up as King Kong.
Just imagine his surprise,
Unless he hears this song.'

# CHAPTER TWO

# THE FRENCH CONNECTION

*Madness, madness*

The current grabbed hold of the little raft, which Peter Rule had made from bamboos lashed together with rushes, buffeted it against the river banks and span it around, so the raft hurtled backwards through the black waters of the night towards Hanoi and the Gulf of Tonkin, still a long way away. Peter Rule wanted action during those long days in Pin-Ku-Yin, a military post high in the mountains, where the cold and damp rotted the huts, the body and the soul, and during months of waiting on the banks of the Nam-Na, just a few miles from the border. He was trained for action, a graduate of a British commando course in espionage, learning to blow up bridges and kill sentries without a sound. He wanted action; now he had it. But it was not quite what he expected. Rule was alone in a hostile environment, where he risked drowning in the water, and betrayal on land. He was now deep into enemy territory, with letters to make contact with the Resistance and plans of bridges along the Hanoi–Saigon railway, hidden in the inner tube of a truck tyre. When he scrambled ashore, sharp rocks sliced through his bare feet and leeches sucked at his blood. He travelled only at night, seeking shelter in the tropical forests by day, where he was attacked by fierce ants. And only at night would he venture, soaking and sore, into the paddy-fields, where the mud came up to his knees. He wanted action. He wanted to do his bit against the Nazis and the Japanese. He hurtled onwards, an insignificant speck on a landscape that would for ever be etched on his mind. Alone, day after day, he pondered his place in the universe, man's place in the universe, and how ridiculous it all was. It made him want to laugh. A typhoon sucked him and his little boat to the bottom of the river and fragments of a life flashed before his eyes.

Pierre Boulle was born in Avignon, France, on 20 February 1912, the son of a lawyer. He studied science at the Sorbonne and worked as an engineer in Clermont-Ferrand. But he hankered for adventure, like the adventures recounted in the works of his favourite author, Joseph Conrad, and in 1936 he pursued his ambitions in an outpost of the British Empire, taking a job as a rubber planter in Malaya. At the outbreak of the Second World War he was commissioned in the French army and posted to Indo-China. When the motherland was occupied by the Nazis and a puppet regime set up at Vichy, Boulle refused to surrender and joined the Free French in Singapore. He is to organize resistance in Japanese-occupied Indo-China. He will travel from Kuala Lumpur to Rangoon and Mandalay, into China, and on into what is now Vietnam. He adopts the name and identity of Peter Rule before entering Chinese territory controlled by Chiang Kai-shek, who is involved in his own struggle against Japanese invaders but does not recognize the Free French. Boulle's strong French accent is explained by the fact that he was supposedly born in Mauritius in the Indian Ocean.

Peter Rule survived his nightmare raft journey. If he had not done so, there would have been no *Planet of the Apes.*

After five days Rule is captured by peasants and handed over not to the Japanese, but to the French authorities at Laichau. He reveals his true identity to the major there, only to be informed by the intransigent officer that the Vichy government is now the legitimate government of France. Boulle is court-martialled, convicted of treason, stripped of his French nationality and sentenced to hard labour. In 1944 he escapes and at the end of the war he is repatriated and decorated for bravery. After another brief spell as a rubber planter, he returns to Paris and moves into a small hotel room, where he will devote himself to writing. In 1950 he publishes his first novel, *William Conrad,* the story of a Pole who acquires a leading position in English literature. Future works will borrow heavily from his own experiences in South-East Asia. His third book draws on his commando training, his rafting trip and his time in a prison camp. The French major he encountered in Laichau becomes a by-the-book English colonel, who believes the surrender in South-East Asia precludes further hostilities. Ordered to build a railway bridge, he determines his men must produce as fine a work of British engineering as possible, to prove themselves superior to their Japanese jailers. Boulle held no ill feelings against the major, but rather tried to understand his point of view, though apparently the major continued to maintain Boulle had been in the wrong, even after the war ended.

*Le Pont de la Rivière Kwaï* was published in 1952 and appeared in English two years later, under the title *The Bridge over the River Kwai*, translated by Xan Fielding. Another remarkable figure, Fielding was a British army major who organized wartime resistance in occupied Crete (dramatized by family friend Michael Powell in the film *Ill Met by Moonlight*), was captured in France and rescued just a few hours before he was due to go before a firing squad. But Fielding's is another story, recounted in his autobiography *Hide and Seek* and other annals of the Second World War. He would later translate *La Planète des Singes* as well.

*The Bridge over the River Kwai* was adapted for the cinema by *High Noon* writer Carl Foreman, who had been blacklisted in America's anti-Communist witch-hunts and moved to England. But director David Lean hated Foreman's script, which he thought reduced the story to a conventional war film, full of offensively false heroics and lacking the absurdity of the original. Lean felt Foreman completely misunderstood the British mentality. 'Monsieur Boulle, on the other hand, knows what he's talking about. We do have an inordinate respect for discipline and the team spirit. We make almost a fetish out of doing a job well.' Lean also believed Foreman had turned the Japanese commander, Colonel Saito, into a 'stock B-picture villain', whereas, like his British opposite number, Colonel Nicholson, Saito was essentially a product of his culture and its traditions and conventions. Each stubbornly insists his way of seeing the world is right and refuses to consider alternatives, just as Astronaut Taylor and Dr Zaius, who is both Minister of Science and Chief Defender of the Faith, will religiously stick to their predetermined world views in the film *Planet of the Apes*. It is not uncommon for several writers to work on a film script and it was Foreman who recommended Michael Wilson, another blacklisted American scriptwriter, living in Paris. Just as Boulle had to use a false identity in South-East Asia during the war, Wilson assumed a pseudonym to work on the *Kwai* script: John Michael, which appeared on all the paperwork.

Lean and Wilson changed the ending of the novel so that, during the climactic commando raid, Nicholson (Alec Guinness) accidentally falls on the detonator and blows up the bridge, leaving the British doctor Clipton (James Donald) to mutter the immortal line 'Madness, madness'. Wilson would later work on the adaptation of *La Planète des Singes* as well.

Foreman and Wilson's inclusion on the notorious Hollywood blacklist should supposedly have prevented them from working in the film industry. Producer Sam Spiegel wanted to play safe, and not only avoid any mention of their names on the credits, but also avoid pseudonyms. Lean had also contributed to the script and felt he was due some acknowledgement, though ultimately the script probably owed more to Wilson than to either Foreman or Lean. It was a complex and difficult situation, but even Lean was amazed when he saw Spiegel's solution on screen, which was to allocate the writer's credit to Boulle, who had not written a single line of the screenplay. But the on-screen credit for *Bridge on the River Kwai* was not the end of the matter. Spiegel, and a reluctant Lean, had to see it through and maintain the pretence that the script was Boulle's work. The situation was further complicated when the film was nominated for just about every Oscar going, including best adapted screenplay. The world was meant to believe Boulle could write an Oscar-worthy screenplay without any previous experience, even though he needed Xan Fielding's services to translate the novel. Spiegel, one of the slipperiest characters in the history of the movies, explained to journalists that Lean had collaborated on the script with Boulle but did not want a credit – whereas in fact Lean had collaborated on the script with Wilson and certainly did want a credit. Just for good measure, Spiegel claimed to have had a hand in the script too.

At the 1957 British Academy Awards Boulle caused consternation when he admitted he had not written the screenplay, only the novel. Spiegel insisted Boulle was just being modest. Boulle later told Lean's biographer, Kevin Brownlow: 'Since many writers (two or three) had worked on the screenplay, Spiegel decided to give me the credit, the novel being his basis. I accepted without knowing that the real reason was the famous Black List. I found this out when it was too late. But I have never claimed to have written the script. In fact, I did not care a damn about the script!'

Meanwhile stories began to circulate that Foreman was the true author (stories which may well have been circulated by Foreman himself); Lean responded by letting it be known that he 'threw out' Foreman's draft; Wilson eventually defended Foreman, saying he had retained elements of the Foreman version. And Boulle got the Oscar. But he did not attend the ceremony in Hollywood on 26 March 1958. Slippery Sam collected it instead and later that night Spiegel and Lean, who won the director's award, were seen angrily waving Oscars at each other, like a couple of duelling swordsmen. In the words of Dr Clipton: 'Madness, madness', and of Astronaut Taylor: 'It's a madhouse, a madhouse.' Boulle and Wilson had good reason to appreciate the lunacy and absurdities to which mankind might stoop. But there is still one final twist in this particular tale: in 1985, twenty-seven years after the event, the Academy of Motion Picture Arts and Sciences finally awarded Oscars to Wilson and Foreman for their efforts on *The Bridge on the River Kwai*. The only problem was that by that time they were both dead. After all that, perhaps the notion of a planet ruled by apes does not seem that far-fetched.

Boulle drew on his knowledge and experience of Asia for several novels, before adopting the medium of science fiction, to present a series of wry and laconic tales, whose raison d'être is perhaps best summed up by the title of his 1970 collection of short stories *Quia Absurdum (Sur la Terre Comme au Ciel)*, or *Because It Is Absurd (on Earth as It Is in Heaven)*. In various, diverse works by Boulle a whale gets involved in the Falklands war, a message from a distant solar system turns out to be an advertising slogan, and a planet is ruled by apes. He was inspired by a visit to the zoo, where he was impressed by the similarity between the facial expressions of humans and gorillas. This is hardly the place for a detailed text on apes, but a quick definition might be useful. There are just three types of great ape, as correctly represented in the novel and films. They are the chimpanzee and the gorilla, natives of equatorial Africa, and the orang-utan, which is confined to the rainforests of Borneo and Sumatra. They are the premier league; gibbons are the first division, the 'lesser apes'. It was reported on the Internet that Tim Burton's film would include other ape species; someone who pointed out that the newcomers were monkeys was dismissed as a pedant, though a monkey is no more an ape than a chimp is a man, which is exactly the sort of demarcation that excited Boulle in the first place. One basic physical difference between apes and monkeys is that apes do not have tails. There are about 180 species designated as primates and the 'higher primates' – note the hierarchical language – include marmosets, monkeys, apes and man. It is an oversimplification to say they are 'more evolved' than other animals – stick a naked man and a polar bear out on the Arctic ice and see which is better suited to survival in that environment – but they are generally more intelligent, with relatively larger brains.

Apes and monkeys were revered in many ancient cultures. Ancient Egyptians believed they understood human speech and were more intelligent than they let on. They regarded the screeching of baboons at dawn as prayers to the sun god and the Egyptian god of wisdom was sometimes portrayed as an old baboon. In India, Rama's emissary Hanuman was a monkey. Long before Darwin expounded his famous theory, Chinese families were proud to claim descent from monkeys who had abducted and mated with human women. In ancient Greece, Aesop endowed animals with human virtues and failings, in his famous fables. No one knows who Aesop really was; some say the name represents the work of several men, but others have suggested he was an exceptionally gifted baboon, which would, of course, explain his preoccupation with animals. In Christianity, however, the ape got a largely negative press, as a symbol of debasement, imitation and mockery. He gave us the verb 'to ape' and St Augustine called the Devil 'the ape of God' because of his blasphemous imitation of God's kingdom. Considering this long relationship between ape and man, Boulle's imagination took flight and the result was *La Planète des Singes*, first published in 1963. The French word 'singe' encompasses both monkeys and apes – 'les grands singes' – and the novel appeared as *Monkey Planet* in the UK the following year, though it was entitled *Planet of the Apes* in the US.

Both film and literary critics (including Boulle's biographer, Lucille Frackman Becker) would have you believe *Planet of the Apes*, and for that matter *The Bridge on the River Kwai*, bear little comparison with their source novels, with film critics dismissing the novels as inconsequential and obscure, and literary critics dismissing the films as gross oversimplification. 'All philosophical inquiry and all social criticism have been ignored by the makers of the film *Planet of the Apes*,' Becker writes, a contention which is quite simply ridiculous. (She takes a similar stance on *The Bridge on the River Kwai*, irrespective of its seven Oscars.) In fact what is striking about the novel *Planet of the Apes* is just how much is retained in the film version; indeed some incidents which did not make it were dusted down for the sequels *Escape from the Planet of the Apes* and *Conquest of the Planet of the Apes*. The main differences between film and novel are that, in the novel, the hero is French rather than American; the novel's ape planet is in the solar system of Betelgeuse – though when the hero returns to Earth he discovers it too is run by apes; and Boulle's ape society is more technologically advanced. The theme of nuclear warfare is, however, unique to the film. And then there is the tone and format of the novel, which is strong on ideas and philosophical inquiry, but not on descriptive detail. It is written, in short chapters, in the first person in the style of much eighteenth- and nineteenth-century literature, including *Gulliver's Travels* and *Frankenstein*, both of which might be deemed science fiction, and some of the stories of the great French master of science fiction, Jules Verne. Although it is obvious, the point that public and indeed some critics consistently fail to appreciate is that films and books really are two very different media. They have different forms and demands, and you cannot use a novel as a film script any more than you can use a restaurant menu or a copy of the *Daily Mail*.

The novel *Planet of the Apes* begins with a couple of tourists, Jinn and Phyllis, holidaying in what is literally a spaceship, complete with sail, when they come across a message in a bottle – a neat use of an old cliché. The message begins: 'I am confiding this manuscript to space, not with the intention of saving myself, but to help, perhaps, to avert the appalling scourge that is menacing the human race. Lord have pity on us!' The manuscript recounts the story of journalist Ulysse Mérou, who appears to have taken his name from the wandering hero of Homer. Accompanied by the brilliant scientist Professor Antelle, his assistant Arthur Levain and a chimp called Hector, he sets off on man's first interstellar flight, in the year 2500. They are headed for Betelgeuse, 300 light years away, though it will take only two years to get there. 'At top speed, time will almost stand still for us,' Antelle explains. For the human body, speed is not such a problem, it seems, as acceleration. 'To reach the speed at which time almost stands still, with an acceleration acceptable to our organisms, we need about a year. A further year will be necessary to reduce our speed ... Between the two, only a few hours, during which we shall cover the main part of the journey.' The travellers leave their spaceship in orbit and descend to an Earth-like planet in a launch vessel. At a lake and waterfall, they strip and swim, find a human footprint and encounter a beautiful, mute, naked woman, though how she possesses such a 'perfect body' while living rough in open countryside remains a mystery. Ulysse names her Nova, because he is 'able to compare her appearance only to that of a brilliant star'. Remember, this is Ulysse's senti-ment, not Boulle's. The heavenly creature then meets Hector ... and strangles him. Other humans set upon Ulysse and his colleagues, but are pacified by the destruction of the newcomers' clothes, weapons, equipment and launch, leaving the visitors naked and helpless.

Next morning the humans' forest encampment is disturbed by a terrible noise. 'It was a strange cacophony, a mixture of rattling sounds like a roll of drums, other more discordant noises resembling a clashing of pots and pans, and also shouts.' There are gunshots, too, and Ulysse comes face to face with the exact nature of the threat – the humans are being hunted by gorillas. Levain is shot dead and Ulysse scooped up in a net. Ulysse notes the gorillas have the manner of aristocrats – they are 'correctly dressed' for hunting – and he even describes the attendant 'lady gorillas' as elegant. The gorillas are photographed alongside their 'game'. Ulysse and Nova are taken by truck to a medical or scientific establishment, where Ulysse determines he must demonstrate his superior intellect, introducing himself, rather pompously, with the words: 'How do you do? I am a man from Earth. I've had a long journey.' But the apes fail to recognize this as intelligent language and collapse in laughter, sending Ulysse into a 'towering rage'. Ulysse delights in showing off in various scientific tests for Zira, the female chimp in charge of the depart-ment, and the orang-utan Zaius, the head of the institute. He easily assembles the building blocks to reach food in a basket near the ceiling. Zaius wants Ulysse to mate with Nova, which, after initial reluctance, Ulysse does: 'I, one of the kings of creation ... the ultimate achievement of millennial evolution, in front of this collection of apes.'

Ulysse convinces Zira of the extent of his intelligence by seizing her notebook and drawing geometrical diagrams and a map of space, which Zira hides from Zaius. He teaches Zira French, she teaches him the simian language and they discuss evolution. 'It used to be thought that species were immutable, created with their present characteristics by an all-powerful God,' she tells him. 'But a line of great thinkers, all of them chimpanzees, have modified our ideas on this subject completely. Today we know that all species are mutable and probably have a common source ... Many orang-utans, however, still insist on denying this obvious fact.' She explains that 'in principle' the three ape species, chimps, gorillas and orang-utans, are equal, but chimps are the innovative thinkers, gorillas are particularly good at organizing and at physical labour, while orang-utans have a tremendous capacity for book learning and represent 'official science'. Ulysse is certain the apes will accept him as their equal, but Zira warns him they may both be in danger if they are not careful, as claims about his capabilities could be regarded as 'scientific heresy'. Ulysse visits a zoo and finds Professor Antelle has apparently regressed to the level of the planet's other humans, and he studies ape society and achievements, which include electricity, cars, planes and space satellites but not interplanetary travel. There is world peace and no armies. Finally he addresses a major scientific congress, becomes a celebrity, is pampered by a tailor – 'the most famous of all, [who] had the most noted gorillas in the capital as clients' – and gets drunk in an ape nightclub, where he is besieged by female apes.

Ulysse accompanies Zira's fiancé, Cornelius, another scientist, to distant archaeological ruins, where they uncover a human doll that speaks the single word 'Papa', the same in simian language as French, and evidence that man once had his own civilization on the planet. Ape scientists get men to talk by applying electrodes to the brain, thereby releasing race memories of a time when humans were masters and apes servants. The apes rebelled (a story fleshed out in the film *Conquest of the Planet of the Apes*) and humans slipped back down the evolutionary scale. Nova gives birth to Ulysse's son and Ulysse sees himself as an instrument of human regeneration on the planet, once more failing to recognize the inherent danger of the situation (one which is reversed when Cornelius and Zira come to Earth and give birth to Caesar in *Escape from the Planet of the Apes*). Once more it takes Zira to warn Ulysse of the likely reaction to the prospect of a new race of intelligent humans. The child is to be taken away and put in the care of orang-utans and Ulysse is likely to be lobotomized or 'eliminated'. 'It's not possible!' he storms. 'I who believed myself entrusted with a semi-divine mission!' Cornelius and Zira arrange for Ulysse, Nova and the baby to take the place of three humans who are due to go into space in a satellite (a direct reversal of the situation on Earth, where chimps were sent into space before humans). The scientists will pretend the mission was a failure, while Ulysse is able to reach his own spacecraft. He returns to Earth after an absence of 700 Earth years and finds Orly Airport in Paris little changed. His craft is approached by an old-fashioned truck, an officer steps out of it and is revealed as a gorilla. The book concludes with Phyllis and Jinn's reaction to Ulysse's tale. Phyllis was moved by it, but adds: 'Rational men? Men endowed with a mind? Men inspired by intelligence? No, that's not possible; there the author has gone too far.' For, of course, Phyllis and Jinn are also apes. Apes have taken over not just the Earth, but the entire universe.

'The characters you see in *Planet of the Apes* have nothing in common with the fantastic beings that populate works of science fiction,' said Boulle. 'The apes ... are as like humans as two peas in a pod; they are in fact human beings. The novel is really a satire.' Boulle was neither the first nor the last to give apes human characteristics. Because of their resemblance to man – the very name orang-utan means 'man of the forest' – apes have figured prominently in literature, often in satires, from *Aesop's Fables* to Will Self's 1997 novel *Great Apes*, in which the narrator is a chimpanzee psychologist whose patients include another chimp who thinks he is human. In an author's note Self presents himself as a chimp and explains he wrote the book to promote a deeper understanding of humans. The American academic Marion W. Copeland described it as a 'clever and affecting satire, a kind of updated *Planet of the Apes*.' Back in the sixteenth century, Monkey was one of the key characters in Chinese stories about a monk who goes to India in search of the sacred scrolls of Buddhism and an adaptation was a hit on UK TV in the late seventies and early eighties and retains a cult following on video. Scholars have argued that Shakespeare conceived the character of Caliban in *The Tempest* as an ape and, much later, in the early twentieth century, it was apes who were entrusted with bringing up the young Lord of Greystoke, in Edgar Rice Burroughs's enormously popular and influential Tarzan stories, which introduce the concept of ape society, albeit one that is latterly lorded over by a human.

There are similarities between Boulle's novel and George Orwell's *Animal Farm* (1945), in that an animal underclass inherits the world. And in the film *Planet of the Apes*, Taylor adapts the famous slogan 'All animals are equal, but some animals are more equal than others' to suggest that some apes are more equal than others, a comment the orang-utans interpret as evidence of his lack of reasoning. But, whereas Orwell's voice is angry and very obviously political, with the farm animals driving out the farmer, Boulle's stance is one of wry bemusement. *Animal Farm* is very specifically a satire on Stalinism, as the animal revolution starts to go awry under the pigs' tyrannical leadership. Like Boulle, Aldous Huxley was a writer who fused science fiction and satire. His best-known works are *Brave New World* (1932), in which he presented a dystopian future for mankind, and *The Doors of Perception* (1954), the hymn to mind-bending drugs from which Jim Morrison's band took their name. *Ape and Essence* was published in 1948, just three years after the Americans nuked Japan, at a time when many believed nuclear war against the Soviet Union was almost inevitable. The story is set in the year 2018, in Los Angeles, where Huxley worked as a scriptwriter. In a world that has been laid waste by nuclear holocaust, man has regressed to a primitive, animal state and has been overtaken on the evolutionary ladder by baboons. Readers might find the book difficult because of its structure – that of a screenplay – and its surrealism, which includes two baboon armies facing up to each other, each with an Albert Einstein on a leash, while *Land of Hope and Glory* plays on the soundtrack.

*Planet of the Apes* is closer, in its style and its tone of philo-sophical inquiry, to the fourth and final part of Jonathan Swift's *Gulliver's Travels* (1726), in which Gulliver visits a country occu-pied by the Houyhnhnms, a race of intelligent horses, and the Yahoos, brutal, disgusting creatures, to whom Gulliver, unfortu-nately, bears a striking physical resemblance. The Houyhnhnms consider Gulliver inferior, but he learns much about virtue and reason from them, and when he finally returns home he finds his fellow man repellent. The two books share a sense of the absurd, and yet the idea of talking apes is perhaps not quite as absurd as the idea of rational, virtuous, talking horses. Boulle's story seems more credible because he opts for the species closest to us in the evolutionary chain. And, unlike Huxley, he presents a story which can be read quite literally. It might just happen. Maybe. There are no Einsteins on leads to reassure the reader that this is just a fantastic nightmare, a warning, a parable, rather than something which is really happening. Boulle sets his story in the far future and includes a lot of solid, scientific detail – the discussion of time and space travel has the air of Verne and Wells, who explored the idea of time travel and the regression of the human race in his novel *The Time Machine* way back in 1895.

Boulle's vision cannot be traced to a single book or even a single experience, whether it be a visit to the zoo or being forced to consider the meaning of life when faced with death on a bamboo raft on a river in Indo-China. One less obvious novel that comes to mind – my mind anyway, for I have not seen it cited by any literary critic or scholar – is *Robinson Crusoe*. Ulysse, like Crusoe, finds evidence of other humans in the form of a foot-print, but that is just one of a series of echoes from Daniel Defoe's story, which first appeared in 1719, just a few years before *Gulliver's Travels*. Shipwrecked, Crusoe seeks solace in the Bible, while demonstrating the patience, perseverance, industry and ingenuity that rescued the world from barbarism. In the 1975 novel *Man Friday*, Adrian Mitchell rewrote Defoe's classic from the viewpoint of Crusoe's black companion. Instead of allowing himself to 'be civilized' by Crusoe, Friday questions and under-mines Crusoe's values. Eventually Friday is happily reunited with his people and Crusoe commits suicide. (The book was filmed with Peter O'Toole and Richard Roundtree.) The French writer

Michel Tournier performed a similar exercise in his award-winning 1967 novel *Vendredi, ou les Limbes du Pacifique* (published in English as *Friday*). Boulle, like Mitchell, turns the natural order (or what seems to be the natural order) upside down. Time and again Ulysse demonstrates the same cultural and racial arrogance as Defoe's hero, and sometimes the same self-pity at his plight. 'The good Lord does not shoot dice, as a certain physicist once said. Nothing happens by mere chance in the cosmos. My voyage to the world of Betelgeuse was decreed by a superior consciousness. It is up to me to show myself worthy of the choice and to be the new saviour of this human race in decline.' The evidence around him should force Ulysse to question his values and prejudices, but he lacks the detachment to do so. He identifies with the ruling class, whichever species they may be, while at the same time seeing himself as some sort of messiah for a 'human race in decline'. Yet this 'king of creation', this 'ultimate achievement of millennial evolution', has to rely on sympathetic apes to explain the dangers to which his arrogance blinds him, and to provide his means of escape – for what it is worth.

Ulysse is no classic hero, though he may see himself as such, and he may even have passed as such in previous times. But the irony in much of his account of his adventures was inescapable to readers in the second half of the twentieth century, as it now is in the twenty-first century. The fact that he finds a certain contentment with 'one of the loveliest girls in the cosmos', even though she has an intellectual capacity comparable to a chimp on Earth, is an indictment of certain male attitudes to women, as are the 'thundering slaps across her beautiful face' that Ulysse delivers when Nova shows signs of jealously in Zira's company. And it seems Nova had some justification for being jealous. Ulysse describes one encounter with Zira in the following terms: 'I put my hand on her long hairy paw. A shiver went down her spine … When she returned me to my cage, I roughly rebuffed Nova, who was indulging in some sort of childish demonstration to welcome me back.' And later, just before Ulysse takes off: 'We are about to kiss like lovers when she gives an instinctive start and thrusts me away violently … "Oh, darling, it's impossible. It's a shame, but I can't, I can't. You are really too unattractive."' *Brief Encounter* goes ape.

The novel mixes satire and philosophical discussion, with science fiction and adventure, exotic colour and a modicum of humour, but it is very literary, and incidents and ideas that work on the page do not always work on the screen. 'I never thought it would be made into a film,' said Boulle. 'It seemed to me too difficult and there was the chance of it appearing ridiculous.' But Arthur P. Jacobs thought otherwise. A former publicist, he had until recently been responsible for Marilyn Monroe's public image. After Marilyn, a bunch of apes did not look too daunting.

# CHAPTER THREE
# ARTHUR

*'Arthur Jacobs is so difficult and slippery a character
to deal with, I hardly know where to begin.'*
Charlton Heston, *The Actor's Life: Journals 1956–1976*

In the days before video, Arthur P. Jacobs had a little cinema in
his house in Beverly Hills and he would regularly invite friends
over to watch a film with him, sharing the enjoyment and anticipation that generation after generation has experienced as the
lights go out and the screen flickers to life. But, quite apart from
size and location, there was one big difference between the
Arthur P. Jacobs cinema and the local Roxy. Often the faces in the
audience at Jacobs's shows were the same faces as on the screen.
Marilyn Monroe was not the only celebrity guest. Jacobs loved the
movies and he loved the movie business. Movies were his work,
from the days when he was a messenger boy at MGM through to
the point where he was running his own public relations
company, with offices on both coasts, and a roster of clients and
friends that included Monroe, Gary Cooper, James Stewart,
Marlene Dietrich and Gregory Peck. When Monroe overdosed
one fateful night in August 1962, Jacobs was one of the first
summoned to the scene, long before the police. 'He had them
all,' says Mort Abrahams, a long-time associate who would later
become his right-hand man after Jacobs set up his own film
production company, Apjac. Movies were also his passion. Like a
teenager compiling a cassette of favourite songs, he would cut out
parts of his favourite films and edit them together in a sort of
personal greatest hits. He especially liked the song-and-dance
numbers from the classic musicals of the studio where he once
delivered messages, and his compilations were reputedly the
inspiration for *That's Entertainment*. Movies were his whole life.
Born in Los Angeles in 1922, he studied cinema at the University
of Southern California, long before such studies established
themselves as an accepted route into the industry.

His home movies also reflected another passion – he loved compiling lists. Lists of actors who might suit a particular role flowed as a stream of consciousness into his little notebook. He made up lists of films and he made lists of jobs to do around the house on his day off, sorted on colour-coded cards to indicate the nature and importance of the task. He even wrote down the details of his marriage ceremony on an index card, and he had it in his breast pocket the night before the wedding, just so he would not forget what he had to do. Jacobs was a physically slight man, with dark hair, cut short, and darting, restless eyes. Fragile health forced him to cut down on some of life's luxuries and he eschewed the big, phallic cigars flourished by many movie moguls in favour of slim cigarillos. By August 1963, when the former publicist was producing his first movie, he reckoned he had the perfect subject for his second and sat down to draft an outline that would include a list of potential stars and a list of classic movies with which he felt the project shared certain features. His debut film, *What a Way to Go!*, would not be in cinemas until the following year and he wanted to keep up the momentum. *What a Way to Go!* was a musical comedy that he had been developing for Monroe and Dean Martin at the time of her death. The loss of the world's biggest star would have been a crushing blow for even the most experienced producer, let alone one who was just starting out. But for Jacobs, Monroe's death was nothing more than a temporary setback. He had an irrepressible spirit and a habit of viewing every closed door as an opportunity to develop new openings. Within a few short months Shirley MacLaine had stepped into the breach, and Jacobs was also able to call on the services of Martin, Paul Newman, Gene Kelly, Dick Van Dyke and Robert Mitchum, the last of whom he supposedly talked into working for nothing as a tax dodge. Now Jacobs had another project to pitch – 'a rip-roaring horror story – a classic thriller utilizing the best elements of *King Kong, Frankenstein, Dr Jekyll and Mr Hyde, Things to Come, The Birds* and other film classics'. One of the easiest and most effective ways to describe a film is to tap into images, memories and emotions evoked by the mention of other movies. And Jacobs's list mined a rich seam of images, memories and emotions – the nightmare future world of *Things to Come,* the H.G. Wells film that prophesied the aerial carpet bombing of the Second World War; the beast struggling with the civilized man within a single protagonist in *Jekyll and Hyde*; man tampering with nature and the concept of life in *Frankenstein*; nature gone awry in Hitchcock's chilling classic of animal revenge *The Birds*; and the terror and tragedy of the giant ape in *King Kong*. But what if you had more than one ape? What if you had a whole Planet of the Apes?

One of the first executives Jacobs approached was the head of Twentieth Century Fox, Richard Zanuck, who, at twenty-eight, represented a new generation of movie-mogul talent. Zanuck speaks highly of Jacobs and his vision today. 'He was a kind of Barnum and Bailey showman,' he says, 'the Mike Todd of the time, and he had great ideas and he was very energetic.' Zanuck's comments reflect a widespread, though not quite universal, appreciation of those qualities in Jacobs. 'I loved the idea right off the bat,' he adds during a break in filming the new *Planet of the Apes* movie, in the Mojave Desert, on which he is producer. But it is not that simple. Memories play tricks, and more than thirty-five years later accounts differ, and often conflict, on just about every aspect of the movie. 'He didn't have to be persistent with me, because I loved the idea right off the bat,' says Zanuck. But that is not how Mort Abrahams remembers it. And it would take Zanuck three years, from the initial approach, to give the film the green light; three years in which Jacobs, and latterly Jacobs and Abrahams, tried every other studio in town, repeatedly, and even tried to raise finance in Europe. Abrahams remembers Zanuck threatening to throw them off the lot if they ever mentioned *Planet of the Apes* again.

*King Kong* was one of Jacobs's favourite films. He liked it so much he wished he had made it. Other film producers were looking for the new Marilyn Monroe or the new James Dean. Jacobs wanted to be the man to discover the new King Kong. He was a determined man, but not the sort who had only one project on the go at any one time. There were other ambitions too, other movies to be made, other lists to be compiled. In 1963 a series of meetings about potential projects for his fledgling production company took him to Paris, where an agent was trying to interest him in a new novel by Françoise Sagan. Jacobs was showing little enthusiasm in the book when the agent decided there was nothing to lose with a change of tack. 'Speaking of *King Kong*,' he said,

'I've got a thing here, and it's so far out, I don't think you can make it …' Jacobs did not speak or read French, but the agent outlined the story of Pierre Boulle's new novel, *La Planète des Singes*. Jacobs was one for grand visions, rather than fine detail. He did not procrastinate. He was not bothered with such niceties as actually reading the book. At the end of the agent's outline he did not hesitate. 'I'll buy it,' he said.

Jacobs was working in tandem with J. Lee Thompson, the Englishman who directed *What a Way to Go!* and who had a considerable track record on stage and screen, particularly in the field of action-adventure films. He had recently been nominated for an Oscar for the war film *The Guns of Navarone* and other credits included *Cape Fear, Ice Cold in Alex* and *Northwest Frontier*. The duo sent galley proofs of the English-language version of the novel to several studios and commissioned a series of sketches of characters and scenes from the book which they hoped would help executives visualize the story. 'I thought it would be quite difficult to get a studio to make it,' says Thompson. 'It was very different from the kind of films that studios were making.' Their first choice for the role of the astronaut was not Charlton Heston but Marlon Brando, who, along with James Dean and Montgomery Clift, had introduced audiences to a new type of film anti-hero, a brooding, highly charged, highly sexual rebel, the very antithesis of Heston's wholesome screen characters. While Heston had been playing prophets, Brando had been playing bikers, boxers and wasters. When asked what he was rebelling against in *The Wild One*, he famously replied: 'What've you got?', though after the triumphs of *The Wild One, A Streetcar Named Desire* and *On the Waterfront*, his career had expensively stalled with the remake of *Mutiny on the Bounty* and he had chosen to stay on in the South Seas, so Jacobs sent a copy of Boulle's novel to him in Tahiti. He suggested Brando join forces with him and Thompson, and that the film could be a joint production involving Apjac, Thompson's company Orchard and Brando's Pennebaker, which Jacobs, never one for the fine detail, misspelled as 'Pennybaker' in his letter to Brando. As if a proposed three-way co-production was not enough, Jacobs also had a deal with Jerome Hellman, who later produced *Midnight Cowboy*, and it was intended that Jacobs's *Planet of the Apes* and Hellman's *A Fine Madness* should be co-productions involving Hellman's company.

Brando may have been the first to receive a formal approach, but Jacobs knew enough about Brando not to bother waiting for his reply before discussing the film with Paul Newman, with whom he was working on *What a Way to Go!*, and ascertained that he was interested. Newman was another of the new breed of young anti-heroes – contemporary, complex and often confused, selfish and sexual. While Brando wore leathers, Newman was more likely to be found in blue denim in films like *The Hustler* and *Hud*, drawing on traditional images of the cowboy and updating them. Jacobs, a great believer in the value of having at least two birds in each hand, also discussed the role of Zira, the chimpanzee psychologist, with *What a Way to Go!*'s female star, Shirley MacLaine.

Jacobs and Thompson drafted out a pitch for studios, outlining what they saw as the strengths of the project. The document might also be termed, in today's parlance, a mission statement. After presenting the project as a 'rip-roaring horror story' and comparing it to *King Kong* and *The Birds*, Jacobs ran through a number of key points and objectives:

'The sole object in doing this is to entertain and thrill, nothing more.

'We see this not just as a film but rather as an attraction which will appeal to all ages and all audiences.

'It should be talked about on a world-wide basis as the most unusual movie ever made!'

Jacobs was nothing if not ambitious, and although he seems to be downplaying anything other than the entertainment value, he goes on to say that he thinks the social satire requires no comment because it is inherent in the material. In case studios might be wary of any such highfalutin idea, he quickly adds the film will also feature adventure, comedy and pathos.

Already in these earliest documents, Jacobs and Thompson have clearly identified the strengths and weaknesses of the book in terms of its potential as a Hollywood movie, beginning with turning the hero from a Frenchman into an American, though at this point he is still called Ulysse. The floating bottle – which contained Ulysse's story in the novel – has been jettisoned, the astronauts are to get to their destination much more quickly than in the book, the big scene in which the humans are hunted by gorillas is to be retained, but a chase sequence is also proposed for the middle of the film. 'We envision a chase where he is hunted down by ape citizens, ape policemen, ape children etc,' wrote Jacobs and Thompson. The hero's escape with Nova and their child was to be turned into a third major action sequence, 'a miniature version of *The Great Escape*', before they arrive back on Earth, possibly at Los Angeles International Airport, where they will find the entire airport 'peopled' by apes. The apes were to be dressed in contemporary human clothing, would drive motor cars and live in familiar houses, while humans would wear only the scantiest of costumes. 'We have had considerable discussions with top make-up artists and there is no problem envisioned in getting the results we have indicated in our sketches,' say the film-makers, with breathtaking, offhand confidence. 'In regard to the language for the simians, we feel we have come up with a method of handling this which is completely plausible and further which is a bonanza in regard to the world market. When we first hear the apes, they speak in a deep guttural language which would somewhat resemble a combination of Russian, Polish and German. We, of course, do not understand what they are saying nor does our hero. Then little by little as Ulysse is able to speak certain words, such as proper names, ie [sic] Zira, our hero's over-screen narration finally tells us that he has been able to master enough of the language to converse with them. He then has his initial conversation with Zira, but as he is now able to understand their language, therefore our audience is able to understand the language as the language becomes English at this point. Obviously this is a great asset for us, as in Japan the language then becomes Japanese, in Spain, Spanish etc.'

The three actors proposed for the role of Ulysse at this juncture are Brando, Newman and Burt Lancaster. Three 'newer stars' are also mooted – Steve McQueen, George Peppard and Rod Taylor. But Jacobs and Thompson add: 'We do not feel they would give it the prestige the picture should have.' Sean Connery was suggested in a slightly later version of the same document. Their first choice for Nova was Ursula Andress, 'or possibly we would unleash an international search (as there is no language barrier) for the most fantastic beauty to be discovered for films'. Jacobs, who died in 1973, was a great showman, but he could also be quite secretive at times. Abrahams, who was to become his trusted lieutenant and closest friend, did not know of Thompson's early involvement on the project until I told him. Even though Abrahams and Thompson subsequently worked as producer and director on another Apjac film, *The Most Dangerous Man in the World* (aka *The Chairman*), it seems neither Jacobs nor Thompson mentioned it. Thompson obviously had an input into these early proposals, but in early 2001 he admitted it was Jacobs who was the driving force, and that it was Jacobs, as producer, who made the rounds of studio executives. Jacobs worked out a budget on the basis of fifty days' shooting in black and white, with as many as 500 ape extras at the medical convention, which would ultimately become a tribunal in the final film. He costed it at $957,600, a figure that looks suspiciously as if someone was determined to keep it under $1 million. Paramount, however, budgeted the film at almost $3 million, and a budget, worked out with Fox executives for Zanuck and finalized on Christmas Eve 1963, put the figure at $1.7 million. Jacobs had already received knock-backs from several studios, including United Artists, who believed the story stretched credibility way beyond breaking point and that the book was essentially unfilmable. Nevertheless, Jacobs believed deals were imminent with Fox and Newman. Jacobs did meet Boulle, but most of his dealings were with Boulle's agent, Alain Bernheim, and a long correspondence developed between the two, with Bernheim pleading to be kept up to date and Jacobs forever reassuring him that a deal was just around the corner. Bernheim claimed to be wearing out his shoes pacing up and down. In response Jacobs addressed his letters and cables 'Dear Pacer' and signed off with 'keep pacing' and 'love and kisses'. Jacobs went to Acapulco for the holidays, but continued firing off cables from Mexico. Then it all went worryingly quiet. On 8 January, Bernheim was on holiday at Klosters, in Switzerland, pacing with fingers crossed, and begging Jacobs to get in touch. On 9 January, Bernheim still had heard nothing from Jacobs, and was complaining that his silence put him in a difficult situation with Boulle. Bernheim finally got hold of Hellman, who gave him the impression the deal with Fox was now nothing more than a formality. On 22 January, Jacobs and Hellman wrote to Bernheim to say Fox had turned them down.

Their communication was no brief cable, but a long, three-page letter, updating Bernheim on other avenues Jacobs had already investigated and the many that still remained to be explored. They said Fox would not authorize a budget of more than $1 million. Paramount had apparently indicated it might be interested if the budget could be brought down to $1.5 million. Jacobs had already been back on to them, only to be told: 'Paramount has lost all interest in the subject matter, and there is no point in having a meeting and taking your time.' Paramount was determined that, this time, Jacobs should get the message. There had also been a 'stormy meeting' with United Artists. Jacobs felt none of the studio bosses had the imagination to recognize the film's potential. But, far from calling it a day, he simply intended to change targets, and get a star, a writer and a director, and then use their names and reputations to help secure finance. Jacobs believed that, if he had gone to a studio with a package of Paul Newman, director Tony Richardson or Blake Edwards and writer John Osborne, he would have got his money. 'Even this may be wrong, but at least it's an approach,' he wrote, which is as close as Jacobs ever comes to sounding pessimistic. Stanley Kubrick was another possibility for director. The letter from the two film-makers goes on: 'Arthur is told, through his cutter on his Fox picture [*What a Way to Go!*], that Fritz Lang is ecstatic about it and would like to direct it – an interesting idea, but we don't know if he's financeable.' The German expressionist director of the arche-typal sci-fi silent movie *Metropolis* and Hollywood thrillers such as *Scarlet Street* and *The Big Heat*, was now in his seventies. The letter even suggested going to England and making *Planet of the Apes* on the cheap with Hammer director Terence Fisher. The names of Fred Zinnemann, who directed *High Noon* and *From Here to Eternity*, Bryan Forbes, director of such gently ironic English tales as *The League of Gentlemen* and *Whistle Down the Wind*, and Sam Peckinpah, the man who turned violence into an art form, all appeared in Jacobs's notebook around this time.

J. Lee Thompson had moved on to other projects, which were going to tie him up for almost two years, and Hellman too was about to depart the scene, leaving Jacobs to battle on alone. 'He asked me to help finance the option on the book,' says Thompson. 'I thought it would be quite difficult to get a studio to make it. It was very different from the kind of films that studios were making. The kind of message we were getting was "Are you crazy – a lot of talking apes? What is this?" They couldn't believe it … It was looking pretty grim at one time, so I very stupidly sold my share back to Arthur … Naturally I wish I'd stayed with it, but I didn't.' Thompson refuses to discuss the financial details. A letter from Bernheim to Jacobs, in January 1964, agrees to Jacobs's request for a four-month exclusive option on the book – effectively the right to buy the film rights. Neither Jacobs nor Bernheim refers to it as an extension of an option; in fact Bernheim says: 'Because it is Boulle and because of the stature of his work, you must understand that I have never given an option to anyone. If you do think you need an exclusive option, I will make an exception for you because of your enthusiasm and past work. However, you will then have to put up some money.' The figure was set at $3,000. So are we to believe no money at all had changed hands up until this point? Or at least that no money had departed Jacobs's hands, because Thompson claims to have put up cash, though he will not say how much? Without attracting the popular notice that the studio bosses attracted, Jacobs was undoubtedly one of Hollywood's greatest wheeler-dealers, and several years down the line Charlton Heston would note in his diaries: 'Arthur Jacobs is so difficult and slippery a character to deal with, I hardly know where to begin.'

Two weeks later Jacobs had lunch with Blake Edwards, the director of *Breakfast at Tiffany's* and *The Pink Panther*. Edwards gave him a firm commitment to direct *Planet of the Apes* and there seemed to be a fair chance that Edwards could get it made at Warner Brothers. Jacobs was still ducking and diving over the $3,000 option on the book, suggesting it should start on 1 March – if he still did not have a definite deal with a studio by then – which, of course, would bring with it a much bigger, six-figure payment for Boulle, straight from the studio. By the beginning of March, Jacobs had his deal with Warner. Rod Serling, creator of the hit *Twilight Zone* TV sci-fi series, was hired to write the script, Shirley MacLaine was to play Zira and production was scheduled for January 1965. 'Now that the pacing is over I just want you to know how happy we all are,' Jacobs wrote to Bernheim. 'It was a tough battle, but we made it!'

How wrong he was. The pacing had just begun.

# CHAPTER FOUR
# ROSEBUD

A team of American astronauts crash-lands on a barren planet. They set off to explore the desert terrain, but ultimately only one of them will still be around to learn the terrible truth. He scrambles over a ridge and … 'His eyes suddenly narrow,' wrote Rod Serling, arguably the finest science-fiction screenwriter of his day, or indeed any day. What has he seen? No, not the Statue of Liberty. Not yet. 'The camera begins a giant sweep down the other side of the mountain until we're on a long shot of a four-lane, concrete highway. A sign in the foreground reads: "Reno, Nevada, 97 miles"… Then down the highway rolls a big truck, and after a few moments in the opposite direction a big, flashy convertible. The camera stays on this, establishing it for a long moment, then sweeps back up for a long angle shot looking up at Corey, who starts to cry and laugh at the same time. COREY (shouts): "Hey! Oh my dear God … Oh my dear God. I know what happened. We never left Earth."' It is not quite the *Planet of the Apes* ending that established itself in popular culture, but the basic idea is there.

Serling was originally approached to adapt *Planet of the Apes* by the King Brothers film company, who envisaged it as a cheapie, with actors in gorilla masks. Instead he joined forces with Arthur P. Jacobs and developed the film for Warner Brothers in 1964–5, before other writers took over and guided it towards production at Twentieth Century Fox a tortuous two years later. Two names share on-screen credit for the script, *Twilight Zone* creator Rod Serling and Oscar-winner Michael Wilson, but three other writers, including Pierre Boulle, also had a go. The film's release in 1968 prompted a debate on authorship that has persisted to this day, with bitter arguments between fans and academics over who was responsible for what, and particularly who could claim credit for the twist ending in which Taylor discovers he has been on Earth all the time. One thing is certain: the script did not emerge fully formed from Boulle's book, nor from Serling or Wilson's typewriter, but was constantly changing, developing and evolving. Serling's scripts, like the novel, envisaged a technologically advanced ape society and even his biographer, Joel Engel, attributed the film's shock ending to Wilson. But he was wrong.

Rod Serling wrote more than thirty versions of *Planet of the Apes*. But our opening paragraph came from none of them, even though, if you replace the road sign with the Statue of Liberty, the scene would play just like the final film. Serling wrote it all right, but not for *Planet of the Apes*. It comes from a Serling script called *I Shot an Arrow into the Air*, which he wrote for his *Twilight Zone* series in 1959, four years before Boulle's novel was published. What *I Shot an Arrow into the Air* does establish is that the *Planet of the Apes* ending is not merely characteristic of Serling's work, with its final twists and philosophical hammer blows, but was actually incredibly close in detail to, as they used to say on *Blue Peter*, 'one I did earlier'. The final shooting script for *Planet of the Apes* bears only one name, that of Michael Wilson, and yet it includes the earlier foundations laid by Serling. It also includes uncredited, last-minute changes from a certain John T. Kelley, a little-known writer whose name carries none of the cachet of Serling or Wilson and is virtually forgotten. We will come to his contribution later. Gordon C. Webb, an assistant professor in the television and radio department at Ithaca College in New York state, home of the Rod Serling Archive, wrote, in an article called '30 Years Later – Rod Serling's Planet of the Apes', first published in *Creative Screenwriting* in 1998: 'As far as the film's ending is concerned, evidence gathered on both coasts over a period of nearly five years leaves little doubt that Rod Serling dreamed up the concept of "a world turned upside down" by nuclear disaster, and an astronaut – thinking he's millions of miles from Earth – who finds out he never left home.' Associate producer Mort Abrahams told me unequivocally: 'Rod broke the back of the book. It's impossible to put that book on the screen. He came up with the basic plot line, including the Statue of Liberty.' Abrahams is dismissive of Wilson's contribution – but Abrahams did not join the project until after Serling had completed his draft scripts. But – another but – the Statue of Liberty was already there in the script by the time he joined. Does that mean it was Serling's idea? The evidence seems overwhelming, but is it?

Rodman Serling was born on Christmas Day 1925 in upstate New York. During the Second World War he served in a paratroop demolition platoon in the Pacific Ocean and was wounded. He subsequently worked in local radio, he was an accomplished light-weight boxer and he combined the two interests when he won a national contest for a radio script about a prize fighter dying of leukaemia. He graduated to writing for television in the early fifties, though, with his sparking eyes, dark, wavy hair and urbane good looks, he might have made a career on the other side of the cameras. Serling had been excluded from a college fraternity because he was Jewish, and he developed an acute sense of social injustice and prejudice, which showed in his work. He won the first of a string of Emmy awards for his play *Patterns*, a portrait of greed in corporate America. This was the golden age of television drama and *Patterns*, shown in 1955, was immediately adapted for the big screen. Serling scored one of his biggest successes in 1956 with *Requiem for a Heavyweight*, with Jack Palance as a boxer on the slide. The BBC version the following year proved a turning point in Sean Connery's career and led to a film contract. A movie version appeared in 1962 with Anthony Quinn as the boxer, Mickey Rooney as his trainer and a supporting cast that included Cassius Clay.

Serling is best known, however, for *The Twilight Zone*, the series of twenty-five-minute sci-fi dramas that he created, wrote, produced and hosted. Imaginative, thoughtful and provocative, they had an enormous influence on a generation of young Americans, including Steven Spielberg, who directed one of the segments in a film version in 1983, eight years after Serling's death. The show was also revived on television and retains a huge cult following. Other writers also worked on the original series, but Serling's own scripts were often allegories. A liberal, Serling was forced into allegory by the conservatism of the television stations. In 1959, the year *The Twilight Zone* began, he said: 'If you want to do a piece about prejudice against Negroes, you go instead with Mexicans, and set it in 1890 instead of 1959 ... If you want to do a play about a man's Communist background as a youth, you have to make him instead a member of a wild teenage group.' Arthur P. Jacobs may have believed that the sole object of *Planet of the Apes* was 'to entertain and thrill', but it seems unlikely Serling saw it in such simplistic terms. He once said that in almost everything he wrote he was exploring man's 'seemingly palpable need' to dislike those who were different from himself.

While Serling worked on the script, Jacobs returned to one of his favourite activities, making up lists of candidates for the main roles. The principal astronaut's name had already been changed from Ulysse to the much more WASP appellation Thomas. Paul Newman, Burt Lancaster, George Peppard and Rod Taylor, star of *The Time Machine*, were all still in the running, but they were now joined by James Garner, Stuart Whitman and Cliff Robertson. For Zira he was considering Patricia Neal, Jean Simmons, Eva Marie Saint, Newman's wife Joanne Woodward, Claire Bloom and Jean Seberg – Shirley MacLaine having dropped out. An unknown was now his favoured option for Nova, followed by Ursula Andress and Yvette Mimieux, who made her debut in *The Time Machine* and, curiously enough, would go on to make *Monkeys, Go Home!*, a 1967 Disney film about a man who trains animals to work on his farm. For Cornelius, Jacobs had only two names – Roddy McDowall and Barry Nelson. He was looking for a heavyweight actor and star name for Zaius. Peter Ustinov, at the height of his fame and popularity after *Spartacus*, Laurence Olivier, Yul Brynner, José Ferrer, Orson Welles, Alec Guinness and Edmond O'Brien were all in the frame.

Serling, whose status within the business was reflected in a then astronomical fee of $125,000, delivered a complete first draft on 22 May 1964, by which time Jacobs had already made a series of sharp observations on the early pages. He wanted gorillas, rather than orang-utans, in the hunt, and he had serious reservations about the tempo and tone of the opening scenes, which he thought lacked gravity and suspense. 'Take for example *King Kong*,' he wrote, 'which in my opinion today is still a classic. There was a tremendously long build-up ...' He then goes into a long explanation of how Serling might use *King Kong* as a template. Serling's official first draft begins in the spaceship, just like the final film, the astronauts crash-land on the planet, they find a human footprint and meet the locals – 'There are men, women and children dressed, if at all, in loin cloths and animal furs.' Dodge is shot dead during the hunt and Thomas shot in the neck. However, the ape hunters are dressed in 'white garb and pith helmets' and sound like English gentlemen. 'Good show,' says one. 'Not a bad bag at that,' says a second. Serling was a great storyteller, but never a master of natural dialogue, and Jacobs had good cause to be worried – this was not exactly a scene that would strike horror into the hearts of the audience, not as written, anyway. Thomas is taken to Zira's lab, visited by Zaius, escapes and is recaptured. His first words are 'No! Get away! Let me alone!' They do not have quite the same impact and venom as 'Take your stinking paws off me, you damn dirty ape!'. Zaius observes: 'He has told us much of Earth. Its perennial wars … God help us if he's our superior.' Thomas becomes a celebrity, gets tipsy in a bar, as in the novel, and when asked to speak says: 'Bow wow.' Jacobs feared parts of the script were too light-hearted. He might also have had some cause for concern about the bar scene in the hands of his director, Blake Edwards, who had a penchant for slapstick and comedy that would become ever broader as the years went by and the *Pink Panther* series continued. Serling not only has Nova learning to talk, but serving tea as well, quite the little housewife. Nevertheless, the essential structure and characters in his earliest drafts do bear a close resemblance to the structure and characters of the final film, but then the characters were really established in the novel.

Serling had been working on a version of the script that followed Boulle's plot, with Thomas and Nova returning to Earth, to find it populated by apes. But, by the time he submitted the first official draft, a decision had been made to cut out the return journey to Earth and end with the revelation that the mystery planet was Earth. In this version the archaeological dig has thrown up, not just a talking doll, but also film of a nuclear explosion, which it is made clear was produced by the US Air Force. 'What was that film, Mr Thomas?' asks Cornelius, who is exceedingly polite. 'A hydrogen bomb,' says Thomas, and, after a long monologue, he concludes: 'This is Earth.' The apes plan to kill Thomas and claim he never existed. They will say he was nothing more than a hoax and produce a robot man to substantiate the claim. But Thomas and Nova escape (again), retrieve his landing craft and join the mother ship in orbit. The revelation that Thomas had been on Earth all the time was a typical Serling twist, straight out of *I Shot an Arrow into the Air*, except Jacobs and Edwards felt, quite rightly, Serling was throwing the ending away by simply having Thomas announce: 'This is Earth,' as if he were a bus driver telling a visitor he had reached the required neighbourhood and it was time to get off. They determined to come up with an alternative.

In 1971, just a few years before his death, Jacobs told *Cinefantastique* magazine: 'It's funny, I was having lunch with Blake Edwards, who at one point was going to direct it, at the Yugo Kosherama Delicatessen in Burbank, across the street from Warner Brothers. I said to him at the time: "It doesn't work, it's too predictable." Then I said: "What if he was on the Earth the whole time and doesn't know it, and the audience doesn't know it." Blake said: "That's terrific. Let's get a hold of Rod." As we walked out, after paying for the two ham sandwiches, we looked up, and there's this big Statue of Liberty on the wall of the delicatessen. We both looked at each other and said: "Rosebud" [a reference to Citizen Kane's mysterious dying word, revealed at the end of Orson Welles's film to have been the name of Kane's boyhood sledge]. If we never had lunch in that delicatessen, I doubt that we would have had the Statue of Liberty as the end of the picture.' Abrahams says: 'I never heard that story. I don't know how to say this diplomatically – it doesn't seem to ring true.' Serling told *Cinefantastique*: 'The book's ending is what I wanted to use in the film, as much as I loved the idea of the Statue of Liberty. I always believed that was my idea.' It is not exactly a resounding rebuttal, but maybe Serling was being diplomatic. Interviewer Dale Winogura commented: 'I'm beginning to think, from all the interviews I've done, that the end of the picture was a combination of about four or five people thinking exactly the same thing at about the same time.' Serling replies: 'That's very possible.' If Winogura was having trouble pinning down the truth in 1971, imagine how much more difficult it is thirty years later.

But the truth may lie in records from the time, now held at Loyola Marymount University in Los Angeles. There are huge stores of movie papers at UCLA, kept in conditions that resemble Fort Knox, but it was to this little university, 'in the Jesuit/Marymount tradition of academic excellence', on a surprisingly peaceful hillside campus, not far from Los Angeles International Airport, that Jacobs bequeathed his papers. And there, in a letter to Blake Edwards, dated 14 October 1964, Jacobs refers to the idea of 'selling' a new ending to Serling, which he outlines in considerable detail. 'Cornelius and Zira steal a helicopter to transport Thomas and LaFever [the third astronaut, later renamed Landon] to the site of the ship. Once they are in the air and halfway to their destination, Cornelius discovers via space radio that they are being pursued by gorillas on order of Zaius, and it is known they are in a medical helicopter. Cornelius then says that they have recently discovered a strange statue at a location, which is near the site of Thomas's ship. There are several helicopters belonging to the scientific expedition there. The gorillas are coming closer in pursuit. Cornelius suggests they land at the site, put Thomas and LaFever into another helicopter – Thomas knows how to operate it. Thomas will then safely go back to his ship, while Cornelius and Zira, in the medical helicopter, become decoys and go in the wrong direction, giving Thomas and LaFever time to get to their own ship, and take off safely. They land at the excavation – the sun is rising, and we see some unidentifiable statue. They say goodbye. Thomas and LaFever's helicopter goes off in the distance to the left, as the sun is rising. Cornelius and Zira in the medical helicopter go off to the right, as the gorillas follow Cornelius in closer [sic] pursuit. As the helicopters disappear in both directions, and the sun rises – camera swings around and reveals "rosebud".' In the letter, Jacobs not only refers to the new ending as 'the 'rosebud' ending', but also, tellingly, as 'our ending', because it was clear at this point that Serling needed convincing.

It was not just with the script that Jacobs was having problems. He had to move from the Fox lot, where he had been based for his first film, to offices on the Warner lot in Burbank, but a row with Warner executives over the supply of furniture went on for months. It may seem trivial, but it got to the point where agents and lawyers were involved. And Warner were querying expenses for everything from design sketches for the film to Xerox charges. Jacobs was told that he must get specific authorization for every individual item of expenditure. It did not bode well for when Warner would consider the cost of the film itself, though that was going to be some way off, as it quickly became apparent that the scheduled filming date of January 1965 had been too optimistic. Paul Newman was still interested, without committing himself, and Jack Lemmon's agents had long discussions with Jacobs, pushing their client's case. Lemmon was hardly obvious casting – he worked largely in comedy and his dramatic characters were typified not by action, but by angst and inaction. He had a working relationship with Blake Edwards, however, having recently played an alcoholic PR man, afflicted by moral doubts, in *Days of Wine and Roses*. And, according to the annual Quigley poll of film exhibitors, he was the biggest male star of 1964 (second only in the overall ratings to Doris Day). Jacobs reckoned he was a good fallback if Newman fell through and also toyed with the idea of casting him as Cornelius. It was also rumoured that Rock Hudson (the third most popular star of 1964) might be interested and on another occasion Gregory Peck's name appeared on the wish list.

Serling was still refusing to abandon the philosophizing and rely on visuals in his script of 17 December 1964. Thomas and Cornelius are in their separate helicopters, when Thomas tells him over the radio: 'Mr Cornelius ... just below me something is sticking out of the ground. Do you see it?' Cornelius tells him he sees some ruins. 'They mean nothing to you,' says Thomas, 'but remember them. And remember what I'm going to tell you now. Because in case I don't get where I'm going ... the following is another chapter in your history book ... When we first landed and looked toward the sky, some of the stars had changed their positions. We assumed we were somewhere out in space and that explained it. It wasn't a question of space ... it was time. Time had altered the look of the sky. When I looked in your telescope, it was almost identical to what I'd seen on Earth. Almost identical ... and again I assumed I was on another planet. Your maps ... again familiar. So damned familiar that it was like trying to stick a piece in a jigsaw puzzle. Here's the last chapter in the history book, Mr Cornelius. The stars are the solar system as I know it. Your map is a map of a world I know. Parts of the land have sunk into the sea. Continents have been split. Jungle has replaced cities, but I've come home, Mr Cornelius. This is Earth ...' The camera pans down from his helicopter to reveal what Thomas saw. 'Protruding from the earth, is the giant metal arm surrounded by its iron picket fence ... It is caught in the blaze of the morning sun revealing it as what it is – the top part of the Statue of Liberty.'

These final scenes were printed on pink pages and headed: 'PLEASE DO NOT REVEAL THE CONTENTS OF THIS PAGE

TO ANYONE.' Six days later there was another script. It was still not quite right, but Serling was getting there. 'I feel the last three pages must be kept a total secret,' said Jacobs, in a letter to Edwards, 'and would like to explore with you some sort of phoney final three pages that we could put in the script for the purpose of everyone except those directly concerned, that would not reveal Earth and the Statue of Liberty.' Jacobs and Edwards were insisting the denouement should be presented visually in the very last shot of the film. Serling was becoming increasingly irritated by the continual demand for rewrites and at one point he amused himself by writing an ending in which Thomas's speech lasts so long that Cornelius's helicopter runs out of fuel and crashes, while Thomas is still blethering away, and the Statue of Liberty is seen raising her middle finger towards him. 'Yep. I knew I'd never left home!' he concludes triumphantly. In January 1965 Serling submitted one final ending, which takes place, not in the air, but on the beach, and which attempts to exploit the full visual and dramatic significance of the world's most famous statue. This time Thomas sees it and delivers a much briefer version of his previous speech. But this time, for once, he does not escape. Like the western gunfighter who has had enough, he tells Cornelius: 'I'm afraid there's no place to run to. I'm afraid there's no place to go … now.' There is the sound of gunfire and he collapses in the sand. His body is carried away by two apes, one of whom asks what he meant when he said there was 'no place to go', and only then does the audience get a proper look at the Statue of Liberty.

Problems with tone had been sorted out. On the hunt scene, Jacobs had written that the film should cut from the first close-up of a gorilla to a 'close-up of blood spurting from Thomas's neck – which will stop any laughs'. For the time being at least, the script was just about there. The next consideration was costs. Warner's experts got down to business and prepared a budget for 128 days of filming, in colour, with locations in Monument Valley, Texas and Hawaii. Paramount had balked at $2.8 million, Fox at $1.7 million. Warner budgeted the film at $7,478,750. And that did not include the cost of the actors, the music, the director or the story, and Serling was already getting $125,000 and Boulle $101,900. Warner reckoned, once everything was added in, the final budget could top $10 million, which was astronomical by the standards of the day.

So that was that. Warner decided it was just too expensive and within a matter of weeks they had pulled the plug on the film. Blake Edwards went off to make the wacky, and now forgotten, comedy *What Did You Do in the War, Daddy?*, marry Julie Andrews and attempt to turn her into a sex symbol in *10* and *SOB*, though sadly the world was not ready for a topless Mary Poppins. If Blake Edwards had directed *Planet of the Apes*, I might not be writing this book today, though he did direct *Breakfast at Tiffany's* – Audrey Hepburn, 'Moon River' and that scene with the cat in the rain – wonderful. Jacobs contacted Boulle's agent, Alain Bernheim, only after receiving a worried communication from him enquiring about a rumour he had heard that Edwards may be pulling out. Jacobs confirmed it was true, but was quick to add that he was now working on alternatives, and signed off: 'Love and kisses.'

Jacobs and Serling both died in the seventies, but Blake Edwards is still around. Perhaps he could offer some light on the origins of the Statue of Liberty ending. 'It was a combined effort between myself and an artist called Don Peters,' he told me. Not Serling? Not Serling. Not Jacobs? Definitely not Jacobs. Jacobs's comments in *Cinefantastique* prompted laughter, but it was the sort of laughter you employ to keep your temper under control. 'That's the biggest ... most elaborate ... lie that could be made! He had nothing to do with the Statue of Liberty. Absolutely nothing. It originated between myself and Peters and, if I had to give anybody most of the credit [in Hollywood no one ever gives all the credit away], as I recall, it was pretty much Don. It's an interesting story and we may have had lunch there, but as far as seeing the Statue of Liberty ... Arthur is a good publicist – I hate to call him a liar.' But Edwards admits he remembers very little about the project: he says Serling came on board only after he had dropped out (which is certainly incorrect), he could not recall exactly why he left the project – 'I just didn't like things that were happening' – and he did not know Jacobs was dead or whether Don Peters might still be alive.

So who is this Don Peters? By this time I was back in the UK, but I remembered I had noted down the name from papers at Loyola Marymount and I knew he was indeed one of the artists who worked on early sketches. Beyond that? Edwards told me Peters worked with him on *The Great Race*. These were the days before everyone, right down to the deputy assistant coffee-maker, got a namecheck on the credits. There was no Don Peters in *Halliwell's* and scant information on the Internet Movie Database. The IMDB listed two Don Peters – a writer who won an Oscar nomination for his first film, *The Naked Prey*; and a second individual who supposedly worked in various capacities on movies, including art director on 'Wild Bill' Wellman's *Good-bye, My Lady* (1956), production designer on Wellman's *Hell Bent for Glory* (US title: *Lafayette Escadrille*) (1958) and associate producer on *The Grip of Fear* (US title: *Experiment in Terror*), a 1962 thriller directed by Blake Edwards. Beyond that the Internet threw up the fact that he came from Indiana, graduated from John Herron Art School, in Indianapolis, in 1950, and worked for Disney in the mid-fifties. There are over 200 Don and Donald Peters listed in California telephone directories alone, but not one registered with the guilds for film artists and art directors. Finally I came across a dealer who was selling signed artwork Don Peters had produced for the 1962 animated film *Journey Back to Oz*. It was a long shot, but it was all I had. 'I haven't talked to him in years,' said Diane Steele. 'He'll be eighty this May ... I hope you find him well.'

'It's the first time anybody has ever asked me anything about what I did on this film,' says Peters, who had retired from movies and was living outside Los Angeles. 'My involvement was, Blake called me one day and asked me if I would like to redesign the world. So I quit a job that I had and went with him, and I worked on it for about a year.' Peters had got his big break after painting pictures of First World War planes for director Bill Wellman, who had been a fighter pilot in the war and wanted them to hang on the walls of his house. Wellman was so impressed he hired Peters as an art director. 'I went from $81 a week at Disney to 750 a week ... I said to Bill one day: "Well, what is it that an art director does?" He says: "Jesus, I don't know, they're always bringing me blueprints" ... So I went to the library and made some sketches.' Peters reckons he produced more than a hundred paintings for *Planet of the Apes*. 'I had a free hand,' he says. He gave the apes tanks and helicopters and at the end of the long trek he thought it might be a good idea if they stumbled out of the mist and found a statue of an ape. He remembers a meeting with Edwards, Jacobs, Serling and Jack Warner. Warner Brothers liked the idea of the film, and his designs, but the budget was prohibitive. 'What happened in the final analysis was Blake backed out of the deal.' He confirms that the relationship with Jacobs was not an easy one. 'Arthur Jacobs was a paranoid schizophrenic. He used to sweat all the time, which should have been a tip-off.' Peters remembers telling Jacobs that he had heard Picasso wanted to make an animated film. Jacobs went to see Picasso, when he was in France, but was turned away at the gate. 'He blamed me for it,' says Peters. 'He was a total neurotic.' Most of Peter's ideas for *Planet of the Apes* never made it before the cameras. And the Statue of Liberty? 'It was my idea,' he says. 'At least three of the paintings I did were the Statue of Liberty.' And no one asked him to do it? Serling? Edwards? Jacobs? 'It was my idea ... I never asked for credits.'

Nevertheless, Peters was in the spotlight shortly after his abortive stint on *Planet of the Apes*; for this Don Peters is indeed the same Don Peters who worked briefly as a writer in the second half of the sixties and won an Oscar nomination for his first script *The Naked Prey* in 1967 – the year in which *Planet of the Apes* was shot. *The Naked Prey* was an adventure film centring on a prolonged hunt, in which the normal order of things is turned upside down when a white hunter (Cornel Wilde) finds himself the quarry, pursued by African tribesmen for sport. Peters came up with the basic storyline for *The Naked Prey* and admits it was co-writer Clint Johnston who turned it into a screenplay. It bears more than a passing resemblance to *Planet of the Apes,* with its long, dramatic and upside-down hunt sequence when the astronauts first see the apes. Peters insists he was not influenced by *Planet of the Apes* – he conceived *The Naked Prey* as a western, with a white man pursued by Indians, and was inspired by a true story he read as a boy. He says it was Johnston and Wilde, who was director, producer and star, who relocated it in Africa. Ideas can indeed be difficult and complex things to pin down ...

Meanwhile Jacobs refused to be downhearted at the knock-back from Warner. He had picked up the $60,000 Warner paid out as his producer fee and he now had a script by Rod Serling, though any other studio taking on the project would have to repay Warner for the money they had spent, a total of $366,000. Jacobs also had another animal project in development, a big-budget musical version of *Doctor Dolittle*, at his old stomping ground of

Twentieth Century Fox. And if he could persuade Dick Zanuck that Rex Harrison was a viable proposition singing to a whole menagerie of animals, in a project that would eventually cost the studio close on $20 million, surely he could talk Zanuck into backing a film in which the hero restricts himself to talking with primates, at a mere fraction of the budget of Sexy Rexy's movie.

But before we close this chapter there is one footnote that should perhaps be added here. It seems anomalous that in his original documents pitching the film Jacobs changed the hero's nationality from French to American, but left his name as Ulysse. This was one of the first and most basic changes that had to be made in Serling's script and the hero's name appears in his first draft as Thomas. It would remain as Thomas, in version after version, for three whole years, right through until April 1967. It was changed just before the film went into production the following month. No one now can remember why. Perhaps it had something to do with Maurice Evans, the British actor who played Zaius, for he must surely have recognized the significance of the name, even if no one else did.

Serling's hero was not merely called Thomas; he was called John Thomas, which is an English slang term for the penis. The name is used in full in dialogue in several scenes, including one in Serling's first draft where the robot announces: 'Good afternoon. I'm John Thomas from the planet Earth.' The name was given a certain international profile when it figured in Monty Python's *Penis Song* in the 1983 film *The Meaning of Life* – 'Three cheers for your Willy or John Thomas, Hooray for your one-eyed trouser snake'. But associate producer Mort Abrahams, who had worked in England, was unfamiliar with its usage until I told him and was mortified, and ultimately highly amused, to learn of the connotations. For all his deep philosophizing, Serling, as we have seen, was not above the odd joke or two ... Which then leads one to wonder just exactly when Arthur P. Jacobs first mentioned his 'rosebud' idea to him. Rosebud was, of course, the name of Citizen Kane's sledge. And everyone knows Orson Welles and writer Herman Mankiewicz based the character of Charles Foster Kane on newspaper tycoon William Randolph Hearst. What is less well known, and what supposedly infuriated Hearst most about the film, is that 'rosebud' was his pet name for his lover Marion

Davies's vagina, or more specifically her clitoris. Serling was asked to accommodate 'rosebud', and did so in a script in which he called the hero John Thomas. Of course, it could just be coincidence. But then we seem to be building up enough coincidences for a Dickens novel, rather than a straightforward historical account of the making of a Hollywood movie.

# CHAPTER FIVE
# JOHN WAYNE VERSUS CHARLTON HESTON

Cinema was in freefall. After the post-war boom years, audiences were deserting the movies in droves for television, bowling alleys, other glossy new attractions and leisure activities. Hollywood was on life support with no guarantee that it would pull through. Studios were forced to gamble big money on big movies to attract audiences away from the box. The 'studio system', which tied stars to long-term contracts with individual companies, had virtually collapsed, and studios had to pay the market value for star names. Fox gambled bigger than anyone. They had a historical drama on their slate, which was due to go before the cameras with Joan Collins in the lead role. But they raised the stakes, believing they had a royal flush in the combination of Hollywood royalty, Elizabeth Taylor and Richard Burton, and the Queen of the Nile. At $44 million, *Cleopatra* cost more than twice as much as any other movie up until that time and Fox had to sell most of its backlot to balance the books. The film dragged on and on and on, and was way over budget. It looked like it might never finish and the studio was teetering on the point of collapse. Desperate times called for desperate measures and in 1962 Fox recalled Darryl F. Zanuck, who had run the company for twenty-one years since its foundation in the thirties. He shut production down and sacked almost the entire staff. He would base himself in New York, and he needed someone to get the studio up and running again in Los Angeles. There was intense speculation about who might end up in the hot seat, but he wrong-footed everyone by appointing his son Richard Darryl Zanuck, a soft-spoken twenty-seven-year-old with handsome, chiselled features and a receding hairline. The cynics reckoned his tan would last longer than his appointment and knives were sharpened in anticipation of the funeral feast. A lamb to the slaughter, Dick moved on to the lot, read through a mountain of possible projects and gave the green light to a film about a singing nun set in Nazi Europe. It would be directed by one of Hollywood's foremost horror directors, would star a twee English actress and was dubbed *The Sound of Mucous* by its male lead. 'We're going all out for the big, family-type show that I suppose you could call pure entertainment,' Dick Zanuck said at the time. The proper title of the film was, of course, *The Sound of Music*, though in the industry it was to take on a third appellation – *The Sound of Money*. In 1963 Fox released the most expensive film ever made and looked like they were about to collapse. Two years later they released the highest-grossing film ever made and effected one of the most dramatic turnarounds in American corporate history.

Zanuck senior raised Dick tough, never allowing him to win at games and sending him to military school. But, as studio bosses go, Dick Zanuck was one of the good guys. 'I'm very much aware that what we do here is seen by millions of people around the world,' he said, soon after taking over. 'My first responsibility is to the company I work for, but I also have a responsibility as a person and as a film-maker to put on things of which I can be proud.' He was, and is, a much more urbane character than his cigar-chomping old man, who once famously snapped at an underling: 'Don't say yes until I finish talking.' Dick worked for his father in his early twenties, when 'DZ', as he called him, was an independent producer. Dick produced his first film, the thriller *Compulsion*, for him when he was twenty-four. When father asked son who he thought should run the studio, Dick had sufficient confidence to reply: 'Me.' His appointment may have been nepotism, but it was not just nepotism. The Zanuck family were the biggest stockholders in Fox, and Darryl Zanuck was not about to appoint his son if he did not think he could do the job. Ultimately, when the studio's fortunes took a dip again, Darryl Zanuck would show his ruthlessness by sacking him, and Dick Zanuck would go on to prove himself as an independent producer, breaking the all-time box-office record again with *Jaws*, again in the face of widespread scepticism, and winning best picture Oscars for *The Sting* and *Driving Miss Daisy*. Darryl Zanuck was a movie mogul, a Citizen Kane, one of the Hollywood tsars; Dick Zanuck was a moviemaker, a producer, who did not want his underlings to fob him off with a simple 'yes' – he wanted their opinions. The father was a man of few words, the son a man of many. 'In the old days,' Dick told John Gregory Dunne, the author of *The Studio*, in 1967, 'my father could staff and cast a picture in minutes from the card file, listing everyone under contract. Nowadays, planning a picture takes longer than making one. Jesus, we spend hours fighting with agents over billing, salary, fringe benefits, start dates, stop dates, the works. DZ doesn't have the temperament for this sort of thing. His inclination was always to throw an agent out of his office. Not me. I like to wheel and deal.' This was a man with whom Arthur P. Jacobs could do business.

Jacobs was wheeling and dealing all over town. As well as trying to get *Planet of the Apes* made, other projects included musical versions of Hugh Lofting's *Doctor Dolittle* stories and James Hilton's happy schooldays tale *Goodbye, Mr Chips* and a First World War aviation movie called *Time of Glory*. He had a deal at MGM, and it was in the MGM canteen that he met up one day, by chance, with his old friend Mort Abrahams, a clever, sharp-minded television producer. Abrahams was as far from the stereotype of a producer as you can get. The son of a stockbroker, he was born in New York in 1916 and came to showbiz via economics and statistics, married his college sweetheart and they were still happily married (to each other) half a century later. The Bank of America had pumped a fortune into films, many of which flopped, and one of Abrahams's jobs was to assess the value of these properties in the new television market. 'I had no idea what they were worth, nor had anyone else,' he says. 'If I'd known you at that time, and had been smarter than I was, I would have called you and said: "Brian, you and I are going to buy the TV rights for a thousand dollars."'

Abrahams did not perhaps appreciate the full value of the television rights to old movies, but he did see a future in the developing medium. He began by writing for it and, in 1950, produced *Tom Corbett, Space Cadet*, America's first science-fiction serial. He worked with Rod Serling on *Tales of Tomorrow* and got to know Jacobs while producing *General Electric Theatre*, which was presented by Ronald Reagan. Jacobs did publicity for the show. Abrahams had his finger on the pulse of the times; he could spot trends and sometimes predict them. *Route 66* was an early sixties precursor of *Easy Rider*, in which two young men cross America in search of adventure, while *The Man from UNCLE* copied James Bond so successfully that it became a phenomenon in its own right and its stars Robert Vaughn and Scotsman David McCallum were mobbed in the streets, like the Beatles. 'Arthur started to talk to me, this luncheon, and it ended up with him saying: "Would you like to join me, because I have this development deal with MGM and I'm trying to work something with Fox?"' Abrahams relished a new challenge and became executive vice-president of Apjac and associate producer (and ultimately producer) of Apjac's movies. Abrahams and Jacobs may sound like a law firm, but they were to become a formidable movie-making team, with Abrahams adding practical experience to Jacobs's vision and persistence, and playing a crucial role in getting his projects from the drawing board on to the studio floor. 'Arthur was an idea man,' says Dick Zanuck now, 'and Mort Abrahams was the production guy, because Arthur didn't know anything really about the mechanics of making a picture.' For the next few years they would be almost inseparable. Abrahams literally became Jacobs's right-hand man.

For most of the time Jacobs was trying to get *Planet of the Apes* up and running, he was also beavering away on plans for a musical based on Hugh Lofting's books about Doctor Dolittle, a veterinarian who can talk to animals. The author's estate had turned down overtures from previous producers. But Jacobs enlisted the support of star Rex Harrison, songwriter Alan Jay Lerner and composer Andre Previn, part of the team that had been so successful with *My Fair Lady*, a musical version of George Bernard Shaw's *Pygmalion*, and he used their names to charm the estate into giving approval. Dick Zanuck originally approved a budget of $6 million, though the film would end up costing three times that. Lerner spent fifteen months on it, but suffered an acute case of songwriter's block and dropped out, to be replaced by Leslie Bricusse, the British songwriter and composer whose works included *Stop the World I Want to Get Off*. Rex Harrison said he was quitting too and *Sound of Music* star Christopher Plummer was signed to replace him, only for Harrison to then say he had not really meant it. *Doctor Dolittle* was a nightmare from beginning to end, but it meant Apjac was back on the Fox lot, with the ear of the studio boss. And, having got the green light for one film, they were determined not to miss the opportunity to remind him of *Planet of the Apes*.

'Every time I came into his office I brought it up,' Jacobs told Dunne in an interview for *The Studio*. 'It got so I never even got the name of the picture out of my mouth. I'd say "Dick, what about ..." and he'd say "No."' It is worth recalling Zanuck's recollections now about the pitch on *Planet of the Apes*. 'He didn't have to be persistent with me, because I loved the idea right off the bat ... I read it, I loved it and I told him that, you know, if we could, if the test turned out successfully that's all I needed ... I thought there was a chance that it could be comical, that apes talking in perfect English, back and forth to one another, could bring the house down in bad laughter, the kind of laughter that we really didn't want to encourage ... It was just, we wanted to see the test. And to do the make-up, as you know, takes a long period of time.' Jacobs had already approached Zanuck in 1963, Fox had worked out a budget and they had knocked him back. Jacobs tried again after the Warner deal collapsed in March 1965. It would be March 1966 before the screen test was shot and September 1966 before Zanuck finally gave the go-ahead for the film.

By this time Abrahams was very much part of the project and he has vivid memories of trying to persuade Zanuck to back the film. 'We had a couple of films in development with Fox, so we were speaking with Dick frequently and every time that I went up, or Arthur went up, or we both went up, to Dick's office, it's true we would say: "*Planet of the Apes*?" The point was reached at which Dick Zanuck called me and said: "I want to speak to you." So I came up and he said: "Mort, I have to tell you, I want to do business with you guys, but, if either of you ever mentions *Planet of the Apes* to me again, that will be the end of our relationship. I'm sorry Mort, but I've had it up to here with that project, so from now on when you want to see me, you have to type out an agenda and tell me what you're going to talk about."'

Pierre Boulle re-entered the picture at this point, with his own version of the screenplay, or at least a partial version of the screenplay. He wrote to Jacobs on 29 April 1965, enclosing 'the result of a few days feverish work on *Planet of the Apes* and of my valorous and perhaps ridiculous attempts both at writing in english [sic] and visualizing that silly sorry [sic] as a screenplay' – Boulle could write, but he could not type. In the opening space-travel sequence he came up with the idea that there should be nothing to remind the viewer of space travel, because travel to another star would be so unlike the space travel with which audiences were familiar. Boulle had been intrigued by reports of a Russian scheme to 'unhang' one of Mars's natural satellites, a body fifteen kilometres across, and use it as a spacecraft. 'Of course, we cannot show that,' he says, though it is unclear whether he is accepting it was impossible to represent such a scheme on film, or whether he had actually been weighing up the possibilities of using the moon itself. But he did think the spaceship should be large enough to accommodate a crew of a hundred men and women, which is strange considering Serling's script had basically duplicated the three men from Boulle's book – Serling did add a fourth man, Stewart, but he is dead by the time they reach the new planet. Boulle's script opens in a commodious living room, with armchairs, curtained windows, a spiral staircase to another floor, and Thomas and Dodge playing chess. The problem in presenting the audience with a depiction of space travel that in no way resembles the popular perception of space travel is that the film wrong-foots viewers for no clear reason (other than a rather dubious scientific logic) and thereby undermines the later impact of the scene in which the film does have to wrong-foot the audience for dramatic effect – the first appearance of the apes.

Boulle wrote thirty-four pages, roughly half an hour of screen time, and he spent half that time in the spaceship, before the astronauts' arrival on the planet, an episode that is neatly dealt with in the pre-credits sequence of the finished film. One of his main points was about Serling's anti-war theme. 'I would not have the "thing" having happened as a result of any nuclear destruction, but as a result of a natural oddity of evolution.' And he anguished over the Statue of Liberty scene, insisting at first that if he were to carry on he would have to 'dismiss it entirely from my mind', then in the next paragraph suggesting it might be accommodated after all, before adding a PS in which he called it a 'cheap unwarranted effect'. 'I have come to consider it as a temptation from the devil: one of those that may seduce for a while cinema stars, a few artists, or intellectuals like us, but that would unmoved [sic] – or even annoy – the last judge, I mean the man in the street – I am definitely against it, from every point of view. Too much sophisticated …' It is clear from his abortive attempt at a screenplay that Boulle, despite his impressive intellect and imagination, had no sense of cinema. Having worked as a script consultant as well as a film critic, I would say that this is one of the worst attempts at a screenplay I have ever seen. And yet this is a man whom history would have us believe merited an Oscar as a scriptwriter.

Jacobs and Abrahams decided that what they really needed was a star. Abrahams saw the central character quite clearly as a representative of mankind and felt that although he might be portrayed as a pioneer of sorts, out there on the final frontier, he was also serving as a representative of mankind and of our civilization. Abrahams believed Thomas should be a figure of authority, almost an establishment figure, rather than an anti-establishment figure like Brando or Newman. Jacobs always thought big, and another big name was beginning to feature in his thoughts. 'We talked, Arthur and I, about John Wayne, for obvious reasons,' says Abrahams. Eventually they decided Wayne was not quite right. 'It would throw the balance of the picture too much. It would be a star vehicle.' They also believed Wayne's image was tied just a little too closely to the Wild West and the lawlessness of that era. 'Heston was American civilization. He fit the frame and he didn't take away. He was a star, of course, but not of the proportions of John Wayne.' The Duke was the most popular star of the sixties (and the fifties), according to the annual Quigley poll of film exhibitors, whereas Charlton Heston never made the top ten, not even for a single year when *Ben-Hur* came out. A handsome, blue-eyed giant of a man, Heston looked like Dan Dare, with a chin that could open doors before the rest of him got there. He had grown up in a hut in the Michigan woods, hunting game and being pulled through the snow by dog-sled, and he seemed to epitomize traditional notions of white American manhood. Yet on screen he represented more than just American civilization. His acting career began with a string of classic period roles on stage and television. And, in movies, he had been President Jackson, Moses and John the Baptist, and had won an Oscar as Ben-Hur. He was most readily associated with historical epics, but he had a history of choosing projects

*Above: Debate has raged for years over the origins of the Statue of Liberty ending. But it was Don Peters, a former Disney artist, who came up with the idea in preliminary sketches when the film was in development at Warner Bros. (picture courtesy of Loyola Marymount University, © Twentieth Century Fox).*

*Above: Don Peters's vision was realised on a secluded beach outside LA. Only the statue's crown and torch were built there – the full-length view was a painting. It became one of the most famous endings of all time, but Peters never received the recognition he was due (picture courtesy of the Kobal Collection, © Twentieth Century Fox).*

Above: Pierre Boulle was a French war hero who attempted to organise resistance in Indochina. He wrote the book that inspired David Lean's classic The Bridge on the River Kwai *and the satirical novel producer Arthur P. Jacobs believed could be turned into the new* King Kong *(© Agence Photographique Roger-Viollet).*

Right: Richard Zanuck, the 31-year-old boss of Twentieth Century Fox, had the courage to back an adventure film about talking apes when every other studio said no. It was a huge hit, but Zanuck was ultimately sacked by his own father when other films flopped (picture courtesy of the Kobal Collection, © Universal Pictures).

*Right: Legendary Hollywood tough guy Edward G. Robinson was the original choice to play the role of orang-utan Dr Zaius and agreed to a screen test to prove audiences would take the make-up seriously (picture courtesy of Loyola Marymount University, © Twentieth Century Fox).*

*Below: As Hollywood's top publicist Arthur P. Jacobs (right) helped craft Marilyn Monroe's legend, before setting up his own film company. He is pictured in front of the Lawgiver statue with (left to right) associate producer Mort Abrahams, Charlton Heston and Edward G. Robinson, who is sporting the beard that ended his involvement in the film (from the personal collection of Mort Abrahams).*

*Left: You put your left leg in... On location on the Utah-Arizona border, director Franklin J. Schaffner outlines his plans to Charlton Heston and Mort Abrahams (from the personal collection of Mort Abrahams, © Twentieth Century Fox).*

*Below: Charlton Heston's spaceship crashes in a landscape he might have recognised from John Ford's classic westerns (from the personal collection of Luiz Saulo Adami, © Twentieth Century Fox).*

*Above: The apes were heading for the record books even before filming began. Scenes needed as many as 200 gorillas, chimps and orang-utans and $1 million was allocated for make-up – more than Arthur Jacobs's original budget for the whole film (picture courtesy of Loyola Marymount University, © Twentieth Century Fox).*

*Above: Apes and humans prove peaceful coexistence is possible with a quick hand of cards between shots (picture courtesy of the Kobal Collection, © Twentieth Century Fox).*

*Above: Ape City was initially constructed in miniature, with inspiration coming from the organic curves of Spanish architect Antonio Gaudi and from caves in Turkey (from the personal collection of Luiz Saulo Adami, © Twentieth Century Fox).*

*Left: The ape civilization was constructed at the Fox ranch in Malibu Canyon, which provided outdoor locations for a string of productions from* How Green Was My Valley *to* MASH *(from the personal collection of Luiz Saulo Adami, © Twentieth Century Fox).*

*Above: These were turbulent times, with violence and conflict across the planet, and Dr Zaius prided himself on keeping up with the news. The cigarette-holder was not an affectation however, but a necessity to avoid ruining the elaborate make-up (picture courtesy of the Kobal Collection, © Twentieth Century Fox).*

*Above: Associate producer Mort Abrahams may be the one with the script,*
*but the ape has the club... and is several steps higher on the evolutionary scale*
*(from the personal collection of Mort Abrahams, © Twentieth Century Fox).*

that stretched him as an actor. Sometimes they stretched him too far. He was too stiff for comedy, though that stiffness, and his monolithic profile, could be made to work well in dramatic context, if the film and role were right and he had a good director. Like John Wayne, the typical Heston character knew right from wrong, and increasingly had to do what he had to do, without sitting around and fretting. He was the polar opposite of Jack Lemmon, almost. David Thomson puts it neatly in *A Biographical Dictionary of Film* when he says: 'But just as he seems slightly musclebound the longer he talks, so as an athletic hero his greatest distinction was the suggestion that he had hankerings to be articulate.'

Heston also had a reputation for fighting for projects he believed in, including the Orson Welles thriller *Touch of Evil* at a time when Welles had lost his sheen; though Heston was certainly not universally popular, because of his increasingly right-wing politics and what many perceived as his personal arrogance. I remember some years ago Heston and I were together at an official function at a cinema in Glasgow, after which I was due to join him, his wife, his son and a few journalists for lunch in a restaurant about half a mile away. Heston, his son Fraser and I were the only ones at the cinema – everyone else was already at the restaurant – and a limo appeared to transport him to the venue. I asked Heston's PR person if I should go in the car too, only to be told that Mr Heston had very long legs and he might need to stretch them. Heston, it seems, is literally a big star, even if he never made the Quigley top ten. In the event it was me who ended up stretching my legs, running along behind the limousine, because I could not get a taxi. Heston was the first person I approached to interview in connection with this book, but, despite encouraging noises from his people, it proved impossible to pin him down to a time, any time, over the course of four months, largely because of his commitments to the work of the National Rifle Association, championing the rights of ordinary Americans to shoot one another. 'Folks do not realize the magnitude of Mr Heston's various projects,' says his publicist, Lisa DeMatteo, 'the hectic schedule he maintains, and the fact that, at seventy-six, he is still working to make America a better place.'

It was as if, having played God, Heston was now encouraged to believe he was God. Stardom, particularly the all-singing, all-dancing Hollywood version, does weird things to people's heads. But Ted Post, who directed Heston in the second *Apes* film, *Beneath the Planet of the Apes*, maintains Heston was always like that, even when he was a complete unknown. Post remembers when he was a theatre director, going to see another actor in a flat in a rundown part of New York in the forties, and Heston meeting him at the door in his underwear and proceeding to tell him just how talented he was. 'I felt a very strong egotist,' says Post, 'who was determined to become an important actor, an important star.' Post, whose work ranges from the pilot episode of *Perry Mason* to the Dirty Harry movie *Magnum Force*, is an astute judge of character, and his impressions tie in entirely with Heston's own recollections of the period in *The Actor's Life: Journals 1956–1976*: 'We weren't crazy about the cockroaches, and our cold-water walk-up had its shortcomings, but our friends had no money and no parts and roaches, too. And you knew you were going to get the parts.' Post says: 'I felt that very strongly, and it offended me a little bit.' It would be more than twenty years before they met again and neither ever spoke about that first encounter, though Post suspects Heston remembered.

Jacobs visited Heston on 5 June 1965, with the trusty portfolio of production sketches that went everywhere with him. Heston noted in his journal that it was 'a damn full day', with two picture conferences, a television interview, a game of tennis and a couple of parties. He was immediately impressed by the sound of *Planet of the Apes*, which was very different from anything he had done before, very different in fact from anything anyone had done before, which was its problem. Science fiction still struggled with a puerile image established by Buster Crabbe in the *Flash Gordon* serials of the thirties and with the recent memory of a plague of fifties monster movies. Apes had also been a staple of thirties serials. Sci-fi cinema began way back at the dawn of cinema in the nineteenth century, and the early years of the twentieth produced Georges Méliès's *A Trip to the Moon*, a twenty-minute film that was inspired by Wells and Verne, mixed live action and pioneering special effects, and includes the classic shot of a moon with a face on it and a rocket embedded in one eye. Early sci-fi films, most notably Fritz Lang's silent masterpiece *Metropolis*, concentrated largely on the technological aspects of science fiction, then Flash Gordon, Ming the Merciless and Buck Rogers took over. In the fifties a string of films, including *Invasion of the Body Snatchers, The Incredible Shrinking Man* and *The Day the Earth Stood Still*, used sci-fi to pose philosophical questions about conformity and individuality (and Communism), man's place in the universe and, increasingly, man's potential for destruction on a massive scale. During the same decade Shakespeare's *The Tempest* was imaginatively remade as *Forbidden Planet*. In retrospect it was arguably the golden age of science-fiction cinema, but these were mainly small-scale, thoughtful pieces, closer in tone to *The Twilight Zone* than to any big-budget blockbusters the studios were turning out. And they were virtually overshadowed by the proliferation of tacky B-movies, churned out by small independent companies to appeal to the teenage drive-in audience. With titles like *Invasion of the Saucer Men, The Amazing Colossal Man* and the notorious *Plan 9 from Outer Space*, they featured a succession of bug-eyed monsters and flying saucers, which really were, well, saucers, not so much flying as thrown in front of the camera. By 1964 sci-fi had sunk to the depths of *Santa Claus Conquers the Martians*. One of the few cinematic sights more risible than a bit-part actor walking around with a funny face and an arthritic gait, pretending to be a Martian, was the same actor in a hairy outfit, waving his arms around, going 'oo-oo-oo', pretending to be a gorilla. *King Kong* used a stop-motion model and proved a one-off. There were occasional movie appearances by real apes, notably in the Ronald Reagan comedy *Bedtime for Bonzo*, though often in the forties and fifties they were played by humans for laughs, in the likes of W.C. Fields's *Never Give a Sucker an Even Break* and Abbott and Costello's *Africa Screams*. In the sixties apes were virtually extinct and horror superseded sci-fi as the teenager's preferred genre. It would be a huge leap from *The Incredible Shrinking Man* and *Santa Claus Conquers the Martians* to *Star Wars* and *Alien*, an inconceivable leap perhaps without *Planet of the Apes*.

Within two days Heston had read the script and the novel and had expressed his interest in playing the arrogant hero. Having noted in his journals that he read the screenplay on a plane to Chicago, he then claims in his autobiography, *In the*

*Arena*, that there was no script, not even a treatment, just sketches and a pitch. 'Still, I smelled a good film in it,' he writes. His recollections inevitably centre around his involvement. He once observed that he was more like the hero of *Planet of the Apes* than any other character he had ever played, though there were differences. Heston did not share the character's cynicism or sense of despair – not only had he played Moses and John the Baptist, but he would go on to make a TV series called *Charlton Heston Presents the Bible*. But Heston was perfect casting, not just because of his film track record as a totem of Western civilization, but because of his towering and unselfconscious arrogance. The film-makers wanted to show how low man could fall, and no man had farther to fall than Heston.

With Heston came Franklin J. Schaffner, who had recently directed him in *The War Lord*, an intimate historical film, a psychological drama, that attempted to break away from epic stereotypes, with Heston as an eleventh-century Norman knight disintegrating in the face of sexual lust and primitive beliefs he cannot comprehend. Schaffner is not a name that exactly leaps off the page. After *Planet of the Apes* he won an Oscar for *Patton*, but his name does not conjure up a mental image of the man, the way the name Polanski might, or even an image of his particular cinematic niche. Even the most inattentive reader must have noticed that Schaffner does not enter the picture until after Pierre Boulle, Arthur P. Jacobs, Rod Serling, Blake Edwards, Don Peters, Mort Abrahams and Charlton Heston have all made some sort of mark on proceedings. And, of course, Dick Zanuck had already flitted in and out of the picture. Schaffner's late involvement, and his relatively low profile in terms of the story of the film, does not exactly provide much evidence for the French auteur theory, which holds that the director is the author of a film. As director, Schaffner had an enormous influence on the finished product, and it would be downright stupid to suggest otherwise. But *Planet of the Apes* surely owes more to the vision of Arthur P. Jacobs than any other individual. And then there were Boulle and Serling. And the contributions of John Chambers, who won an Oscar for the ape make-up, and William Creber, who was responsible for the set design and overall look of the film, were obviously much more important to the success of this film than, say, the contributions of the make-up and design people on *12 Angry Men*. *Planet of the Apes* is the perfect example of cinema as a collaborative art form.

Schaffner, like so many of the key players, is no longer around to speak for himself, but he was cultured, polite, level-headed and quietly effective, without the ego of a Polanski, Huston or Heston, and totally lacking in bullshit. It is a wonder he ever got anywhere in Hollywood. One critic pointed out that *Planet of the Apes* underscored the fear that the world was headed for self-destruction, while *Patton* illustrated the process, and asked him if he was conscious of the philosophical connection. 'No,' Schaffner replied. He curtly dismissed the suggestion that *Apes* was forecasting the future. 'It seemed to me that the story didn't work unless one assumed that the world had been destroyed ... I don't think that anybody is ever pessimistic enough to say that the world will be destroyed. But for purposes of story telling, licence was taken, and therefore one told the story about what was happening on the planet after the world had been bombed out of existence.' Like so many of the individuals in this story, Schaffner came from television. He was born in Tokyo in 1920, to mission-ary parents, but grew up mainly in Pennsylvania. During the Second World War he served with the US Navy's amphibious forces in North Africa and Europe and with the Office of Strategic Services, the predecessor of the CIA, in India, Burma and China. He joined CBS in the early days of television and worked on 400 shows ranging from baseball and political conventions to dramas, and he directed the TV versions of *Twelve Angry Men* (1954), *The Caine Mutiny Court Martial* and Rod Serling's *Patterns* (both 1955). In the early sixties he moved into films and brought with him a reputation for gritty contemporary subject matter. *The War Lord* was a change of direction for him after *The Stripper* and the polit-ical drama *The Best Man*. He saw *Planet of the Apes* as a new chal-lenge and said he would direct it, though he doubted whether any studio would ever back it.

Edward G. Robinson also read the script and expressed an interest in playing Zaius, the sinister orang-utan who serves as Thomas's main adversary in the film. Jacobs now had a script by Rod Serling, probably the best-known writer of screen science fiction in the world at that time, the commitment of Oscar-winner Charlton Heston and Hollywood legend Edward G. Robinson, and a director. And Jacobs and Abrahams were not slow to keep Zanuck informed of developments, despite his threat to throw them off the lot if they ever mentioned *Planet of the Apes* again. Jacobs even managed to get Heston and Robinson to agree to a screen test, to test the ape make-up. It took place at the beginning of March 1966. Everyone agreed the test was a success, but by the end of the month Heston was already writing the film off. Fox budgeted the film at between $3.2 million and $3.4 million – double the 1963 budget, which had been deemed too high. Come the summer Jacobs and Abrahams were once again trotting round the other studios, although this time they had the Fox screen test to back up their pitch. Abrahams had even managed to breathe new life into the old portfolio of production sketches, by linking them together on a 16mm film, made surreptitiously with Fox equipment. Actor Paul Frees (who would later supply the apocalyptic voice-over at the end of *Beneath the Planet of the Apes*) provided a voice-over outlining the story. Every time a new executive was appointed to any studio, Abrahams set off with his little film.

At the same time he was working on *Doctor Dolittle*, which finally began shooting in England in June. Rex Harrison was not the easiest star to work with. And for much of this film he was in a particularly fractious mood, which may have been largely as a result of his treatment from his co-stars, who proved to be no respecters of the Hollywood pecking order. They had their own pecking order. He was pecked, scratched and bitten by everything from a chimp to a squirrel, which needed a stiff gin to calm it down and keep it still long enough to be filmed. Abrahams regularly had to pick Harrison up and dust him down. A million dollars was spent on animals, and a chimp was laboriously taught to cook bacon and eggs, but British quarantine regulations necessitated a second set of animals for the English leg of the production, and the little pig grew so fast that it had to be replaced every month. It rained fifty-one days out of the fifty-six that the production spent on location in England. As if that were not bad enough, Abrahams had to contend with a violent local resistance movement that took a lead from the tactics of the French underground during the war. The film recreated Doctor Dolittle's little fishing village, Puddleby-on-the-Marsh, in the picturesque setting of Castle Combe, in Wiltshire, but Castle Combe was not on the sea, so the village brook was dammed to create a lagoon for the fishing boats. In his autobiography Harrison recalls an attempt to blow it up involving 'one gallant military gentleman'. The gent in question was the young Ranulph Fiennes. The exploit ended his military career, though he later became famous as an explorer. Production would drag on for a year, in the West Indies and California, and went way over budget, but by that time Jacobs and Abrahams finally had a deal with Fox on their other animal movie – the one where the animals could at least be relied upon not to pee on the sets or bite the stars.

On 24 August 1966, six months after the Heston–Robinson tests, another Fox science-fiction film opened at cinemas in the United States and proved surprisingly popular. *Fantastic Voyage* was an offbeat story with Raquel Welch and Heston's *Ben-Hur* co-star Stephen Boyd as part of a medical team who are reduced to microscopic size and injected into the bloodstream of a defecting Czech scientist to tackle a blood clot on his brain. During their adventures they have to contend with hurricanes in his lungs, huge waves in his heart and white corpuscles that regard them, quite rightly, as a foreign body that should be eliminated. It was directed by Richard Fleischer, a Zanuck favourite who directed *Compulsion* and was at that moment working on *Doctor Dolittle*. Box-office reports did not figure quite so prominently in the press then and the studios did not do the same exhaustive analyses of the opening figures that they do now. Jacobs collected cuttings from all the papers, particularly those dealing with box-office figures, and mounted them in a presentation book. 'We went up to Dick with what we saw as the final pitch,' says Abrahams, 'and I said: "Dick, I know of your edict, but this is the last time you will hear about *Planet of the Apes*." And he said: "Come on, out of the office," in a good-natured way ... And I said: "You've got to listen to me and you've got to see this." And we gave him Arthur's book and he looked through it and he said: "I'll tell you what I'll do ..." He said: "If *Voyage* has legs, lets talk about *Apes*." He said: "Come back in three or four weeks and we'll see."'

In September 1966, almost exactly a month after *Fantastic Voyage* opened, Dick Zanuck gave the go-ahead for *Planet of the Apes* starring Charlton Heston and Edward G. Robinson.

# CHAPTER SIX

# THE SHAFTING OF EDWARD G.

Without Edward G. Robinson *Planet of the Apes* might never have been made. Hollywood legend is a much-abused term, but no one would dispute the use of it for the star of *Little Caesar, Double Indemnity* and *Key Largo.* Robinson had been born Emmanuel Goldenberg in Bucharest in 1893, but his family emigrated to the United States when he was a boy. He attended the American Academy of Dramatic Arts, but was hardly typical film-star material. His face was broad and fleshy, and he stood just five foot, five inches tall. He worked extensively in theatre before the role of gangster Rico in *Little Caesar* made him a star in his late thirties. Rico was the first of a string of gangster roles and other tough-guy parts that the wee guy filled as snugly as a hand in a glove. Robinson and Heston were co-stars in Cecil B. DeMille's *The Ten Commandments* in 1956 and were both long past the stage of their careers when they had to do screen tests. But they agreed to a test for *Planet of the Apes* to prove to Twentieth Century Fox that actors would be taken seriously in ape make-up, though Heston's agent advised him against it and Heston himself was having second thoughts. Associate producer Mort Abrahams had adapted a few pages of Rod Serling's script for the purpose, and every page was stamped 'Confidential: Do not reveal contents of this script'. Heston just had to stand around, towering over Robinson and looking butch in a safari shirt. Robinson, on the other hand, had to pontificate on man's place in the scheme of things, while made up to look like an orang-utan – an orang-utan dressed in a shirt and tie and a white lab coat.

The test was budgeted at $7,455, about half of which would be spent on make-up. Zanuck approved it in December 1965, but it did not take place until 8 March 1966, under the direction of Franklin J. Schaffner, in conditions of utmost secrecy. Producer Arthur P. Jacobs wanted the actors made up on the stage itself, so no one would see them, and he made special arrangements to keep the film and photographs in his own safe. It might be embarrassing for Heston and Robinson if it leaked out that they were making a screen test for a film which did not even have an official go-ahead; and Jacobs, ever the publicist, did not want any pictures of his apes appearing in the press before he was ready to maximize their impact in an organized fashion, shortly before release of the film. Robinson's make-up was the work of Ben Nye, head of Fox's make-up department. He would hardly be mistaken for a real orang-utan – what he does look like, with his orange hair and whiskers and flattened nose, is a cross between an orang-utan and Edward G. Robinson. The roles of Cornelius and Zira were played by Fox contract players James Brolin (the future Mr Barbra Streisand) and Linda Harrison (the future Mrs Richard Zanuck), whose make-up was much less effective. With bushy eyebrows and exaggerated chins, they look more like something out of a police Identikit file than chimpanzees. The orang-utan make-up does nothing to diminish Robinson's natural authority, however, as he declares: 'Man here was an animal. He had no civilization. He wore no clothes. He thought no thoughts. He spoke no language.' It is mere speculation now, but this was the sort of role and the sort of performance, at the tail-end of a great actor's career, that might just have won him an Oscar. Robinson once said: 'Some people have youth, some have beauty, I have menace.' Although Robinson was small he still had more menace in his pinkie than Heston had in his whole body. The menace had grown subtler with the passing of the years, but it was still there, under the surface, under the orange hair. Dick Zanuck had been worried audiences would laugh at actors in ape make-up. When Jacobs screened his test footage no one dared laugh at Robinson.

It would be another year before the film started shooting, but *Planet of the Apes* took a huge step forward that day. By the spring of 1967 the script had been polished, new make-up processes had been developed to further improve the look of the apes, and Heston and Robinson had been joined by an impressive supporting cast, including former child star Roddy McDowall, as Cornelius. But in April, just one month before shooting began, Heston would note in his journals: 'Eddie Robinson feels very claustrophobic about the ape make-up … we may move to Maurice Evans.' Narrating the 1998 documentary *Behind the Planet of the*

*Apes,* Roddy McDowall, said: 'With the start of actual filming draw-ing near, the production was hit by the unexpected loss of actor Edward G. Robinson. Voicing concerns over the lengthy make-up process, he decided to withdraw from the role of Dr Zaius.' Heston added: 'He said "My heart's shot, I'm too old," and he said "That make-up just drove me crazy. I couldn't possibly do that day after day."' Correspondence in several archives refers discreetly to the need to resolve 'the Edward G. Robinson situation'. Everyone to whom I spoke told me the same story – Robinson withdrew because of ill health. He was in his seventies and had suffered a serious heart attack in 1962, so that seemed to make sense. Except Robinson did not slink off to the retirement home, but seemed to be working harder than ever. In the biography *Little Caesar,* Alan L. Gansberg says work was flowing in at this time, mentions *Planet of the Apes* briefly, in passing, and then notes: 'In all he had six films released in 1968 [the same year as *Planet of the Apes*], topping his previous highs.' And yet everyone to whom I spoke said he was seriously ill. Or at least almost everyone.

Robinson's contribution to *Planet of the Apes* was invaluable, but his was a supporting role and he was not cheap. His deal was for $150,000 – which made him the second highest paid actor on the film, after Heston, who was to get $250,000 against 10 per cent of the gross. By way of comparison, McDowall was getting $40,000; Kim Hunter, the Oscar-winning actress who played Zira, was on $25,000; and Lou Wagner, who played Lucius, was to get $500 a week, with a guarantee of only one week's work. Following the test scenes, Fox's primary concern was cost. In the summer of 1966 Fox were still prevaricating and Jacobs was growing desperate. In July, Jacobs contacted a production manager in England and took the initial steps towards moving the shoot across the Atlantic to take advantage of a more favourable financial climate, including the Eady Levy, money siphoned off from box-office receipts and used to subsidize new British films. On 24 August, the very day *Fantastic Voyage* opened, he came up with some very specific proposals for Fox to help bring the budget down. Shoot in England. Dump Franklin J. Schaffner. And dump Edward G. Robinson.

Schaffner was costing $75,000 up front and another $50,000 later, and Jacobs and Zanuck discussed the possibility of replacing him with Sidney Furie, director of *The Young Ones* and *The Ipcress*

*File.* One of the problems was that Schaffner was Heston's choice. It was unlikely Heston was just going to stand by while his buddy, who had already directed the test footage, was replaced by someone whose main attraction was that he was cheap. Jacobs had thought of that. In his memo, Jacobs suggests: 'Our excuse (and an accurate one) could be that we need an English director to qualify for Eady.' And then there was Robinson. 'There is an allocation of $150,000 for Edward G. Robinson as Dr Zaius,' says Jacobs. 'I feel strongly that a good English actor should play the Doctor, rather than a recognizable star, and therefore figure that the $150,000 allocated for Zaius should represent $50,000 (or less), and the extra $100,000 utilized to convert the picture from black and white to colour.' In September 1966 when Zanuck gave the go-ahead for the film it was as a UK production, with Eady Levy money. By that point he and Abrahams had got as far as outlining a severance deal for Robinson, with a pay-off and a promise of another film in the future.

But there were fears that it could get messy and end with legal action. Robinson was a Hollywood legend, a Hollywood legend who had dressed up as an orang-utan to help a near-novice film producer get his picture made. The press, and the public, would not take kindly to the idea of a studio replacing a Hollywood legend with an English actor because he was cheaper. When make-up director John Chambers started in January 1967, Robinson was still very much on the picture. Schaffner was still director. And, of course, ultimately the film was shot in California and on the Utah–Arizona border, not in England.

Fox's own Ben Nye was responsible for the make-up in the Heston–Robinson test, but the producers wanted an expert for the film. Overtures were made to Stuart Freeborn, who was working on Stanley Kubrick's *2001: A Space Odyssey*, the other big sci-fi film of the time. *2001* included an opening sequence featuring primitive humans. A formal approach was also made to Kubrick's company, Hawk Films, asking for their co-operation and advice, but Kubrick saw the two films as rivals and Freeborn was ordered not to talk to anyone from *Planet of the Apes*. Instead Jacobs and Abrahams turned to John Chambers, who had a solid track record of creature make-up in sci-fi TV shows such as *The Outer Limits* and *Star Trek*, where he was responsible for the design of Mr Spock's ears. Chambers came from Chicago-Irish stock and trained as a commercial artist and sculptor before serving as a medical technician during the Second World War, working on prosthetics and facial reconstructions. 'When I would get them, they would have ears torn off, side of the head torn off, anything you can imagine,' he told me when I went to visit him early in 2001 in the motion-picture industry hospital in Woodland Hills, California, not far from the Fox ranch, where he worked on *Planet of the Apes* more than thirty years earlier. Chambers was a big, popular, happy-go-lucky individual, noted for speaking his mind, but a stroke had confined him to a wheelchair and he was paralysed on one side.

Working with injured soldiers, he built a reputation as a miracle man, who could do just about anything, but there were limits. 'One time I got a guy: he was driving in a Jeep and he drove over a landmine, and it blew up right under the Jeep, right under him. The floor plate, which was a real heavy metal plate, came up and took a slice of face right off. And the guy is alive, he isn't dead. He can't talk or anything, but he's alive ... They wanted me to make him a whole face, like he was, from photographs ... I told them: "We shouldn't do it, it won't work with his family and it'll make them upset." But I did make the face and it looked like his photograph.' Chambers reconstructed the face, with a false nose and lips and cheeks, so the man looked just the way he did in his photograph. But, just like in the photograph, he could never change his expression. 'This was the impossible thing – no movement. I couldn't, at the time. Today you might get good animation, but this guy ... I says: "I'm not going to tell you that that's going to work." I kept telling him negatively: "This was something that I'm not able to give you." And what he did, he wanted to go home to the mother. She wanted to see him.' Chambers pauses in his story as vivid and painful memories take more definite form in his mind. 'He got home, got off the plane, got down, and the mother was in the crowd waiting for him. When she saw him, she fainted. She was shocked because it was a mannequin. So he turned around and got out ... I never forgot that. It was awful.' It was a morbid business, so Chambers headed west to try his luck in movies and television. An Oscar and numerous other awards sit by his TV in testimony to his success. Many regard him as the true genius behind *Planet of the Apes*. He developed new techniques on that film that would push back the frontiers of make-up. And, like every great, mad inventor, Chambers experimented on himself.

There was a long tradition of actors appearing in Hollywood movies in ape costumes, but usually these were comedies or B-movies: the actors were not appearing in principal roles, nor were they required to speak, just grunt. Previously actors playing apes simply wore masks. Chambers had to devise a new type of make-up in which the ape's lips would seem to form the words that the actor was delivering. Chambers also knew, from his bitter experience with the Jeep driver, that there was a big difference between a mask that covered the whole face and individual false features when it came to the ability of the subject to express emotion. His apes had to be realistic, but at least they did not have to look so realistic that people might mistake them for real twentieth-century apes – over the centuries the apes in the story had taken on many of the cultural attributes of man. There was therefore a dramatic justification, as well as a practical necessity, for building ape features around the human features of the actors. But Chambers believed that, even if they acted like men, his characters should look like ape versions of the actors, rather than just hairy versions. He began with Ben Nye's design for Edward G. Robinson in the test, dismissing the alternative 'Neanderthal' look worn by Brolin and Harrison as 'silly'. 'We carried the evolutionary process only very slightly beyond what you might call "basic ape",' he says. The make-up, at least for actors with speaking roles, was going to have to be glued, piece by piece, to the actor's skin. Chambers began by sculpting prototypes for a flexible rubber jaw, complete with false teeth, that would fit over the actor's own jaw and allow him or her to speak, not grunt or mumble, but speak articulately in a normal voice. The extension of the upper jaw also made the nose look shorter. Chambers experimented on himself and on extras, but was instructed to avoid black actors, because they might be offended at the idea of being used as models for apes. In fact they were offended by the loss of work and the policy was abandoned. Chambers and his team worked round the clock to perfect the designs and art director William Creber tried to help by borrowing a chimp from the set of *Lost in Space* and taking it to Chambers to study.

Having perfected the design, Chambers had to execute it.

'We began by making a moulage, a plaster likeness of the actor's face,' says Chambers. 'We poured a gelatin-like substance over their faces, and this solidifies in a few minutes. Then we removed this and we could thus have a negative face mould. Into this we'd pour artificial stone, a plaster that withstands heat and is five times as hard as plaster of Paris. So now we have an actual three-dimensional bust of the respective actor.' That was the starting point for each individual ape character. Lou Wagner recalls the process in further detail: 'Johnny would take that life mask and he would give it to a sculptor … The different additional parts that they needed to change my face into Lucius were then moulded … My chin had to be higher and my big eyebrows and my big nose, all those additions were then fired every day in the kiln.' The individual features, the make-up pieces, needed to transform human into ape were referred to as 'appliances'. 'It took, like, eight hours to make an appliance, and if something was wrong with that, they had to go right back in and spend another eight hours cooking another appliance,' says Wagner. 'I think I had four, because the main appliance went around my upper lip and my eyes and my eyebrows.' This appliance was a T-shape, which also covered the nose, but left the cheeks and flesh under the eyes bare. This exposed flesh left considerable scope for actors to wrinkle their faces and express emotion, scope they would not have had if they had been wearing an ordinary full-face mask. 'And then the jaw piece was added, that's two, and then my ears, so that's four, and everything else was layered and made up and, of course, the hair was laid over it.'

Chambers had wanted hair from China, because it was particularly strong and wiry, but the authorities refused to allow him to import 'Communist hair', so he had to make do with other Oriental sources. He dismisses the suggestion of actor James Gregory, who played Ursus in *Beneath the Planet of the Apes*, that Fox starlets were having their hair trimmed, on order, to service the film. The actors wore wigs and hair was also pasted on to the face. The naked skin and the rubber appliances had to be painted the same colour, but there was a recurring problem of paint cracking and peeling on the appliances. Chambers looked around for alternative types of paint. 'I would look at a small balloon that has advertising on it. You look at it and you blow it up. And the advertising, from about half an inch, is blown up. And I says: "I've got to know what they put on balloons ..." It's like everything I see, I wondered – does that help me in what I'm doing?' In the course of his work Chambers developed a new paint, in which the particles did not join together, allowing the actor's skin to breathe; he developed a new type of foam rubber, which allowed heat and sweat through; and he developed a new gum. He attributes a lot of breakthroughs to common sense and simply thinking about solutions for what were new problems for make-up artists. 'If you are a plumber, you are meant to fit any kind of pipe,' he says, with characteristic modesty.

Different actors reacted in different ways to the ordeal of being made up as an ape. Wagner was a newcomer, getting his big break, and the whole experience was exciting. Julie Harris, who had co-starred with James Dean in *East of Eden* and was scheduled to play Zira, took one look at the make-up, declared she could not possibly act in it and walked out, never to be seen again. Make-up was a very long process, which initially took five or six hours, and never came down below three or four, even after Chambers hit on the simple expedient of spraying paint on the appliances before they were put on the actor's face rather than afterwards. Ape actors were going to have to turn up for make-up in the middle of the night, so they would be ready to shoot in the morning. 'They would get into the make-up chair and they would doze a little and they would wake up and they would doze again,' recalls Mort Abrahams. 'On the first day Kim and Roddy were being made up, Roddy came in and was absolutely manic. He was jumping around, making the weirdest noises, jumping up and down on furniture, going to the point where I was really worried. This was not just joking around and, when he finally calmed down, I went: "What went on with you?" He said: "I've just had the strangest experience I've ever had. I would see something strange, close my eyes, wake up again, and see something else strange. And then finally, when I woke, when the make-up was finished, there was something in the mirror that had nothing to do with me. I was just flipping out."'

Harris's replacement was Kim Hunter, the New York actress who had won an Oscar when she and Marlon Brando reprised their original stage roles in the film version of *A Streetcar Named*

*Desire*, although she too had problems with the make-up. Abrahams remembers her first day: 'She ran to me and threw her arms around me and cried and cried. She could not adjust at that moment to what was going on with her visage.' Hunter loved the whole idea of *Planet of the Apes*, and the challenge of playing an intellectual chimpanzee, but she found the make-up so difficult that she needed drugs to get through filming, not cannabis, which was beginning to appear on some film sets around this time, but something with an assured source of supply to soothe her nerves. 'I said: "You know it's a marvellous script and I love the role, Dr Zira." But I said: "You know, I mean, they're apes, they're chimps, and how the hell are they going to do that?" And my agent said: "Oh don't worry, Kim. You know, they're smart people. They'll put some fur here and there." Anything but "fur here and there". The appliances for the face were, well, totally, I felt, absolutely enclosed; except for my eyes. And I'm a bit claustrophobic in the first place, so it was not easy, believe me. I came home and went to my doctor and said: "Oh my God I need some sort of pill or something or other to help me get through this." And he didn't believe in such pills at all, except when I told him what I went through, to have to wear these appliances, he said: "I understand." And he gave me some Valium, not a huge dose, but enough to get me through the four hours of preparation to get on set ... I said: "I mean, that's all I want it to last for, because I've got to be alert and 'with it' when we're shooting."' It took another hour and a half to get the make-up off, she says, at which point her own face was a less-than-welcome sight. 'When I got home, my face looked as if I had measles. I learned to put gentle lotions on my face at the end of the day, and that kind of helped. But by the end of the week, no, I had to have days off to let the face recover.'

It was a daunting prospect for any actor, particularly one in his seventies who was not enjoying the best of health, and Edward G. Robinson had good reason to have second thoughts about the film. But Chambers does not attribute his withdrawal to ill-health. Chambers was impressed with Robinson as an actor and liked him as a person, but there were particular problems when it came to his make-up. Robinson cultivated a neat little beard in later years. He grew it for the 1963 film *The Prize*, in which he played a Nobel Prize winner. His biographer, Alan L. Gansberg, managed to trace its creation to Tommy Furlong, the barber at the Hillcrest Country Club, though it was apparently inspired by Commander Whitehead, the international symbol of Schweppes tonics. Robinson considered it statesmanlike and sophisticated, befitting a Nobel Prize winner. He had grown a little vain, and a little cantankerous, with the passing years, and he was not for shaving it off to play an ape.

'He wanted by all means to keep his beard,' says Chambers. 'So I says: "Well, we'll try an appliance." And I says: "It won't work … It doesn't fit."' Chambers told him he simply had to lose the beard, there was no alternative. 'And, my God, he wouldn't.' Robinson would not shave it off and Chambers could not fix the ape make-up – which by now was markedly different from the make-up in the test – on to his beard. It came to a head, so to speak. 'I told the producer he would have to get rid of him,' says Chambers. 'He had to spend two hours with Edward G.' Make-up man versus Hollywood legend? Surely it was no contest. Robinson argued his case, but to no avail. Was he given an ultimatum – the beard goes or you go? 'Yeah,' says Chambers. If he had shaved off the beard, would he have been kept on the picture? 'Sure.' Chambers adds: 'He went to Disney, he was doing something else, and he was talking to the make-up man; he says: "I'll tell you, you've got a tough guy over there, called John Chambers."'

So Robinson was out, and Chambers was the fall guy, if one was needed, not that it was in anybody's interest for the true story to come out. The official line was ill-health, and few knew that Jacobs and Fox's senior management had been plotting for months to replace him with someone cheaper. But Robinson did not simply produce a doctor's note and drop out. He was paid off. The details are outlined in an internal Fox memo, dated 27 April 1967: 'With Richard Zanuck's approval, the following arrangement has been made with Edward G. Robinson. We will pay him $50,000 in settlement of the commitment Arthur Jacobs made with him to play the role of Dr Zaius in *Planet of the Apes*, and by such payment all parties shall be relieved of any further obligation.' Maurice Evans, who replaced him, signed up for a deal worth $25,000, so, even with the $50,000 pay-off, Jacobs saved $75,000. Jacobs wrote to Robinson, saying 'how terribly sorry' he was 'that things didn't work out'. He added that this was due to 'matters beyond my control' and expressed the hope that they might work together in future. They did not. Robinson did, however, work again with Heston, in a chilling little science-fiction film called *Soylent Green*. It was Robinson's final movie, made shortly before his death in 1973.

'Mother of mercy, is this the end of Rico?' Robinson asked in *Little Caesar*. As far as the *Planet of the Apes* story is concerned, Robinson's involvement was almost over, but not quite. The baby ape in *Escape from the Planet of the Apes*, who grows up to become the ape leader in the last two films, was named Caesar. It was a tribute to the Hollywood legend who played a vital role in getting the original film made.

## CHAPTER SEVEN
# HAS ANYBODY HERE SEEN KELLEY?

When he first pitched the idea of a film version of *Planet of the Apes*, producer Arthur P. Jacobs had been thinking about Ursula Andress for the role of Nova, the primitive beauty with whom the spaceman hero becomes involved. It is the lead female role, if you exclude Zira, who is covered in fur, but with the start of filming just weeks away the role remained uncast, at least officially. 'We weren't going for, nor do I think we could have gotten, any major star, or major personality, like a Raquel Welch at the time,' says Fox studio boss Dick Zanuck, 'because it was a part that was showy, but it had no dialogue.' Jacobs's alternative was an international competition to find 'the most fantastic beauty to be discovered for films'. But, with 'the Edward G. Robinson situation' to resolve, the need to recast the key roles of Zaius and Zira, and continuing concerns about script, make-up and costs, Jacobs and Abrahams simply did not have time to organize an international search for a new star. 'Unfortunately we have been so swamped by production problems, we will not have time to come to Europe on this casting job and so we will have to do the best we can by casting here,' Jacobs admitted in a memo to Twentieth Century Fox. 'He always had showmanship ideas like that,' says Zanuck, 'like David Selznick trying to find another Scarlett, but you know that was more talk than any kind of action.' Heston expressed concern in his journals about the continuing absence of a co-star. But a solution was already at hand. Dick Zanuck did what studio bosses, including his father, had done since the movies began. He gave the role to his girlfriend, Linda Harrison, a former Miss Maryland.

'I don't recall quite frankly whose idea it was,' says Zanuck. 'She was a very beautiful young actress that we had put under contract.' Jacobs may have thought he was running out of time to find a new star for the role of Nova, but Zanuck had already promised the role to Harrison even before he decided to go ahead with the film, before she had played Zira in the screen test.

'The heads of the studio are very powerful, and I was his lady,' says Harrison. She had shot her first screen test at Fox less than a year before the *Apes* test, to determine whether she might have a future in the movies. Zanuck decided she did. 'He saw my screen test and he said: "Sign her up,"' she remembers. 'The first time we met in person was actually at the premiere of *The Agony and the Ecstasy*, which was a Charlton Heston film on the great artist Michelangelo. So that's when I first met Dick and he laid eyes on my person and started pursuing me.' She had appeared in a few minor film roles and was 'Cheerleader No. 2' in the *Batman* TV series in 1966, but Nova was to be her first big role. Harrison was undaunted by the prospect of appearing almost naked (or perhaps even naked, for the question of costumes remained a moot point), in a role with no dialogue. 'I would have done anything to get a role in a movie. That's how basically actors are when they're just starting out.' Belying the beauty-queen stereotype, Harrison is candid, articulate and intelligent.

The biggest challenge lay before those actors who were going to play apes. They not only had to act convincingly as chimpanzees, gorillas and orang-utans, they also had to employ a similar style. Lou Wagner, who played Lucius, told me that before his first scene he had a meeting with director Franklin J. Schaffner and Roddy McDowall. 'Roddy showed me the walk that they had worked out,' he says, 'and just by accident it was the exact same walk that I had worked out.' But it was no mere coincidence. The first thing Wagner did when he got the part was go and study the chimps at LA Zoo. Meanwhile McDowall was doing the same in San Diego and Kim Hunter was doing her best to strike up some sort of rapport with a chimp in New York. Hunter was an old girl of the Actors Studio, the famous New York establishment that pioneered 'method' acting in American movies and plays, the approach in which the actor seeks to become, rather than simply play, a character. Hunter and McDowall were both hugely experienced actors. Hunter had been on stage since her teens; McDowall started even younger, making his film debut in his native England, in *Murder in the Family* in 1938, at the age of nine. Darryl Zanuck spotted him and turned him into a major child star at Twentieth Century Fox. Early hits included *How Green Was My Valley* and *Lassie Come Home*. His co-stars were often of the animal variety, but he was still playing teenagers in his mid-thirties. He broadened his range on the New York stage and returned to movies in adult character roles. Hunter's career was even more up-and-down and she made her mark in the movies after a transatlantic journey in the opposite direction, playing the American wireless operator with whom RAF pilot David Niven falls in love in Powell and Pressburger's *A Matter of Life and Death* (aka *Stairway to Heaven*). She returned to America and the role of Kowalski's much put-upon wife Stella in both the stage and screen versions of *A Streetcar Named Desire*. Her career stalled when her name appeared on the Hollywood blacklist and she made very few major films in the decade preceding *Apes*.

Suddenly ape houses across the United States were full of actors, all taking notes – and the apes did not necessarily like the attention of their celebrity visitors. 'I went to our Bronx Zoo and found a chimp, bless his heart, and we didn't get along, let me put it that way,' says Hunter, with just a hint of regret in her voice. 'First time seeing him, he was fine, kind of watching how he moved, that sort of thing … After I came by to watch him, two, three times, he became very self-conscious. And in fact, after about the second time, I think it was, when he saw me coming into the room he just turned his back on me, like "would you get out of here". I learned to follow groups of kids that would be coming in to see all the apes, and I'd kind of hide behind them. But he found me and then he'd always turn his back on me and everybody as well. And I understood it completely when we were shooting because people are … they don't consider that the ape may not be happy at all. I couldn't believe it, what they were doing with us. These studio people would bring people in, because it was a marvellous sort of film they were making, it was all different and everything … These people come up and would kind of grab your ears and say: "Oh that isn't real, that isn't your ear, is it?" and poke at it, and so forth, not considering we were people under all this.' Suddenly she empathized with the chimp in the zoo and his dismay at being treated like a painting in an art gallery. 'The fact that I could see that behaviour and believe it, and know what he was feeling, made it very much easier to treat our chimps not as storybook characters. They were real characters, and behaved the way real – you want to say human beings, but I don't mean that, I mean live creatures – would behave under various circumstances. And that's what we were.'

Edward G. Robinson was replaced in the other main ape role by Maurice Evans, a distinguished Welsh Shakespearean, who was best known for acting and producing on stage, but had recently worked with Heston and Schaffner on *The War Lord*. The producers deliberately plumped for mature theatre actors to bring authority to the roles of the other orang-utans, though James Whitmore, who played the president of the assembly, had been the tobacco-chewing sergeant in *Battleground* and also appeared in the film of *Oklahoma!*. One legacy of Robinson's screen test was the policy of deliberately hiring small actors as apes – Lou Wagner, for instance, was only five foot two. Heston would tower above them and his treatment at their hands would be all the more humiliating. Neither Jacobs nor Fox was ever going to take on board Boulle's belated idea of a spaceship with a crew of a hundred men and women, but the suggestion did cause Jacobs to consider the nature of the crew and how it should reflect humanity in the distant future. It was decided to make one of the astronauts a woman, very much a token gesture as she was dead on arrival on the planet, and another was to be black, though Jeff Burton's character would not last much longer than his female colleague. Jacobs was aware not just of the civil rights movement and advances black Americans were making in society, but of the growing black audience and the need to give them a character with whom to identify, however briefly. Black people had made advances, but there were still very few black Hollywood actors, and Jacobs was never going to get Sidney Poitier, so he had to look beyond the usual talent pool to fill the role of Dodge. Jeff Burton's day job was as a Los Angeles parole officer. Heston was on $250,000 plus profits, the character of Dodge was budgeted at $6,750, but Burton signed for $2,890. More money saved.

Concerns about costs and script ran hand in hand. When art director William Creber, who was to be responsible for the 'look' of the film, joined the production the story was set in a technologically advanced civilization. 'My initial idea was to go to Brasilia,' he says, 'because at that time it hadn't been used much in a film.' The ultra-modern Brazilian capital had been inaugurated only a few years earlier and Creber believed he could adapt it to fit the descriptions in Serling's scripts and Boulle's novel. One possibility was the addition of overhead monkey bars, which simian pedestrians might use to pass over the traffic. When the apes were not swinging on bars, they were flying around in helicopters and it was all beginning to look prohibitively expensive. When the producers finally did opt for a futuristic urban setting in the fourth *Apes* film, *Conquest of the Planet of the Apes*, it would be in Century City, right on Fox's doorstep, on land it had once owned, rather than in South America. Michael Wilson, a highly experienced and accomplished writer, was brought in to rework Serling's script, with a specific remit of relocating it in a more backward, and cheaper, society, and trying to make the dialogue more realistic.

Wilson was not, however, the first to rework the script after Zanuck gave the film the go-ahead in September 1966. Almost immediately Jacobs hired a young American writer called Charles Eastman, with whom he and Schaffner had already had lengthy discussions. They wanted him to develop the main characters and build up the suspense. But instead of reworking the existing drafts, Eastman took the film in a completely different direction. He opens in the spaceship, but the skeletal corpse in a spacesuit, at the controls of the craft, is more reminiscent of *Alien* than the previous *Planet of the Apes* scripts. The crew emerges from hibernation chambers as before, but Thomas is now called Command 60 Maddox. He has the dead captain's computer chip installed in his head. His colleagues include a professor called Elite 25 Petchnikoff, who is blind and has a pet monkey, and the randy Index O'Toole. Their purpose apparently includes colonization of other planets and O'Toole is keen to get started. Before long, O'Toole and a 'sleek astronette' named Index 53 Reverse Maryanne 'energetically make love on the floor'. It is weird stuff, and possibly more promising than it sounds, but the one thing it is not is *Planet of the Apes*. Eastman did a lot of research on apes and took a lot of photographs at the zoo, but he never actually wrote about them. In December he submitted twenty-seven pages, in which the crew never quite manage to leave the spaceship, and was promptly replaced by Michael Wilson.

There is a Charles Eastman registered with both the American writers' and directors' guilds. He wrote the 1970 film *Little Fauss and Big Halsy*, a story of two motorbikers, played by

Robert Redford and Michael J. Pollard, directed by Sidney Furie, whom Jacobs had considered as a cheap alternative to Franklin J. Schaffner for *Apes*. Eastman also wrote and directed *The All-American Boy*, a 1973 boxing film with Jon Voight, before more or less disappearing off the movie scene. Even his business manager did not know of any possible involvement with *Planet of the Apes*. But Eastman later phoned me to confirm he was the same young writer who struggled with *Planet of the Apes* for a few weeks in the autumn of 1966. 'I remember going in to see Arthur Jacobs, and his enthusiasm,' he says, 'and he had wonderful illustrations.' Eastman accepted the assignment, but when he got home the only way he felt he could make sense of it was to play up the comedy and turn it into a spoof. It was his own decision to go off in a different direction. 'I remember the reason Arthur didn't want to pursue it with me was I took a rather light approach, and his explanation was he needed Charlton Heston, and Charlton Heston didn't have a sense of humour ... To tell you the truth, I think I was lost.' Eastman was to have a recurring problem matching his vision of films to that of producers. 'Generally I took them a little too far afield for the people.' His last film credit was on the Hal Ashby movie *Second-Hand Hearts*, which was released in the US in 1981, having lain around for a couple of years. Its original title gives an indication of Eastman's offbeat perspective on life and movies: it was originally called *The Hamster of Happiness*.

After three years of trotting round the studios with his sketches and arguing with an endless line-up of executives, Jacobs finally had a green light from Fox. At the end of September 1966 Zanuck set the start date as 15 May 1967, giving Jacobs just seven and a half months to polish the script, while John Chambers worked on the make-up and Bill Creber designed the ape civilization. Three months had now been wasted in which the writer took it upon himself to turn Jacobs's 'rip-roaring horror story' into 'a spoof'. The clock was ticking and Jacobs could not afford any more mistakes, no more gambles with untried young writers. Michael Wilson was an Oscar-winner, who had proven he could empathize with Pierre Boulle's offbeat sensibilities without descending into the dangerous realm of mockery. He was the principal writer on the film version of *The Bridge on the River Kwai*, but had to work on it in secret, as he was on Hollywood's political blacklist, and he could only look on in bemusement as the Academy of Motion Picture Arts and Sciences awarded his Oscar to Pierre Boulle, as described in Chapter Two.

Wilson already had one Oscar, for the 1951 film *A Place in the Sun*, a searing adaptation of Theodore Dreiser's *An American Tragedy*, with Monty Clift as a poor young man wooed away from plain mill girl Shelley Winters by the rich and beautiful socialite Liz Taylor. But even as that film was released, the mood in America was changing. Wilson, who served his country in the Marines during the Second World War, refused to answers questions before the House Un-American Activities Committee and his new film, *Salt of the Earth*, a drama about striking miners, was denounced by a Screen Writers' Guild official as 'Communist propaganda'. Wilson, the film's star Will Geer, its producer and director were all blacklisted. He fled to France and worked on European films. But he was too good for Hollywood to ignore and under a pseudonym he worked on a number of Hollywood films, including *Lawrence of Arabia*. Critic Jay Boyer argues that after his blacklisting his films were 'much less charitable toward human nature'. He and Dalton Trumbo, one of the Hollywood Ten who went to jail for their refusal to answer HUAC's questions, did get screen credit on Vincente Minnelli's 1965 romance *The Sandpiper*, though in retrospect they might have wished they had not. Wilson was not cheap – he would be almost as expensive as Rod Serling, but the producers felt they had no choice. They say that if you pay peanuts you get monkeys, but on this occasion Jacobs was going to have to pay a lot more than peanuts to get his monkeys.

Wilson regarded Serling's script as 'science-fiction melodrama, solemn and earnest in tone'. Like Eastman, he wanted to add an element of comedy, 'a measure of mordant wit and sardonic comment', but without compromising Jacobs's perception of the film as a 'rip-roaring horror story'. Wilson, like Boulle in the original novel, perceived the comic elements as satire rather than spoof, and cited *Gulliver's Travels* and *Animal Farm* by way of comparison. Wilson did, however, retain the Statue of Liberty revelations, which he saw as both satiric and tragic. By March 1967 Wilson had completed several new drafts, and it seemed that only the exact details of the ending were still under discussion. He had long arguments with Jacobs, who wanted to stick with Serling's ending, in which Thomas was killed. Jacobs managed to elicit the support of both Schaffner and Abrahams. Wilson argued that it would be anti-climactic to kill Thomas after the revelation that he was on Earth, and more effective to keep him alive, facing a grim future as 'a second Adam'. Ultimately Wilson got his way, or at least part of his way. He hated the title *Planet of the Apes*, claiming it was 'the sort of thing one might expect to see on the late show of Channel 13'. He lobbied Jacobs, Abrahams and Schaffner to change it to *The Survivors*. Or *Our Second Adam*. Or *Adam II*. Or *The Last Seed*. Anything but *Planet of the Apes*. At that point the film ended with Nova pregnant. Wilson told *Cinefantastique* magazine in 1972: 'Virtually all my work was in the final film.' The main omission, he said, was the pregnancy, though Nova's pregnancy had not been Wilson's idea, but came from the novel. Serling, with considerable input from Jacobs and, of course, the book, had already established the structure of the film. The main areas of concern which Wilson had to tackle were pacing, characterization, dialogue and tone. Critic Jay Boyer argues, in the writers volume of the *International Dictionary of Films and Filmmakers*: 'His chief weakness is his dialogue ... Never does it ring to the ear like a conversation between two individuals. But then neither does Wilson really offer us individuals ... Wilson is at his best when he's exploring the dynamics of the group.'

Changes in tone stemmed largely from his belief that the film was a satire and the apes were essentially humans. Wilson was very clear in his own mind as to how he saw the comic elements. A planet ruled by apes? This was not the comedy of Laurel and Hardy, this was the comedy of Kafka; not the comedy of slapstick, but the comedy of nightmare. First and foremost, Wilson politicized the film. He politicized the ape characters and developed tensions between the different ape species. He had baboons in an early draft, who filled the most menial jobs and were not allowed representation on the legislature. When Thomas escapes he passes baboons protesting against discrimination. The baboons did not make the final film, but the inquiry into Thomas's status, and Zira and Cornelius's association with Thomas, took on a new, sinister, heavily political dimension, raising issues of racial and religious intolerance. Accusations of heresy prompt comparisons with the Scopes Monkey Trial, when a biology teacher was charged with illegally teaching Darwin's theory of evolution, and also with the House Un-American Activities Committee's hearings into supposed Communist infiltration of Hollywood. While the Hollywood Ten went to jail, hundreds of others, including Wilson and Kim Hunter, were blacklisted for their beliefs. Make no mistake, this was payback time.

By the mid-sixties Hollywood's moral watchdogs were more concerned with the risk that the nation's youth might be corrupted by nipples than Communists. Wilson's script was sent to the Motion Picture Association of America to ensure it met the Production Code, which regulated what might and might not be shown. The MPAA pointed out that if the producers intended to use 'live animals (in our present sense of the word)' they should consult the American Humane Association. Otherwise they had only one objection. 'According to the stage directions the female "humans" in this story are described as being "bare breasted",' they observed. 'We could not approve this in a finished picture. Their breasts should be properly covered.' Starlet Angelique Pettyjohn, who appeared in the series *Star Trek*, had already posed topless in a make-up test, and Zanuck had thrown a wobbly and ordered a cover-up. In the book Nova was completely naked, and Heston noted in his journals: 'Logically, since the subhumans in the story were animals, they should have been naked,' adding: 'This was not a feasible option in 1967 and would be a distracting choice even now.' But the question remained: 'How naked can she be?' And the MPAA was giving no indication of what might constitute 'properly covered' in these unique circumstances. It was time to dig out the trusty little fur number to preserve Dick's girlfriend's modesty. It would be Heston's nudity that would cause continuing arguments during shooting and editing of the film.

The shooting script would carry just one screenwriter's name, that of Michael Wilson. But he did not write it. He undoubtedly played a major role in shaping the finished film, but he did not write that script. He finished working on *Planet of the Apes* on 28 March 1967. The shooting script is dated 5 May, and was subsequently revised on several occasions. So who wrote it? 'Michael did a fix on it, but I wasn't quite satisfied,' Abrahams told academic Gordon C. Webb in 1994, 'and then I got a third screenplay writer.

[Actually the film was now on to writer number five.] The third writer was Kelly [sic] … I can't remember his first name.'

It was John, John T. Kelley. Don't look him up in *Halliwell's*, he's not there. He had scripted *A Rage to Live*, a would-be racy melodrama, with Suzanne Pleshette as a nymphomaniac. It was panned by critics when it came out in 1965, but Abrahams knew Kelley from his television days, when Kelley worked on *Bonanza*, and the producer admired his style. 'He had a light-hearted approach, which I think the script needed,' says Abrahams. 'It was getting ponderous and he had a lovely sense of humour.' Kelley also had a reputation as what is now known as a 'script doctor', someone who will come on to a project when the screenplay is virtually complete and find a cure for the odd problem here and there. Kelley was hired to work on *Planet of the Apes* in April 1967 and stayed with it until it began shooting the following month. It was during his time on the film that the shooting script, bearing Wilson's name, was produced. Like Serling and Wilson, Kelley is dead now, but Abrahams confirms that that final script was written not by Wilson, but by Kelley – albeit that he incorporated Wilson's work, just as Wilson incorporated the work of Serling and Serling had modelled his script on Boulle's story – another illustration of the collaborative nature of movie-making.

Abrahams recalls the chain of events that followed Fox's green light (forgetting to mention the Eastman contribution for perhaps understandable reasons). 'The next process was to get a rewrite done. I think that's when I went to Michael Wilson. That didn't work out very well. There were some improvements made, but it didn't seem finished to me, particularly the dialogue.' His star was also unhappy. Heston notes in his journals on 16 April that he 'spent some time musing how to get a better script on *Apes*'. It was at that point that Abrahams called in John T. Kelley. 'He was the final one,' says Abrahams, 'though I don't think he got screenplay credit. But he did a very good job on the dialogue polish and also jiggled a few scenes here and there, which didn't seem to be working from the Michael Wilson version. So Kelley did a very good job all told, and that was the final script. There was a little twiddling around that Schaffner wanted done, and he and I worked that out together with Kelley, but basically Kelley's was the final draft.' But why is his name not on the film or even the script? Kelley was not interested in personal acclaim, says Abrahams. 'To my knowledge he never contested a credit.' Kelley's name appeared on just one more feature film, the thriller *Zigzag* in 1970. It was an ingenious, original story, with George Kennedy as a dying man who frames himself for murder so his wife can benefit from an insurance scam. Kelley did not live to build on that success. He died in 1972, at the age of fifty-one. He is now virtually forgotten, while Serling and Wilson are lionized and their supporters argue over which should get the credit. But it was John T. Kelley who wrote the script Schaffner would have in his hands when he called 'action' on the first scene in the Arizona desert in May 1967.

# CHAPTER EIGHT
# SHOOTING APES

*'You know, Chuck, I can remember when
we used to win these things.'*
Stunt co-ordinator Joe Canutt

After years of struggle Arthur P. Jacobs's dream was finally realized in May 1967, when filming began on barren desert terrain on the Arizona–Utah border, near the Grand Canyon and the western location of Monument Valley made famous by John Ford. But the first day's shooting got under way only after a delay in the make-up department. Charlton Heston had grown a beard and the hold-up was attributable to the supply and fitting of false beards for his fellow astronauts. It did not augur well. If there was a delay in dealing with such a routine item as false beards, what hope had the film of sticking to schedule when the first 'apes' arrived on set in a week's time? The sun climbed high into the sky, and temperatures soared to well over 100 degrees Fahrenheit. It was desperately hot on that bleached, alien landscape, particularly for the actors in their spacesuits and for the technicians lugging heavy camera equipment around. First one man keeled over, then another, until it looked like there would be no one left for the gorillas to hunt later in the shoot. On that first day alone five people collapsed with heat exhaustion, including actor Jeff Burton. During those hot, uncomfortable days in the desert, whenever there was a break in filming, cast and crew would all scurry to the sanctuary of trailers and any available shade, all except Heston. While lesser men were dropping like flies, Heston proved his manliness by running in the midday heat.

Franklin J. Schaffner began the film by shooting the astronauts' long trek across the desert. And then the next day he shot the astronauts' trek. And the next. And the next. Day after day he shot scenes of the three men trekking across the empty landscape. And the comment 'Company lost half day due to slow progress' became a regular refrain on the daily production reports that went back to Los Angeles. By the end of the first week the film was already a couple of days behind schedule. It was not just cast and crew who were suffering.

It had been four extremely difficult years for Arthur P. Jacobs since he produced his first film, *What a Way to Go!*, four years of hopes and heartaches. Now he had finally steered *Planet of the Apes* into production and his other big project, *Doctor Dolittle*, had survived the trials and tribulations of English weather, Rex Harrison and temperamental animal co-stars, and was at the editing stage. *Dolittle?* Rarely had there been a more ironic title. In four years Jacobs had hardly had time to draw breath. *Doctor Dolittle* was in the can, but way over budget, and already *Apes* was heading in the same direction. The constant stress was taking its toll. And when the *Apes* crew relocated to Fox's studio on the edge of Beverly Hills, Jacobs would need a golf buggie to get around the set, having suffered a major heart attack. He was only in his forties, but would never fully recover.

Fox studio boss Richard Zanuck was growing increasingly worried about the painfully slow progress on *Planet of the Apes*. It had been a risky project to back and already he sensed he might have made a mistake. In 1964 Fox had rejected the project, having decided a budget of $1.7 million was too high. In 1966 the Heston–Robinson screen test prompted a rethink, but the revised budget was over $3 million. And in May 1967 it had risen to almost $5 million, with $1 million allocated to make-up alone, the largest make-up budget in Hollywood history. In early May, with preparations for filming almost complete, Fox executives took another, last-minute look at the budget, trimmed it by more than $100,000 and cut the shooting schedule from fifty-five days to forty-five. And no doubt they felt very pleased with themselves. But Schaffner never believed he could make the film in that time and he determined simply to carry on regardless. Now all Zanuck was seeing for his money was endless footage of three men walking across the desert. 'Frank shot and shot and shot,' recalls associate producer Mort Abrahams, 'and I said: "Frank, we're running behind here." On the fourth or fifth day I got a call on the set from Dick. He said: "Mort, if I see one more set of dailies with nothing but these guys trekking across a goddam empty landscape I'm going to yank the picture." So I spoke to Frank and said:

"Why are you taking so long?" He said: "OK, sit down, let me explain." He said the whole picture depended on the set-up – we had to see the isolation, we had to feel the isolation, we had to see how helpless they were against the environment, the struggle to get to the Green Zone. He said: "If you don't set this up properly, you don't have a picture."' Schaffner went on shooting Heston, Burton and Robert Gunner tramping across the desert, while Abrahams did his best to placate Zanuck, assuring him that they were on the last mile, that the end was just around the next big rock. Cast and crew scrambled up hills, hoisted equipment up canyons on ropes and shot footage with the actors on one cliff, the crew on another and a deep chasm between. Sometimes they needed a helicopter to reach locations. Heston had complained about how slow veteran cameraman Leon Shamroy had been on *The Agony and the Ecstasy*, and vowed never to work with him again, but he was pleasantly surprised at Shamroy's work rate on *Apes*. There were endless complications and delays, but this time Shamroy, at least, seemed blameless. He and Schaffner quickly established a bond of mutual respect and trust that served the film well. And if Shamroy felt a location was too arduous for him, he would leave it to Schaffner and his assistants.

William Creber had already worked in this area on his first film as art director, the biblical epic *The Greatest Story Ever Told*, though it was not his idea to go back. 'I went and talked to my boss Jack Martin Smith and I said: "Jeez, you know, we've got to really think about this and where to do it," and he just said, right off: "Of all people, you know where to do this movie." He said: "Why wouldn't you go back up there, to the Grand Canyon area?" And I said: "God, you're absolutely right."' Creber had worked with Heston on *The Greatest Story Ever Told* too, but never socialized with him or got to know him well. Heston kept to his trailer when he was not filming, or running, and made it clear that he should be called to the set only when everything else was ready. There were few built sets in the desert and Creber had less work to do there than other heads of department. However, he was given one important extra task on the orders of the film's star. 'What I did do, from time to time, first thing in the morning, was to measure a mile from the set, so that he could jog down the road and back at lunch.' Creber not only had to plan the route, he then had to drive it in his car to make sure it was exactly two miles. 'He just wanted some spot that told him he was half-done. I don't know why I was chosen. It was like, once the set is ready your department doesn't have a lot to do.'

The scene in which the astronauts emerge from their spaceship was shot at nearby Lake Powell. The craft was about the size of a bus and would be seen in the water as the crew climb out, but it is never seen in flight. It is meant to hurtle across the landscape at enormous speed, a scene that would have been very difficult to realize effectively with models or special effects. Creber suggested it might be easier and cheaper to shoot the entire sequence from the crew's point of view – showing on screen what the astronauts would see if they were looking out of the window. Schaffner had a pilot fly over the landscape and lake, with a camera on his plane. He made runs in two different planes. Schaffner also had a man in the lake shooting film, and the intention was to combine the two. But the camera on one of the planes had not worked properly and the diver had not shot enough film. Today, on a big film, they would probably just go back and do it all again. But in those days the footage was handed over to the studio's optical specialists, to see if they could salvage anything. Between them L.B. Abbott and editor Hugh Fowler managed to stitch together a sequence in which images are repeated, reversed, turned on their side, turned upside down, turned every which way, to disguise the fact there is insufficient material in focus to run the sequence as a single piece of film, and it all merely adds to the impression of speed and the excitement. Creber remembers another film which was shooting 'day for night' (in which exposure is adjusted to make daytime look like night), but the cameraman got it wrong and the film was entirely black when it was developed. Abbott performed such an effective rescue operation that the cameraman won an Oscar and was thereafter considered a specialist at that particular look.

Kim Hunter, Roddy McDowall and Lou Wagner joined the production after the completion of the trek sequence, but did not get out of Make-up on their first day until four o'clock in the afternoon. They quickly worked out how to express themselves through the make-up, after Schaffner had a quiet word in their ear. 'He said: "It looks like a mask … You've got to keep it moving all the time" and so that's what happened,' says Hunter. The ape actors could never allow their faces to remain stationary, they had to keep raising their brows or wrinkling their noses or opening and closing their mouths. 'We felt silly really doing it, but we did. We just kept our facial muscles moving whether we were talking or not, and particularly when we weren't talking.' Shamroy had to select his angles carefully to make sure he avoided showing the second set of human teeth behind the ape teeth. McDowall and Hunter had no way of knowing then that they were to become the Astaire and Rogers of ape movies, continually reuniting for one more dance, though they got on well from the outset. 'Roddy was a marvellous man,' she says. 'I miss him a lot.' (McDowall died in 1998.) 'But Heston I didn't have much … We had what we had in the film and not really any relationship out of that or beyond it. In fact, every time I've seen Heston since the film, he doesn't know who the hell I am.' Lou Wagner, however, remembers being impressed one day when Heston volunteered to run two miles to get him a straw. 'They had forgotten straws for us for water. It was very, very hot, and Franklin Schaffner and quite a few of the crew fainted from the heat, it was just so hot, and we needed water and there was no way to drink it, because we couldn't mess up our make-up, otherwise it would be another eight hours' make-up, and Chuck ran back to the base camp and brought straws back for Roddy, Kim and me.'

Two lengthy story segments were shot in the desert – the opening scenes and the sequence near the end when Taylor, Nova, Zira and Cornelius return to the Forbidden Zone. At the end of the early trek sequence, the astronauts hear water and the camera cuts to a pool in which they cool off with a swim. In reality the film was cutting from the Arizona–Utah desert to the Fox ranch hundreds of miles away in California, to a waterfall that had been created the previous year for *Doctor Dolittle*. It was heightened for *Apes* with the use of multiple hoses. The bulk of Creber's work was in Los Angeles at the Fox studios and the sprawling ranch in Malibu Canyon. I met him in a coffee shop in Santa Monica, where he was living in 2001. A tall bearded man in blue jeans and turtleneck, he sketched out a map to help me track down the site of Ape City, that lost civilization from an era that now exists only on the screen. Malibu Canyon Road winds up from the Pacific Coast Highway into the mountains and the old Fox spread, where apes once shared the hills and valleys with cowboys and Indians. *Planet of the Apes* was shot at the same time as the *Custer* and *Daniel Boone* television shows. But it was the Indians who were there first. They hunted there for hundreds of years before businessmen bought the land at the beginning of the last century and opened the Crags Country Club. Fox took it over in the forties and the ranch provided scenic locations for a string of films and television series over four decades, serving as Wales in *How Green Was My Valley* and Korea in *M*A*S*H*. The state bought it in the seventies, along with the adjoining Reagan and Hope ranches, and created Malibu Creek State Park, which now occupies 10,000 acres of the Santa Monica Mountains. The official map warns of rattlesnakes, poisonous plants and ticks. 'Some ticks do carry diseases (Lyme disease for example),' says a warning on the official park map. 'Learn how to recognize ticks and check your clothing and exposed skin,' it advises helpfully. A notice board points out that a tick is the size of a pinhead and suggests you avoid wandering off the trails and touching any plants at all, because apparently the wee creatures hang there on the branches just waiting for unsuspecting passers-by to jump on. Before long the trail I am following up a steep hill has vanished to virtually nothing and I am down on my hands and knees scrambling upwards, through thick vegetation, with the sweat pouring off me (in January), and visions of ticks dropping in their hundreds on to my exposed skin for an unexpected feast. 'I can't remember when we last saw anyone up this way, Ronnie Flea.' 'Not since those film people cleared out, Bob Flea. Mind you, I remember when these hills were full of apes.' I manage to clamber over the hill and descend to a little lake, deserted, but for the occasional waterfowl. It was created for boating, fishing and duck hunting, when the country club dammed the creek in 1901, and is now silted up and little more than a muddy pond, though it bears the grand title of Century Lake.

It was here, at Century Lake, that Creber built his simian civilization, inspired by Spanish architect Antonio Gaudí's curves, which twist almost organically, like tree trunks, and by photographs of cave dwellings in Turkey, which turned out to be homes not of people, but of doves. Creber developed the look with colleague Mentor Huebner, who had been responsible for some of the earliest design sketches, when Jacobs first tried to arouse studio interest. There was a long-running dispute over Huebner's fees and Abrahams proposed his name should appear on the film's credits as 'production illustrator'. But the proposal was ruled out by Stan Hough, one of the top men at Fox, who said: 'God knows we have enough credits on the screen today as it is.' Creber took their designs to one of Fox's set builders. 'He built a chair out of cardboard … and then he got inside and he shot foam inside of it, and then peeled the cardboard off, and it gave it a strange, concrete look, and I said: "That's the look."' They used much the same process for the ape buildings. 'We used what they call pencil-rod. Pencil-rod is just a metal rod about the diameter of a pencil… It was all welded and we got it so it would stand up.' It was covered in cardboard, like the chair, 'and then the guy got in with a mask and tanks and everything, and sprayed the inside with foam, through the metal, up against the cardboard, and we would peel the cardboard off.' The ape houses even had air-conditioning installed to keep the actors comfortable during filming.

One of Creber's biggest challenges was to provide six-foot-high corn for the dramatic hunt scenes in which the humans flee through the field from an initially unseen enemy, when Taylor and his men first lay eyes upon the gorilla huntsmen. Creber had only three or four months to produce a field with corn or grass high enough for a man to hide in. He hedged his bets and planted more than one variety, planting in wide strips that would give the field an irregular look. 'In a few weeks it was doing pretty good,' he says. 'It got up about thirty inches. And then it would-n't move.' Schaffner could not have people fleeing from an unseen enemy through two and a half feet of corn. 'After a couple of weeks the production department decides it's not going to be tall enough, so they send everybody all over California, looking for corn, but they couldn't find a corn field that didn't have power lines in it or houses or whatever. Finally the weather changed: we had a warm night. And I had sticks marked and dated and I came in one morning and everybody was laughing and smiling and it had grown three inches in one night. And someone said it should do it if the weather holds. So the next day, three more inches. I calculated out, if it keeps this up, and we have three or four weeks left till we shoot, it's going to be higher than we would want it … Finally I went out there, and it's a week before shooting, and some of the corn was eight feet high. And I went to Franklin Schaffner and I said: "Well, Frank, you've got your corn. It's going to be plenty high," and he says: "Well, how high?" And I said: "Well, most of it could be eight feet." He says: "I told you I wanted it six feet." And I said: "Well, what do you want me to do?" He says: "Mow it. Mow it to six feet." And I looked at him. He had this wry smile and he smoked a cigar. I said: "Screw you, you're going to have eight-feet corn."'

In early June the company moved back to Los Angeles, for work in the studio, at the ranch and at local locations. They opted to shoot from ten in the morning until seven at night. Heston was unhappy about the late finish, but there was little choice, because the apes spent so much time in Make-up, and their hours were much longer. It took over an hour to gently peel their make-up off, with the help of an alcohol solution, though the principal ape actors had fresh appliances every day. Maurice Evans said it was his favourite part of the day. 'It takes so long to get it off that one finds oneself inhaling the fumes … and you get quite a buzz,' he told one interviewer. McDowall, however, preferred just to rip his make-up off and get away quicker. Some scenes demanded as many as 200 apes and sometimes there would be eighty make-up artists and hair stylists on set, leading to shortages on other films. The ape actors had to drink through straws and smoke cigarettes through elegant cigarette-holders, like a simian Noel Coward, and they were very restricted in what they could eat. Apes in background shots were given masks, but those in the foreground needed appliances, like Hunter and McDowall. 'The adhesive was good, but not that good,' says make-up director John Chambers. 'If you made it too good, you would have pulled the skin off them. I would say to them: "We've put the toughest kind of adhesive on you, but … you can move it too much and you can have it pop off, so don't eat any solid foods, and eat just with the straw, and eat milk shakes and everything like that, and mush …" They don't listen to anyone. They figure: "Well, they've given me a part, I'm in it now, they're going to keep me anyway." So these guys with the nice appliances on, they come back into Make-up and I said: "How's it working?" And I look at them. Oh Jeez, here's the chin hanging off. There's a pocket between the [human] chin and the rubber. And they say: "Look at what happened to it," and "I didn't have anything much to do with it." And there's peas in it, in this little pocket.' It quickly became obvious each species was sticking to its own at meal times, chimps with chimps, gorillas with gorillas, orang-utans with orang-utans, and Heston by himself. Obviously it was impossible for the apes to simply blow their noses and some actors took pills or inhalers to dry them out.

It was the middle of summer, but one of the few actors to catch a cold was Charlton Heston, who seemed to spend a lot of time soaked, for one reason or another. The cold contributed to the angry rasp when he first gets his voice back, after being shot in the neck, and talks to the apes. The apes' language was still under discussion, even with shooting under way, and Heston noted in his journals at the time that he was called to a meeting with Schaffner and Zanuck to discuss whether his character should comment on the fact the apes spoke English. He also notes: 'Maurice, Roddy and Kim are excellent. Linda H has problems, but Frank's keeping her nearly immobile in her scenes, which works.' It was a baptism of fire for the former Miss Maryland. *Apes* was not exactly *Lear*, but she was joining a heavyweight cast. Her character was described in the script as 'hauntingly lovely and hauntingly stupid' and she was not called upon to express much in the way of emotion, but that in itself was a challenge, and her leading man did little to put her at her ease. 'He basically kept to himself ... He wasn't into small talk.' But she, like everyone else it seems, got on very well with Roddy McDowall. 'I think I was very well accepted, because I was Richard Zanuck's lady ... I might have got a little special treatment, being that I went home and slept with him, so they all wanted maybe a good report.' She might have been Zanuck's girlfriend, but cast and crew found her very easy-going and she was genuinely well liked.

Schaffner suggested that one way of humiliating and dehumanizing Heston's character would be to strip him naked in the tribunal scene. In his diary Heston notes: 'It's the first time I've ever done a nude scene, even photographed from the rear.' And in his autobiography he adds: 'One of the girls supplying coffee on the set said archly, "Mmmm, nice buns". I suppose I could nail her for sexual harassment for that today.' His second nude scene followed in quick succession, at the Fox ranch, when he and his fellow astronauts bathe in a pool and first encounter the local human population. But Jacobs was less impressed with the unexpected sight of Heston's bum than the coffee girl had been. 'We've got to give the impression of nudity without seeing Chuck's ass,' he said. Schaffner ignored him, as was his wont. Otherwise the dailies – the footage of each day's shooting – were looking good, though Fox executives voiced concern about a blood transfusion scene in which a tube is simply run from Harrison's arm to Heston's. 'You can't make blood flow from arm to arm like that,' said one. But Zanuck felt if audiences were going to accept talking apes, they were not going to quibble about the mechanics of blood transfusion. 'What the hell,' he told them, 'maybe that's how an ape does it.' Zanuck's biggest concern was not the blood transfusion. Nor was it Heston's bottom. It was the elusive bottom line, as the film fell further and further behind schedule and overtime payments soared. Increasingly dismayed, he fired off a memo to Abrahams, pleading with him to try to bring Schaffner to heel. 'No matter how good a film you make, I'm afraid that we're reaching a point where the cost of the picture is so excessive that we may never be able to recoup.' Fox executives were poring over individual items of expenditure and queried Heston's personal use of the helicopter five times in a fortnight, at $250 per flight.

Back in the studio, Schaffner shot scenes inside the spaceship, and Heston noted that they provided an octogenarian actress with the rare chance to play an astronaut, though it was hardly very glamorous work, made up as the corpse of Taylor's dead colleague Stewart. Heston and the surviving members of the crew spent a day being sprayed with water from off-camera for shots that would be slotted in with those taken at Lake Powell. 'There's hardly been a scene in this bloody film in which I've not been dragged, choked, netted, chased, doused, whipped, poked, shot, gagged, stoned, leaped on, or generally mistreated,' Heston confided to his diary. 'As Joe Canutt said, setting up one of the fight shots, "You know, Chuck, I can remember when we used to win these things."' The film was shot in conditions of tight security. Buck Kartalian, who played the gorilla guard Julius, later compared it to 'top-secret government work' and admitted he had a difficult relationship with Schaffner, who allegedly said virtually nothing to him over two weeks and always referred to him as Julius, making Kartalian suspect he did not know his name. On one occasion Schaffner announced he would begin a scene with a shot of Julius. 'I said: "Mr Schaffner, since your camera is going to open up on me in this scene, why don't I smoke a cigar?" And he looked at me, and gave me a dirty look.' Beyond that there was no comment on Kartalian's cigar idea. 'So I kept quiet, didn't say anything,' says Kartalian. 'We had two rehearsals and he said: "All right, we're gonna shoot the scene now. The camera's ready … Somebody get Buck a cigar."' Some of the more humorous lines and moments, which would get a mixed response from critics and audiences, were conceived during filming. Mort Abrahams suggested each member of the orang-utan tribunal should at one point be seen to cover his eyes, ears or mouth, as if they were the three wise monkeys – see no evil, hear no evil, speak no evil – and it would introduce a moment of whimsy into a long, serious scene. Schaffner had reservations, but Heston suggested they shoot it just for the dailies, to give everyone a laugh. There was a dramatic justification for some other humorous scenes, such as the one in which Julius says 'human see, human do', because the ape language was English, and if they had inherited the language they might have been expected to have inherited and adapted some of its clichés for their own use. Schaffner felt the three wise monkeys was a cheap gag, without dramatic justification, and that it did not fit into the film. But everyone who saw it thought it was hilarious, and there was considerable resistance to dropping it, making Schaffner wish he had never filmed it in the first place.

It was four years since Arthur Jacobs had first presented his initial pitch, three since he, Blake Edwards, Don Peters and Rod Serling had come up with the Statue of Liberty as the closing scene. But, with just a week of shooting left, the film-makers still had not made a final decision about how to end the movie. The Statue of Liberty was definitely going to be in it. But, beyond that, everything seemed up for grabs. What would Taylor say when he saw the statue? Should Nova be pregnant? Should Taylor be given the chance to recreate mankind in his own image? There is a famous precedent of a film whose ending was not decided until the last minute, but which then went on to become a classic. That look of pain and confusion on Ingrid Bergman's face in *Casablanca* is genuine, because she really did not know with whom she would finish the movie. Linda Harrison might have been forgiven for a certain rosy glow towards the end of *Planet of the Apes*, because they did shoot a scene in which it was revealed she was expecting Taylor's baby. It would disappear in post-production, whereas the Statue of Liberty's full-frontal scene was added at that point.

The full length view of the Statue of Liberty was a painting, by studio artist Emil Kosa, which was superimposed on to the film. 'The ending, as written, was a cut to Heston, and a cut back to the statue,' says William Creber. 'And Frank and I were at Lake Powell, we were filming the beginning of the movie and he said to me: "You know the ending of the movie – we've got to work on it. Can you think of any ideas that we can use to extend the revelation of the statue? Just a couple of cuts that we don't quite know what is going on." Most designers carry a pen and I started drawing on a napkin. I said: "Well, what if we did a shot over the statue, looking down at the beach … It will be the torch, but we won't quite know. It's something familiar, but not. And then we can zoom down the beach … Then we see these spikes come in and we move past them and then we get a nice framing and we go back … Then you go over Heston and you see him, and then we will pull back and include Heston." And he said: "We'll do all three." So those shots were my ideas, and I still have the napkin.' Creber found a secluded spot at the appropriately named Point Dume, just off the Pacific Coast Highway, beyond the Malibu Canyon turn-off, where he reconstructed the statue's torch and crown. 'The camera was actually seventy feet up a tower. We had twenty feet of dolly track [rails over which a camera runs smoothly] up there, and then below that was the torch. And then we went down to another level. At forty-five feet we had another twenty feet of dolly track on a tower, and then we had the head down at ten feet below that, at thirty-five feet, because we figured out all the angles of the real statue … To make the shot the cameraman would go up there, an assistant director would go up and Frank hands me the megaphone and he says: "You built it, you've got to help me do this." So I went up, and we had a camera operator, and a dolly grip, and Frank and I were on the tower.'

Filming was delayed at Point Dume because of fog and boats that kept wandering into shot – it may have been the Forbidden Zone for the apes, but it was a busy shipping channel as far as local Californians were concerned. Hunter remembers going for a nap while waiting for fog to lift. The only way she could sleep in her make-up was on her back. She awoke in a cold sweat from a nightmare in which she had the head of a chimpanzee and could not see the rest of her body. The film was a continuing nightmare for Fox too, as costs kept edging upwards. And there still remained that final scene to sort out. In the shooting script, all Taylor says, when he sees the statue and realizes he has been on Earth all the time, are the two words 'My God'. Heston himself worked up the speech to include the line 'God damn you all to hell'. But his suggestions prompted memories of another classic film, *Gone with the Wind*, which ran into censorship arguments over Clark Gable's ground-breaking use of the D-word. Abrahams and Fox feared *Planet of the Apes* might lose the child-friendly certificate at which it was aiming if Heston said 'God damn you'. They wanted to shoot several different versions of the ending. Heston, however, insisted Taylor was not swearing or blaspheming, but was in fact literally asking God to damn mankind. Heston got his way and only his version was shot. So who was responsible for that final scene? Don Peters? Jacobs and Edwards? Rod Serling? Bill Creber? Charlton Heston? What about the director, Franklin J. Schaffner, the quiet man who gave Arthur Jacobs's vision shape? And what about the mural on the wall of a Burbank deli? Like *Citizen Kane*'s rosebud, it is difficult to pin down. The truth is probably all of them. That's movies for you.

*Planet of the Apes* wrapped on 10 August 1967. And, such is the nature of film-making, it finished by shooting the very first scene – Taylor's monologue on the spaceship, with Heston, Jeff Burton, Robert Gunner and Dianne Stanley, as the uncredited actress playing Stewart before she withered away. It was 'an ideal kind of scene', Heston wrote in his journals. 'Everybody else lay mute and motionless while I had all the words. More than three minutes of them, for that matter, and they were pretty well worked out too, after the usual intense effort with a red pencil.' There was a feeling on the set that the film could be a hit, but you can never be certain. If morale at the end of a film is low, you can be sure you have a dud, but that does not mean the opposite is also true. Many is the film that has finished on a high, only to sink without trace at the box office a few months later. Jacobs was still unhappy about the nudity, but his attention was divided between *Apes*, *Dolittle* and *Goodbye, Mr Chips*, which he was setting up at MGM. *Doctor Dolittle* cost three times as much as *Planet of the Apes* and Fox were pulling out all the stops in an attempt to recoup their investment, with a big Oscar campaign planned in the United States and a royal gala premiere in England. Heston's nude scenes and the three wise monkeys moment both stayed in the picture. There was some concern about the length of the trek and the tribunal scene. Jacobs was by this point hoping to produce a film that would appeal to critics, as well as a mass audience. 'My major concern at the moment is that we do not get too intellectual or lean too heavily on long conversational scenes that will make the "mass audience" squirm,' he said in a memo to Zanuck. But, even in its final form, the tribunal sequence still lasts twelve minutes. The one big change during the editing stage was the deletion of any reference to Nova's pregnancy. Michael Wilson told *Cinefantastique* magazine that he had heard it was deleted on the orders of 'a high-echelon Fox executive' who found the idea of sex between a twentieth-century man and a primitive subhuman distasteful. It was Zanuck who ordered its deletion, though he can no longer remember that Nova was pregnant, let alone why he would have ordered the scene chopped. Abrahams says it muddied the waters and detracted from the impact of the Statue of Liberty and the sense of hopelessness its appearance conveyed.

And still the debate raged over the ending. While Heston gloated in his journals about having come up with the best closing speech and there being no need to record an alternative, Mort Abrahams was suggesting they might have to drop the speech completely because Heston was so bad in it. 'He resorts to that special grin of his, which for me undermines the impact of his speech,' Abrahams said in a memo to Schaffner. 'I would even cut out the lines in favour of eliminating this moment of poor performance.' Schaffner, however, managed to find an alternative take and the result is one of the most effective endings of any movie ever. Of course, I say that with the benefit of more than thirty years of hindsight. Dick Zanuck sat and watched the finished film, and he still could not make up his mind whether he had a hit or a turkey on his hands. Heston was upbeat, noting in his journals that the film was 'different'. But still no one knew for certain how audiences would react to an action-adventure drama about talking apes. *Doctor Dolittle*, with its songs and lighter, whimsical tone, looked a more likely bet. All Zanuck could be sure about was that *Planet of the Apes* had ended up fourteen days behind schedule and $1 million over budget. The film he considered too expensive at $1.7 million, had ended up costing him $5.8 million. He had stuck his neck out for this movie, and he did not know whether to expect the sweet touch of a garland or the sudden trauma of descending steel.

# CHAPTER NINE

# RELEASING THE BEASTS

*The revolution's here*

Arthur Jacobs and Dick Zanuck returned to Arizona, not to the barren northern locations where Franklin Schaffner spent day after day shooting three men walking across the empty landscape, but to Phoenix, a bright, modern metropolis that had expanded hugely since the Second World War. With them they brought the end result of Schaffner's endeavours. Zanuck was now quite happy with the footage of Charlton Heston in the desert. It was the rest of *Planet of the Apes* that he was worried about. As they took their seats in the air-conditioned auditorium and prepared to watch the film with an audience of ordinary people for the first time, the studio boss turned to the producer and said: 'Arthur, I know the first fifteen minutes of the film will be fine, because it's just Heston and the crash and all of that, but let's just pray we survive the first ape exchange.' Thirty-two years later Zanuck was back in Arizona again, producing a new *Planet of the Apes* film, but he still remembers that night and his feelings of uncertainty about how the audience would react. 'We had no idea,' he says. 'It was a big gamble actually at that time, because my original concerns or questions that audiences would accept apes talking to one another in perfect English, some with English accents, whether that would be accepted or not. So not until our first preview in Phoenix did we really know.'

Even before the opening credits, Charlton Heston has explained to the audience – by way of a 'final report' resembling James Kirk's 'captain's log' in *Star Trek* – that he is about to leave his spaceship in the control of computers and join his colleagues in hibernation. 'According to Dr Hasslein's theory of time in a vehicle travelling nearly the speed of light, the Earth has aged nearly 700 years since we left it, while we've aged hardly at all,' he says, and his instruments appear to provide confirmation, showing the ship's year as 1972 and Earth's as 2673. Heston's character Taylor is dressed in the traditional white spacesuit with which audiences had grown increasingly familiar over the past few years, though the uniform still retained an image of danger and adventure. Those that wore them were the new pioneers, the new heroes, and in little over a year's time Neil Armstrong would make that final 'giant leap for mankind' when he stepped out on to the moon. Heston's voice is laconic and manly, and he smokes a cigar – the film's expenditure on cigars was one of the items queried by Fox executives. He insists he left the twentieth century with no regrets, though he turns all wistful as he reflects upon the vast emptiness of space and his place within it. 'The men who sent us on this journey are long since dead and gone. You who are reading me now are a different breed, I hope a better one … Does man, that marvel of the universe, that glorious paradox, who sent me to the stars, still make war against his brother, keep his neighbour's children starving?'

Audiences knew the answer to Heston's questions. The United States had been sucked into a war in Vietnam, and it was about to take a decisive turn for the worse. Shortly before the film opened, in February 1968, the supposedly demoralized Viet Cong exploited the traditional new year truce to launch a series of devastating attacks in what became known as the Tet Offensive. The war would drag on for years and claim the lives of thousands of Americans and Asians, including many teenagers and children who, in 1968, would be sitting in a cinema in Los Angeles or Chicago, or maybe Phoenix, listening to Heston's monologue. War in Pierre Boulle's old stomping ground of Indo-China continually threatened to escalate into global conflict.

Although he is listed on the closing credits as George Taylor, his first name is never mentioned in the film, which seems curiously apt. He is not a man for small talk or bland pleasantries. Soon after they crash-land on a barren, unknown planet, one of the other astronauts, Landon, accuses him of despising his fellow man and of running away. 'I'm a seeker too,' insists Taylor. 'But my dreams aren't like yours. I can't help thinking somewhere in the universe there has to be something better than man. Has to be.' He will shortly find out the answer. And his little speech about man making war against his brother will be reprised at the end of the film. 'He will murder his brother to possess his brother's land.' But it will not be Taylor who is making the speech this time. It will be an ape.

The spaceship crashes into a lake, with the clock reading an Earth date of 11–25–3978 and the crew's only female member, Stewart, aged and withered in her hibernation compartment – the film's first visual shock, following on quickly from the excitement of Abbott and Fowler's roller-coaster ride across the desert. With the spaceship sinking, a now-bearded Taylor reflects with a smile that they are there to stay. He laughs with mocking exaggeration when Landon plants a tiny American flag in the dust, the sort of flag children put in sandcastles at the beach. The needle between the two develops as they trek across the seemingly endless and empty desert. 'Your loved ones are dead and forgotten for twenty centuries,' Taylor tells Landon. 'Even if you could get back, they'd think you were something that fell out of a tree.' The journey establishes the natural hostility of the world on which they have landed, and their isolation, just as Schaffner intended. Their past is ancient history and their future looks bleak, to say the least. Yet while Landon is understandably morose, Taylor does not seem to care. It is more than twenty minutes into the film before the audience catches a glimpse of figures secretly watching and following them, on a ridge, like Indians in a western. The first sign the astronauts see of intelligent life, however, is strange, unnatural figures, like scarecrows, but not in the familiar crucifix stance – more like men hung upon St Andrew's crosses. Immediately afterwards the astronauts come to a pool, strip off and swim – just as in Boulle's novel. And, as in the book, they find footprints and their clothes and equipment disappear, but, unlike the book, they manage to retrieve the former, in rags, and put them on, ensuring that, whatever other problems they might encounter, they should not run into too much bother with the censors.

They discover a tribe of mute humans, dressed in animal skins, which may maintain decency, but perhaps unintentionally gives the impression that the film's humans are more intelligent and advanced than in the novel, not that Taylor is impressed. 'If this is the best they've got around here, in six months we'll be running this planet,' he declares smugly, and somewhat prematurely as it turns out. The mute humans freeze in alarm. There is a wonderful, chilling sound like a cross between a lion roaring and a jet plane passing overhead, and the tribe flees through the corn, with the astronauts running alongside. Unseen pursuers beat the corn with long shafts and there is the sound of hooves. Shots are fired, though the faces on the hunters remain unseen, until at last they are revealed as gorillas, dressed in leather tunics and carrying rifles, a frightening combination of animal intelligence, strength and aggression, underlined by Jerry Goldsmith's weird, staccato assembly of strings, woodwind and percussion, seemingly all scurrying in different directions. Goldsmith's soundtrack owes more to Stravinsky and Bartók than to any Hollywood composer. The third astronaut, Dodge, is shot dead, so although Taylor's party included a woman and a black man, they were the first to die in this brave new world. As the group's scientist, Dodge did at least provide a positive role model, albeit briefly. As in the book, the gorillas are photographed alongside their 'game', while surviving humans are rounded up and taken away in cages on carts. Taylor is caught in a net, escapes, is shot in the throat and then taken to a medical establishment, where he is attended by chimpanzees, who speak English, a major departure from the book, but not from cinematic convention, which would have everyone from Apache Indians to German Nazis speak the same language, differentiated only by accent and maybe the occasional native word. He receives a blood transfusion from an attractive young woman he noticed before the hunt, whom he will name Nova. The operation is supervised by Galen, a chimpanzee surgeon, who complains about the smell of the 'animals'. Much of the film's impact and humour derives from turning the usual relationship and attitudes between humans and animals upside down.

His colleague Zira, an animal psychologist, has tried to improve Galen's lot by speaking to their superior, the orang-utan Zaius, but Zaius apparently 'looks down his nose' at chimps. 'But the quota system's been abolished,' says Galen. In Boulle's novel the three ape species are equal, in theory at least. But the idea of racial division – or species division – is established, very specifically in the film, in one of the first dialogue scenes involving apes, with a reference to 'quota systems'. The US had had quotas for Jewish immigrants, who, like the chimps in the film, were sometimes perceived there, and in Europe, as highly intelligent, perhaps threateningly so. Similar quotas also operated elsewhere in American society. These quotas were not 'positive discrimination' targets, but maximums, to keep the number of Jews down. Obviously this historic detail was familiar to the film-makers, many of whom came from Jewish backgrounds, which simply reflected the huge Jewish contribution to the development of movies in Hollywood. The differentiation between ape species is crudely underlined by Morton Haack's costume designs, which colour-coded the apes. Chimps are in green pyjamas, orang-utans in tan and gorillas get the best of the deal in cool black biker leathers.

Zira notes that Taylor is trying to talk, but Zaius dismisses it as mimicry. 'Man has no understanding. He can be taught a few simple tricks, nothing more ... Experimental brain surgery on these creatures is one thing ... Behavioural studies are something else again. To suggest that we can learn anything about the simian nature from the study of man is sheer nonsense. Besides, man is a nuisance: he eats up his food supplies in the forest, then migrates to our greenbelts and ravages our crops. The sooner he is exterminated the better. It's a question of simian survival.' Later in the animal compound, Zira shows Taylor to her fiancé, another chimp, an archaeologist called Cornelius, from whom she steals a kiss. Taylor is arrogant and cynical, while Zira and Cornelius are forever darting affectionate glances at each other and touching each other.

Taylor attempts to write in the dust, but Nova obliterates the letters, which leads to a fight in the cage. Zaius deliberately finishes the job Nova started. This orang-utan is an altogether more intelligent and sinister individual than the Zaius of the novel. Boulle's Zaius was pompous, no great intellectual, and the subject of mockery behind his back. This Zaius is more like the shadowy individuals in *The X-Files*, clever, devious and dangerous. We know he knows more than he is prepared to admit, but we are never entirely sure of the extent of his knowledge. Taylor finally manages to prove the extent of his intelligence to Zira when he snatches her notebook and writes: 'My name is Taylor.' He manages to convey the idea to her and an incredulous Cornelius that he came from another planet and landed in an area which, it transpires, is called the 'Forbidden Zone', though in the film, unlike Boulle's novel, flight is regarded as a scientific impossibility – not so much because of the physics as the budget. The relative intelligence of the humans in the film, evidenced by their clothing, and the technological backwardness of the apes does have the effect of bringing the species closer together on the evolutionary scale than in the book.

Zira, bubbling with enthusiasm, believes Taylor could be the living proof of Cornelius's potentially incendiary theory that 'the ape evolved from a lower order of primate, possibly man'. Cornelius discovered evidence of a civilization older than the Sacred Scrolls during excavations in the Forbidden Zone. But he is more cautious by nature than Zira and is concerned about his future career. He complains that if Taylor were a 'missing link' then the Sacred Scrolls would not be worth the parchment on which they were written. They are visited by Zaius, who crumples up Taylor's paper aeroplane, and who later orders that Taylor should be 'gelded'. Taylor is still unable to talk, but not unable to hear. Learning of his intended fate, he makes a desperate bid for freedom. He interrupts a funeral, where an ape minister of religion is assuring mourners the deceased has found peace in Heaven, and he finds Dodge stuffed and mounted in a museum – as if a black man were so unusual on this planet that he merits exhibition in a museum. In his book *Planet of the Apes as American Myth: Race, Politics, and Popular Culture*, Eric Greene goes so far as to suggest this scene 'raises the question of whether the other races had been wiped out by white humans before the apes came to power'. This was the time of Martin Luther King and Malcolm X, Black Power and Black Panthers. Black Americans were beginning to demand their rights. Many whites not only wanted to resist these advances, and keep the black man in 'his place', but felt threatened by Black Power, as if the alternative to white domination was not equality but black domination of the white races, a fear that dates back to slavery and slave revolts.

Taylor is stoned by the crowd, whipped by guards and once again caught in a net, prompting Taylor finally to break his silence with the immortal line: 'Take your stinking paws off me, you damn dirty ape!'. Our man fights back. And you can imagine the cheers echoing around the cinema at matinee screenings. It seems that, for all his disillusionment with man, this is not the 'something better' for which Taylor was hoping. He lapses into what sound like playground insults, resorting to accusations over personal hygiene, delivered with every ounce of venom he can muster. After all, he has just been pursued, stoned, whipped and caught up in a net, again, like a tiger, or a tadpole. Subsequently Nova is removed from his cage while he is held back by a water hose, familiar from recent news reports as the weapon of choice in dealing with student unrest. 'Now I don't even have you,' he reflects, and he remembers that on Earth there was 'lots of love-making, but no love', though he becomes almost tearful at the memory of Stewart. There is rarely any great shading in Heston's acting. He is at his best when swinging between extremes – bombastic and wistful, self-important and self-pitying, up and down, and it fits the character of Taylor perfectly.

A high-powered tribunal meets to inquire into the case and decide Taylor's fate. It consists of three orang-utans – the President of the National Academy; Dr Maximus, Commissioner for Animal Affairs; and Zaius. They object to the smell of Taylor's rags, which are ripped from him, leaving him naked. However, the tribunal, and Schaffner, having made their points, Taylor once more wraps the rags around himself to preserve his decency and the film's family-friendly certificate. Zira claims Taylor has a right to know if there are any charges against him. Honorious, the state representative, points out that as a man he has no rights. Zaius says Taylor is not on trial, but scientific heresy is. 'My case is simple,' says Honorious. 'It is based on our first Article of Faith – that the Almighty created the ape in his own image, that He gave him a soul and a mind, that He set him apart from the beasts of the jungle and made him the lord of the planet. These sacred truths are self-evident. The proper study of apes is apes. But certain young cynics have chosen to study man – yes, perverted scientists who advance an insidious theory called evolution.' He alleges that Zira and Galen tampered with Taylor's brain to create a 'speaking monster'. He seeks to prove it by exposing Taylor's lack of intellectual reason, with a series of questions which hinge on his understanding of their religion and culture. To the question as to why all apes are equal, Taylor responds by suggesting some are more equal than others. Honorious, being unfamiliar with the original Orwellian context, quite rightly dismisses the answer as ridiculous.

In attempting to be smart, Taylor just appears stupid. Despite his arrogance, or rather because of it, his behaviour is continually misjudged and inappropriate. An inspection of other survivors from the gorilla hunt reveals Landon has apparently been the subject of brain surgery and is now no more responsive or intelligent than his companions. Zaius claims Landon had a fractured skull and was saved by the fine work of veterinary surgeons. Taylor flies into a rage, accusing Zaius of destroying Landon's memory and identity, at which point the President of the Academy orders that Taylor be gagged. Cornelius and Zira argue that he is a 'missing link'. It is Zaius who persuades the tribunal to let them have their say, as if he were the champion of free speech. And it is Zaius who initiates the charges of heresy when they have spoken.

Race is an important subtext in the film, though it was hardly touched upon in the book – but it is no more than a subtext in this first film. There is no big speech about interracial, or inter-species, harmony, although the lengthy 'court-room' sequence – probably the longest ever in an action-adventure family film – echoes a number of court cases, beginning with the Dred Scott case of 1857. Honorious says that as a man Taylor has no rights. Dred Scott was a slave, who was taken by his master, a US Army officer, from the slave state of Missouri to the free state of Illinois, where he lived as a free man, before returning to Missouri when his master was sent back there by the army. The master died and Scott was deemed a slave again. His case went to the Supreme Court, which ruled that no slave or descendant of a slave had any constitutional rights, because their ancestors fell outside the terms of the constitution, and therefore Scott must remain a slave. The court did rule that constitutional rights were being violated in one respect – they ruled that constitutional rights to property were being violated by measures to prohibit slavery in northern states. The rulings intensified divisions within the US, divisions that would plunge the country into civil war, with brother killing brother, just four years later.

The more obvious parallel is with the Scopes Monkey Trial of 1925, in which a young biology teacher, John Scopes, was charged with breaking a law that expressly prohibited the teaching of evolution in schools. The trial, in the little Tennessee town of Dayton, turned into a long debate on Darwin's theory of evolution, on the one side, and the biblical version of Creation on the other. The Monkey Trial judge refused to hear scientific testimony. But the defence lawyer, Clarence Darrow, called to the stand his opposite number, William Jennings Bryan, a former presidential candidate, and tore his fundamentalist interpretation of the Old Testament apart. Scopes was convicted, because he had taught evolution (though the verdict was later overturned on a technicality), but the overall impression was that evolution had proven its case. In the 1960 film based on the case, *Inherit the Wind*, Spencer Tracy played the liberal lawyer, Fredric March was the character based on Bryan, and Claude Akins, who would later play the gorilla general Aldo in *Battle for the Planet of the Apes*, was a fundamentalist preacher. But the cries of heresy in the *Planet of the Apes* 'trial' echo not just the Scopes trial, but also the much more recent McCarthy hearings into supposed Communist infiltration of Hollywood.

The tribunal scenes raise questions of race, personal belief, religion and science, and the film looks very specifically at the relationship between the last two. Many believed science was undermining religion. In the film Zaius manages to combine the posts of Minister of Science and Chief Defender of the Faith, though at one point Taylor accuses him of being 'Guardian of the Terrible Secret'. *Planet of the Apes* was made before Watergate, but it was becoming apparent that President Johnson had misled the country over American involvement in Vietnam, and there was a growing distrust in the US of the Government.

In private Zaius speaks to Taylor for the first time as something like an equal, albeit an adversary, explaining how he was useful in facilitating the case against Zira and Cornelius. Of course, Taylor is too stupid to have realized what was happening, and would probably not have cared even if he had realized. Zaius more or less admits that Landon could speak too before the surgeons got hold of him, and he threatens Taylor with brain surgery and castration unless he tells him where they came from. Taylor insists he is telling the truth. 'I know who I am,' says Taylor. 'But who are you? How in hell did this upside-down civilization get started?' With the help of Zira's nephew, Lucius, Taylor once more escapes. Taylor, Nova, Zira, Cornelius and Lucius flee to the Forbidden Zone, to look for the evidence that will prove Cornelius's theory of evolution. They are pursued by Zaius and his gorilla soldiers, who catch up with them on the beach beside the excavations. Taylor manages to identify mystery artefacts, including a pair of spectacles, but the clincher is a human doll that speaks, uttering the single cry of 'Mama'. Taylor argues that it is proof that man 'was here before you and he was better than you are.' It is a typical piece of Taylor yah-boo arrogance, with no logical connection between the two points. Zaius asks Taylor: if man were superior, well, what happened? Taylor speculates on meteors or a plague, and suggests Zaius has known the truth all the time. 'What I know of man was written long ago,' says Zaius, 'set down by the wisest ape of all – our Lawgiver.' He has Cornelius read from the Sacred Scrolls: 'Beware the beast man, for he is the devil's pawn. Alone among God's primates, he kills for sport, or lust or greed. Yea, he will murder his brother to possess his brother's land.' How can Taylor argue, for the words echo his own observations in the pre-credit sequence? 'Let him not breed in great numbers, for he will make a desert of his home and yours. Shun him. Drive him back into his jungle lair. For he is the harbinger of death.'

Before Taylor escapes (again) he asks Zira if he might kiss her. 'All right,' she says, 'but you're so damned ugly.' She is clearly moved, but although the moment is both touching and funny, there is none of the sexual undertone of the book. Zaius admits he has always known about man's past. 'From the evidence, I believe his wisdom must walk hand in hand with his idiocy … The Forbidden Zone was once a paradise. Your breed made a desert of it, ages ago.' Taylor maintains that he still does not know the reason why, on this planet, apes should have evolved from men, describing it as 'a puzzle with one piece missing'. 'Don't look for it, Taylor,' says Zaius. 'You may not like what you find.' And Taylor rides off along the beach, to find his 'destiny', in the form of the Statue of Liberty and the terrible realization that he is on Earth, an Earth that has been laid waste by nuclear warfare, sending evolution into reverse.

'Not until the apes start talking and the audience sat riveted and enjoyed every bit of it, did we realize that it was working,' says Zanuck. 'I think they were startled to see apes on horseback and to be thrust into that world where humans were running around

being slaughtered and all of that, because that first audience had
no idea what they were seeing. In those days we had real previews
with real audiences, not recruited, in which you have to recruit by
giving them a bottom-line synopsis of what the picture's about. In
those days we would just pick a similar-type picture that was playing in the theatre and use that audience, but they had no idea of
what they were going to see and I think you get a truer reaction
by that way of doing it, rather than a recruited audience.' More
than half the audience at a test screening in Phoenix in January
1968 rated *Planet of the Apes* as excellent, another quarter considered it good and only one in twenty ranked it poor. Zanuck and
Jacobs still did not realize just how big a hit they might have. 'I
just knew after that screening that audiences would sit still for
talking apes,' says Zanuck.

Children loved the colour, action and adventure. So too did
adults. But the film's deeper meanings and allegorical echoes
were noted by critics from the outset, at least in the United States;
their English colleagues were not quite so sharp. *Variety* set the
tone on 1 February 1968, with a long review that opened: '*Planet
of the Apes* is an amazing film.' It was a producer's dream review.
'Murf' called the film 'a political-sociological allegory, cast in the
mould of futuristic science-fiction'. 'Rather precise parallels exist
in the allegoric writing to real world events over, say, the past 20
years. Suppression of dissent by fair means or foul; peremptory
rejection of scientific data by maintainers of the status quo;
double-standard evaluation of people and events. It's all here.
Screenplay probably could not have been filmed ten years ago,
and the disturbing thought lingers that it might not be possible in
another ten years, when engineered public and political opinion
again swings into another distorted extreme.' But it was not all
heavy allegory by any means. 'Strong entertainment assets for
general audiences, plus concurrent – and perhaps controversial –
appeal to more sophisticated viewers, add up to excellent box-
office prospects.'

The review appeared alongside another report, headlined, in
typical *Variety* fashion: 'Dolittle Boff 26G Frisco Bow', which
roughly translated means *Doctor Dolittle* was doing well in San
Francisco. It seemed Arthur Jacobs's films were a bit like buses –
you wait ages and then two come at once. *Dolittle* premiered at the

end of 1967 to qualify for Oscar consideration and Jacobs master-minded a huge campaign to woo voters. Special screenings were preceded by a champagne reception and dinner, and the film duly picked up nine nominations. You could argue Jacobs and Fox made the best of a bad job, after reviews and public reaction fell short of expectations. On the other hand there were suggestions that the level and nature of campaigning brought the awards into disrepute. *Dolittle* lost out on the best picture award to *In the Heat of the Night*, a brilliant dramatization of racial prejudice, at a cere-mony that was postponed because of the assassination of Martin Luther King. *Dolittle* always looked a little incongruous on a list that included *The Graduate* and *Bonnie and Clyde*. It was like one of those IQ tests – spot the odd one out. But it won Oscars for L.B. Abbott's special visual effects and for best song, though there were cries of 'No' in the auditorium when it was announced that *Talk to the Animals* had beaten *The Bare Necessities* and *The Look of Love*. The film's biggest problem (apart from the very subjective question of quality) was cost. It was always going to be very difficult to recoup an outlay of over $17 million, and the film was no *Sound of Music* or *My Fair Lady*. With *Dolittle* beginning to look like it might live up to its name at the box office, despite that 'boff bow' in Frisco, *Planet of the Apes* became even more important for its makers.

By the middle of February the trade press was reporting that audiences were going 'ape' over the film. It broke house records in Los Angeles, New York and London, where it opened the follow-ing month without the critical acclaim that accompanied its US release. Pauline Kael, America's pre-eminent critic, reviewing the film in the *New Yorker* magazine, reckoned it was 'often fancy-ironic in the old school of poetic disillusion', but suggested audiences just sit back and enjoy it. 'At times, it has the primitive force of old *King Kong*,' she wrote, a reference which especially delighted Jacobs, who, you may remember, had deliberately set out to find a new *King Kong*. She made it her lead review and urged readers to see it before some spoilsport gave the ending away. Cue David Robinson. He made it his last review, in the *Financial Times*, devot-ing only four paragraphs to the film, but still found room to tell everyone what happens at the end. He spotted allusions to the Scopes Monkey Trial and to the Bible, and considered it 'a brave effort at an extremely difficult (and, one would think, somewhat uncommercial) theme'. Penelope Mortimer, in the *Observer*, thought there was too much talk and too little action. 'I had a fleeting dread at one moment that it was all something to do with Black Power; but I don't really think so,' she concluded.

But the film caught the mood of the time perfectly, a time when everything was possible, from the conquest of the stars to annihilation of the species. *Easy Rider* and *Midnight Cowboy* were still more than a year away, but there were signs that the old order of musicals and period dramas, and middle-class, middle-aged values, was under siege. Franco Zeffirelli's *Romeo and Juliet* took the radical step of casting two teenagers, Leonard Whiting and Olivia Hussey, as Shakespeare's star-crossed teenage lovers, and the film came complete with a nude bedroom scene; while Lindsay Anderson's *if....* presented a new spin on Tom Brown and other tales of harsh, but happy schooldays, with Anderson's boys machine-gunning the masters in a climactic bloodbath worthy of Peckinpah. It began shooting shortly before French students barricaded the streets and took control of sections of Paris. Thunderclap Newman caught the spirit of the age in their chart-topping record of 1969 *Something in the Air*, when they declared 'the revolution's here'. Shakespeare besmirched by naked teenage lovers, teachers slaughtered by revolting schoolboys, a sequel in the French capital to the events of 1789, but what could be more revolutionary than a world ruled by apes, with Charlton Heston kept on a leash? This is the guy who was Moses, for God's sake. This is Western civilization. In the course of the film he is gagged, stripped, stoned, whipped, burnt, shot, hosed, put on a leash like a little dog and threatened with both lobotomy and castration. Short of being buggered by the gorillas, what more could the film do to him? The film-makers were going to kill him and be done with it, but decided that seeing his civilization laid waste would be more effective ... and it is. Oddly, in the film, by contrast with some of the earlier scripts, there is no concrete evidence that man lost his place in the evolutionary pecking order as a result of nuclear war, as opposed to a natural disaster like meteors or the plague, as Taylor suggests. It is Maurice Evans's authority in his insistence that man is a killer and Heston's despairing reaction to the sight of the Statue of Liberty that hammer the message home, and brook no other interpretation of events. And because of the impact of those final scenes, audiences might also overlook the glitch in the Sacred Scrolls when they claim that man is alone among God's primates in killing for sport. What were the gorillas doing the first time we saw them?

Joseph Morgenstern, in *Newsweek*, detected influences from Darwin, the Scopes Monkey Trial, *Star Trek*, *King Kong* and even Galileo and Joan of Arc. 'The film catches us at a particularly wretched moment in the course of human events, when we are perfectly willing to believe that man is despicable and a great deal lower than the lower animals.' The two great superpowers had come to the brink of a third world war over the Cuban missile crisis in 1962. The United States was riven by internal division as well, with race riots and political protests. Social values and Christian beliefs were being questioned and undermined not just in the United States and France, but across the Western world. Young people were rejecting the values of their parents, looking to Indian religion (any variety of Indian would do) and even to nature for spiritual salvation. On the one hand individuals in some Western countries enjoyed new personal wealth and social and sexual freedom, and America and Russia competed in the space race, sending men to new frontiers. On the other hand many people felt hopelessly adrift in such uncertain times and the super-powers continued the arms race, stockpiling nuclear weapons and threatening to end it all by blowing the Earth to smithereens.

Pauline Kael reckoned the film was 'an enormous, many-layered black joke on the hero and the audience' and pointed out that 'what seem to be weaknesses or holes in the idea turn out to be perfectly consistent'. She does not go into detail, but the most obvious 'hole' that turns out to make sense is, of course, the apes' use of English. Only in retrospect do we realize that this is not mere cinematic convention, but has a certain conceptual logic, given that these apes live in the United States, or at least what used to be the United States. Kael adds: 'Part of the joke is the use of Charlton Heston as the hero. I don't think the movie could have been so forceful or so funny with anyone else. Physically, Heston, with his perfect body, is a god-like hero; built for strength, he's an archetype of what makes Americans win.' Erwin Kim, in the biography *Franklin J. Schaffner*, later wrote: 'Heston is most shrewdly used in the film, and is effective both for those who like him and those who do not.' Taylor is arrogant, cynical, self-important, just begging to be cut down to size by the little guys from the jungle, the guys in the pyjama suits.

'The object of the picture was entertainment,' Zanuck told me. 'We weren't trying to send any profound messages, most of which have been concocted and interpreted as time has passed.' But contemporary reviews prove critics saw various social and political messages in the film at the time, and Pauline Kael, for one, was aware of the ironic use of Heston and his image, even if the actor was not. Heston was attracted to *Planet of the Apes* primarily because he thought it was an unusual and imaginative adventure film, though it seems to have gradually dawned on him during filming that there might be more to it than that. John Gregory Dunne, in his book *The Studio*, noted comments made by Heston after watching the dailies, when he said: 'I think we've got something more than mere entertainment here … We've got entertainment and a message in this picture.' Heston suggests in his journals that the 'comment' in the film might boost its prestige with critics, but there is no indication as to what he thinks that comment might be. He would clarify this in an interview with Dale Winogura for *Cinefantastique* magazine in 1972 in which he said: 'What Schaffner and I were trying to say with it is that man is a seriously flawed animal; he must learn to deal with his flaws, that it's not something you can eliminate. I suppose the outstanding example of the same comment is Swift's *Gulliver's Travels*, which curiously works in the same way. It can be published as a boy's book of adventure, just as *Planet of the Apes* can be enjoyed as a fantastic adventure film.'

Heston's comments in *Cinefantastique* perhaps have an air of retrospective wisdom about them. But it would seem, even four years later, that he saw the film in terms of rather vague philosophical comment, rather than specific political comment. Yet the film is clearly making a statement about war and the lunacy of war in a nuclear age. And it was making it at a time when nuclear war seemed entirely possible, and indeed had happened two decades earlier when the Americans bombed Hiroshima and Nagasaki, and thereby avoided the need for Charlton Heston to invade Japan. Heston notes in his autobiography: 'I'd volunteered for my own war as we were supposed to do … I'd also given

God heartfelt thanks that two atom bombs had cancelled my scheduled inclusion in the invasion of the main islands of Japan.' He has always taken a keen interest in politics and social issues. He was president of the Screen Actors' Guild, as was Ronald Reagan, and he marched with Martin Luther King, but over the decades his politics have moved further and further to the right. As president of the National Rifle Association he has campaigned vigorously for the 'right' of ordinary Americans to own firearms, to protect themselves and their democracy, arguing that it would be absurd to allow the police and military to carry arms, but not individual citizens. His views have brought him into conflict with Hollywood liberals, including Barbra Streisand. His politics are clearly not the politics of *Planet of the Apes.*

'At the very beginning of my involvement I wasn't concerned with the social issues, I was concerned only with the mechanics of the screenplay and the dialogue,' says Mort Abrahams, the film's associate producer. 'As we began to go into it with Michael [Wilson] first and then with John [T. Kelley], I realized what was going on. We were evolving, really, a political piece ...'

Some actors recognized the political dimensions of the film at the outset. Kim Hunter had been on the Hollywood blacklist and she recognized it as a political film. 'The script to me was absolutely fascinating ... It's sort of as the world is today, and of not liking, sometimes being terrified of, creatures who are not like you, that are different.' Lou Wagner had no doubt that he represented the spirit of youthful rebellion. 'I represented free thinking, I represented the fair way ... I was just so proud to be a part of what a film like that said about war ... We just were playing with toys that we shouldn't be playing with, you know. And, of course, on all the different other levels, the social levels of racism and religion. There were just so many levels to that. A father of a child came up to me after the film one day and said, after seeing *Planet of the Apes,* his five-year-old child told his dad he was going to be kinder to his animals now.'

Whereas Boulle's novel was satirical, the film is much more obviously political, touching on many of the concerns of the day – youth revolt, race relations, the arms race, and even free love, but not, curiously enough, women's lib. Although Zira is a feistier character than in the book, she is the only prominent female, apart from Nova, who brings a very literal meaning to the expression 'dumb beauty'. Of course, the writers, producers and director were all male. Taylor's crew includes a woman, but the central character always had to be a white male, the prototypical white Western male, because he most readily represents the values of Western society, and it is these values that the film-makers deconstruct and challenge, whether by deliberate design or happy accident. And it is this challenge to Western society's values that so effectively touched a nerve within the audience. Linda Harrison says: 'Dick saw it as pure entertainment, so I kind of went along with that ... But what was seeping through all our consciousness is the era in which we were living, which was fear of Russia, fear of the Bomb. It was very real in the sixties ... It certainly reflected the times, civil rights, the black issue, the race issue and all sorts of issues ... I think it reveals what a lot of us were feeling, but couldn't talk about, and that was the race issue, which was very strong, and the apes, with the dark skin, were dominant over us whites, and somehow we were put in the position that maybe the blacks felt they were being put in, and held back and brutalized.'

One of the most remarkable reviews appeared in *Life* magazine in May 1968, when Richard Schickel had the guts to admit he had underestimated the film when he first saw it. 'I should have trusted my instincts, stood up and proclaimed my affectionate regard for the thing right off. Any sensible child, as I will shortly demonstrate, would have done so automatically. But there are times when a critic cannot or will not respond as a child ... Two factors contributed to my sense of guilt about this error. One was the slowly dawning conviction that *Planet* is the best American movie I have seen so far this year ... Care is taken to develop all the implications of its basic premise – the whole sociology of a world run by simians is exhaustively laid out for us ... Director Franklin Schaffner, screenwriters Rod Serling and Michael Wilson and their cast are in no way tempted to let us know that they feel superior to the fairy story they're telling ... Creative people no less than critics are concerned to keep their cultural credentials in order, mostly by winking broadly at us, nudging us furiously in the ribs and saying, at least by implication, "Just kidding, folks, I'm really Shakespeare in drag." The other, and more important, reason for this tardy recantation was my daughter's response to

*Planet.* She's only four, but her buddies down the street liked the movie so much that they had to see it a second time – twenty-four hours after their first exposure – and she was invited along ... Sure, they hooked her with the excitement of a crashing rocket, the exploration of desert and mountains, all those hairy, scary creatures tormenting Charlton Heston and chasing him all over the place and so on. But they also taught her something – that animals, and by implication all creatures different from her, are capable of feeling. It taught her, she tells me in her own way, that they can be scared of the unfamiliar and therefore as foolish and as prejudiced as more familiar beings can be. I have preached this to her and she has been exposed to it as she watched bland kid stuff of the Lassie-Gentle Ben variety. But no one has had the wit to vivify it by a simple, radical reversal of the kind we see in *Planet of the Apes* ... By the way, Erika just wandered by and asked me what I was doing. When I told her, she asked, "Are you writing about how we gotta see it again?" The answer, of course, was "yes".'

*Planet of the Apes* was not the prestige project that *Dolittle* had been. Musicals dominated the Oscars in the sixties, and science fiction did not figure prominently, if at all, in the thinking of Academy voters. But *Planet of the Apes* was not the only significant sci-fi film of the year. *2001: A Space Odyssey*, Stanley Kubrick's epic journey from the dawn of man to the space age and beyond, opened just weeks later. *Paths of Glory*, *Spartacus* and *Dr Strangelove* (another film about the insanity of the arms race) had established Kubrick as one of cinema's leading practitioners. A prestige project, *2001* cost more than $10 million. And, unlike *Apes*, there was no possibility of overlooking its philosophical dimension. Unlike *Apes*, it did not bother with a story: all it had was spectacular visuals, some nice waltz music and its philosophical pomposity, with woolly thinking posing as intellectual depth. It became a favourite with stoned students. The fact there were two such high-profile sci-fi films in one year helped focus Academy voters' minds, though they did not exactly go overboard with the nominations. *2001* was short-listed for four Oscars and *Apes* for two, for Morton Haack's costumes, which several reviewers had singled out for criticism, and Jerry Goldsmith's music. In later years, when sci-fi's critical respectability was more firmly established, Heston and, more especially, Hunter might have been contenders for the acting awards. In the event Haack and Goldsmith both lost.

There was no make-up Oscar in those days. Undaunted, however, Arthur Jacobs knocked off a personal letter to the Academy president, his old buddy Gregory Peck, proposing a special Oscar for John Chambers. It was only the second time the Academy had awarded an Oscar to a make-up man – the first was to Bill Tuttle for *7 Faces of Dr Lao* a few years earlier. And it was only right that they got a chimpanzee to make the presentation to Chambers, jointly with Walter Matthau. 'I knew about it before-hand, so they had a rehearsal,' says Chambers. 'They had a little, young chimp and he was a smart little bugger … He was going to come out on roller skates, wear a tuxedo and have the Oscar. I would say it weighs six to eight pounds. I says: "Jeez, the monkey is a strong little guy, but that's heavy and he might drop it" … so I made them take the skates off the guy.' Walter Matthau got off lightly from his simian encounter, compared to Charlton Heston, but he did not escape the rehearsal totally unscathed. 'He takes the chimp and he had him in his arms,' says Chambers, 'and the chimp pissed, because he's scared of everything … He was awful wet.' Still, it was, as they say, all right on the night, with Matthau, Chambers and chimp all immaculately turned out and perfectly dry in their tuxes.

It was all right on the night for *Planet of the Apes* too. It was Fox's highest-earning and most profitable film of 1968, with $15 million in North American rentals. Rentals was the money that went back to the distributor, as opposed to the gross figure taken by cinemas. It was the standard measurement of a film's perform-ance in those days. Very roughly the gross figure might be around double the rentals. *Planet of the Apes* earned almost twice as much as Fox's next most successful film, *The Boston Strangler*, with *Dolittle* limping home in fourth place with $6.2 million.

# CHAPTER TEN

# PLANET OF THE APES REVISITED

*or Vaguely Kept in Mind*

There were broad smiles on the faces around Dick Zanuck's table as Fox executives reviewed the early figures for *Planet of the Apes*. It was just as well for producers Arthur Jacobs and Mort Abrahams that it had been so successful, following *Doctor Dolittle*'s performance. And it was as well the two films were not conceived as a package, otherwise the losses on *Dolittle* would have wiped out the profits on *Apes*. But in Hollywood you are only as good as your last picture, and *Dolittle* was the picture before last, ancient history – for everyone except the accountants and the shareholders, that is, and it would come back to haunt Dick Zanuck before too long. But in the spring of 1968 Jacobs and Abrahams were now welcome faces in Zanuck's office, welcome to chat about apes any time they wanted, just as long as they did not mention the Great Pink Sea Snail. Abrahams was producing another film for Fox, under the Apjac company banner, a James Bond-type secret agent film with Gregory Peck, which would appear as *The Chairman* in the US and *The Most Dangerous Man in the World* in the UK, while Jacobs was concentrating his efforts on his grand musical version of *Goodbye, Mr Chips*, which was going ahead at MGM, with Peter O'Toole as the dotty old schoolteacher. After all the lean years, the future was looking bright.

As Jacobs, Abrahams and Stan Hough, Fox's head of production, walked away from Zanuck's office, it was Hough who suddenly stopped and said: 'Why don't you do a sequel?' Jacobs and Abrahams were taken aback. Sequels and series were traditionally the stuff of children's matinees and B-pictures, but there were exceptions. James Bond had recently proven audiences were prepared to pay to see the same character again and again as the main attraction. But the Bond films were based on a series of books, whereas *Planet of the Apes* stemmed from a single novel, it had been planned as a one-off and the ending of the film had seemed so final. There had already been one sequel to *The Magnificent Seven* and a second was on the way, though it seemed contrived to keep making films about a gang of seven gunfighters when the membership kept on having to be renewed, due to the nature of the business, to keep it at the artificial magic number. Bond could always find new adventures in new locales, but the Seven seemed simply to relive the same adventures against similar backdrops – they could hardly go to Russia or Japan. And where could Taylor go next and what could he do, except perhaps keep running away from apes, continuing the cycle of capture and escape? No one had any idea how to carry the story forward. They did know one thing, however – the Bond films had not only gone on making money, but *Thunderball* had outgrossed the first three. The first *Apes* film began with a vision of an upside-down world in which apes ruled and man was an animal, and Jacobs held fast to that vision through thick and thin. The second *Apes* film began with a vision of making money, pure and simple, and Jacobs clung to that vision just as tightly. There was no story, no concept, no title, no nothing, just a determination to cash in on the success of the first film. And in doing so, Jacobs truly proved himself a Hollywood visionary, ahead of his time.

Just to complete his happiness, Arthur P. Jacobs was in love. He first met Natalie Trundy in the mid-fifties when she was just fifteen and had a supporting role in the Marlene Dietrich film *The Monte Carlo Story*. Jacobs, who was there as Dietrich's publicist, was charmed by the young lady, who came from a moneyed Boston background and had worked as a model and actress since the age of nine. He apparently told Trundy's mother that he intended to marry her when she grew up. Kirk Douglas cast her as the lead in *The Careless Years*, a drama about troubled youth, but her career was put on hold while she attended college and 'came out' into New York society, winning the accolade of Debutante of the Year. Jacobs and Trundy met up again in 1966 when she was in London with a mutual friend, Vanessa Mitchell-Clyde, and Jacobs was working on *Dolittle*. When Mitchell-Clyde mentioned the friendship to Jacobs, he supposedly replied: 'She is the only girl I ever wanted to marry.' And indeed it is exactly the sort of thing he would have said. Mitchell-Clyde arranged for them to meet and Jacobs went on to prove it was not just studio executives who were susceptible to his sweet talk. Jacobs and Trundy married in London in May 1968. Once again Jacobs proved he could juggle several projects at once and he was back at work on *Goodbye, Mr Chips* within hours of the ceremony.

By this time both Rod Serling and Pierre Boulle were involved in discussions about a possible sequel. Serling suggested a plot in which Taylor and Nova find the remains of a city, along with weapons and a plane, which he uses to fight his ape pursuers. Just when it looks like all is lost, another spaceship arrives from Earth, like the Seventh Cavalry. Taylor has the chance to return home, but chooses to stay and try to lead humanity to a better tomorrow on the planet of the apes. Ironically this story would have restored the image of Heston that the first film had gone to such lengths to undermine. Serling subsequently suggested that, instead of discovering a plane, Taylor finds a spaceship and travels to another planet, which would also be ruled by apes, as in Boulle's novel; or alternatively he would travel through time to an unrelated adventure, in the manner of Doctor Who.

Boulle came up with *Planet of the Men*, a story in which Taylor becomes the leader of a new human community and teaches humans to talk again. Cornelius runs for political office against Zaius on a platform of reconciliation with humans, but Zaius wins and plans a war of extermination. Cornelius, Zira and Lucius go to warn Taylor, who orders his people to avoid unnecessary bloodshed. But his son Sirius (which was his baby son's name in the novel) hates apes and leads his forces in a slaughter of the simian army and a massacre in the ape city. Taylor is killed by other humans when he tries to protect Cornelius and Zira and they commit suicide. The film ends with the apes reverting to their previous animal state, and with Zaius in a circus struggling to say his name for a lump of sugar. It is a clever and ironic tale, but is essentially literary, rather than cinematic. Zanuck was blunter in a cable to Jacobs. 'Not good enough stop' was his verdict. 'It doesn't have the shocking and surprise twists the original picture had ... I have always felt that we need some major new elements in the sequel.'

It was Mort Abrahams who devised a storyline that would marry special visual effects and a third 'racial' grouping – mutant humans (though mutant apes were also considered). They would have the mental power to conjure up visions of earthquakes and fires. The story was built up around these two basic ingredients. Serling was unavailable for further work, Boulle had now proved beyond all doubt that he had no cinematic sense whatsoever, John T. Kelley's name was thrown into the ring again, but the writer with whom Abrahams was to collaborate in the coming months was Paul Dehn, an English poet and scriptwriter obsessed with the dangers of nuclear holocaust. Abrahams and Jacobs were regular visitors to England – *Doctor Dolittle, The Most Dangerous Man in the World* and *Goodbye, Mr Chips* were all shot there, and Abrahams thought an English poet could bring a fresh and slightly offbeat approach to the project, particularly to the language. Dehn was not just a poet. He had been a film critic for many years; served as a major during the Second World War with the Special Operations Executive, a forerunner of the SAS; wrote musicals; in the early fifties he acted in Herbert Wilcox's *Odette,* served as lyricist on John Huston's *Moulin Rouge* and earned an Oscar for his first film script *Seven Days to Noon,* in which a demented scientist threatens to blow up London unless the government get rid of nuclear weapons. Recent film credits included *The Spy Who Came in from the Cold, Goldfinger,* which also featured a nuclear threat, and the Burton–Taylor film of *The Taming of the Shrew,* in which Petruchio silences Katharina by dropping an H-bomb into her ever-open mouth … That's a joke, but only just – Dehn did actually adapt nursery rhymes to feature nuclear devastation and mutants.

Abrahams and Dehn's mutants would live underground in the ruins of New York City and would worship a nuclear bomb, with all the pomp and ceremony of a high mass – the bomb was housed in a set representing St Patrick's Cathedral in Manhattan. They worked their ideas up into a story outline entitled *Planet of the Apes Revisited.* The ape army and mutants are destroyed by the bomb in the underground city, leaving Taylor, Nova, Cornelius and Zira to usher in a new era of harmonious ape-human co-existence. There was even a half-human, half-ape child, to symbolize the extent of the entente cordiale, and the hybrid offspring got as far as a make-up test before going into turnaround. But no sooner had they got the script into some sort of serviceable order than Charlton Heston made it clear he did not want to do a sequel.

Franklin Schaffner, who directed the first film, had gone off to make *Patton: Lust for Glory*, for which he won a best director Oscar. Don Medford, a television director who had worked on *The Twilight Zone*, came and went, replaced by Ted Post, who had directed more than a hundred stage plays and episodes of *The Twilight Zone*, *Perry Mason*, *Wagon Train* and *Rawhide*, before the Clint Eastwood western *Hang 'em High* brought him to the attention of Hollywood's top producers. Post claims his new agent, William Morris, pressurized him to accept *Planet of the Apes Revisited*, to advance his career, though Post liked neither script nor star. Nevertheless, he felt the film simply would not work without Heston and threatened to quit too.

Zanuck was furious that Heston was refusing to appear in a sequel, when he had stuck his neck out for him, backing a film that had been turned down by every studio in town, and that had made Heston a fortune. 'The only story you could tell had been told,' says Heston in his journals, 'anything further would just be adventures among the monkeys.' Heston offered to appear in the opening sequence, if they would kill his character off. The script had to be rewritten again to introduce a new hero and accommodate a cameo from Heston. Dehn and Abrahams came up with the idea of having him appear at the beginning and then killing him at the end. Heston never let anyone forget he was taking part under duress and later, in his autobiography, he revealed he had never watched any of the sequels. It was hardly the best way in which to develop a coherent screenplay. Instead of creating an entirely new central character, Dehn simply introduced a mark-two version of Taylor, another American astronaut. Brent has followed Taylor's route from twentieth-century Earth to the planet of the apes, meets Nova and picks up where Taylor left off. Dehn and Abrahams even considered a romance between Brent and Nova, before deciding the audience might think ill of such infidelity on her part.

Burt Reynolds was in the process of moving from the small screen to the big one, following his success in *Riverboat*, *Gunsmoke* and *Hawk*, and seemed poised to do *Planet of the Apes Revisited*, but the deal fell through. Whoever took the role was going to be compared with Heston, who, although he was not going to star in the film, would pop up at the beginning and end to facilitate direct comparison. Abrahams was finding it very tough to attract a star name with such a proposition. Abrahams's background was in television and Jacobs too knew the value of recruiting actors and directors from TV – they had experience, the actors brought with them some sort of celebrity status, and both were relatively cheap. They settled on James Franciscus, one of the stars of *Naked City*, the cop drama with the legendary sign-off line 'There are eight million stories in the Naked City: this has been one of them.' Franciscus was reasonably happy with the story of *Planet of the Apes Revisited* – happier than Heston or Post – but was dissatisfied with his character, or rather his non-character. 'He was led around by the nose, saying yes and no,' he said. With the help of a writer friend, he rewrote his part. 'He didn't rewrite his part,' corrects Abrahams. 'He rewrote the whole damn screenplay.

'It was really something. We signed him and then I woke one morning and went for the mail and in the mailbox was this big envelope. I opened this envelope and here's what turned out to be a total rewrite of the script, and unfortunately terrible. I had no inkling that he had gone out on his own and hired a writer and done a total rewrite, top to bottom. I didn't have the faintest clue. When I got this, before I read it, I called Jim and I said: "Jim, what is this thing I've got in front of me?" And he hums and haws. And I said: "Look, Jim, if you're not happy you come to me and you say: 'I'm not happy' and we talk about it like civilized people. I'm really pissed off that you didn't do this." He said he was sorry, he apologized and then we had a long talk, and I said to him: "I want to read this," which I did. I don't know who wrote it, but it was quite bad.' Abrahams says Franciscus got on with making the film without further complaint, and none of his amendments were adopted into the script. Franciscus is another actor who is no longer around, but he was quoted in *Starlog* magazine in 1986, as saying: 'I turned the character from a man being chased, to a man in jeopardy – and confused, but still a man' – whatever that means. His rewrite still exists – he not only rewrote his part, he expanded it, with a lot of hip dialogue. He claimed many of his suggestions were taken on board, a point confirmed by Ted Post, who worked on the script with him. 'When I get to his home, all the papers were on the floor, and the writer was on the floor, and he was on the floor,' says Post. 'I liked Jimmy very much. Jimmy was very sincere … and determined to fix his role as best as he could, so that he could understand it.'

Post wanted to hire Michael Wilson again, but he was ruled out as too expensive. Post remembers Paul Dehn came to Los Angeles to work with him on the script, but Dehn spent the whole time in bed at the Beverly Hills Hotel. 'Every time Mort Abrahams would appear he would get a 104 fever,' he says. 'Mort Abrahams was the one who injected most of the clichéd ideas, working with this English writer who we shocked into a state of paralysis ... I never got to work with him.' Ben Maddow, who wrote *The Most Dangerous Man in the World* and won an Oscar nomination for *The Asphalt Jungle*, did a two-week polish on the script at the beginning of April 1969, just before it went into production with location shooting in the Mojave Desert, but Post was still not happy with the script and Heston was still not happy with the whole idea of the film.

Franciscus was hobbling around, having sprained his ankle playing tennis, and Heston was proving more aloof and difficult than ever, insisting on a helicopter to fly him home to Los Angeles at the end of each day on location. 'He said: "I'll give you twelve days," but he chopped it down,' says Post. 'We had only seven days, I think – "I've got to go to England, I've got to do this, I've got to go to Spain or something." I've got to direct a film. He did everything possible to get in and out and off set as quickly as he could.' Kim Hunter was not keen to do a sequel, but was persuaded to return as Zira. Roddy McDowall was one of the few who was keen, apart from the producers and executives, but he was tied up directing *Tam Lin* (aka *The Devil's Widow*), a Swinging Sixties version of a Robert Burns poem, and the role of Cornelius was turned down by Noel Harrison before the British actor David Watson was secured as a last-minute stand-in. (McDowall appears at the beginning of the film when it reprises the Statue of Liberty sequence from the original, and he would appear in the other three sequels and the television series.) Linda Harrison came back as Nova and Jacobs decided if Zanuck could give his girlfriend a part then he could give his wife one, turning the former New York Deb of the Year into the mutant Albina. The gorilla general Ursus was played by James Gregory, a veteran Hollywood heavy, who had appeared in *Al Capone* and *The Manchurian Candidate*. 'There was a rumour going round that Orson Welles had also been considered for Ursus, but I got it,' he told me. Post had indeed attempted to get

Welles for the part. 'Is it an ape?' Welles asked. Post told him it was. 'Would I have to wear a mask?' Post explained the nature of the make-up. 'You can't act with a mask,' snapped the great one. 'It's insulting.' Post pointed out that in ancient Greece the actors wore masks. 'A-ah,' said Welles, 'but can you name any of them?' Post could not name a single ancient Greek actor, so James Gregory played Ursus, though Ernest Borgnine and Burl Ives were also considered. Fox executive Jack Hirshberg suggested they might get some good publicity by adopting a strategy of casting well-known Hollywood veterans in minor roles and nominated James Cagney, Lon Chaney Jr, Betty Grable, Paulette Goddard and Claudette Colbert as possibilities, but there were two big problems – no one would see their faces and cash was tight.

The film had been costed at just under $5 million and this time it would come in almost on budget, but only after some expensive underwater scenes were jettisoned and the ape army was cut from 300 to 150. Wherever possible in those days, films had to adapt old sets, which was not too difficult if you were making a western. But from which film could you borrow sets if you were making a sci-fi movie about talking apes? The *Apes* sequel managed to make use of two from the Barbra Streisand musical *Hello, Dolly!* The dual staircase on which the mutants stand when they torture Brent had previously served as Grand Central Station. And Streisand's film's Harmonia Gardens became the location for the mutants' bomb in the *Apes* movie – art director William Creber would use that set again on *The Poseidon Adventure*. The ape make-up had been mastered in the first film. Chambers experimented with various looks for the mutants, including twisted faces with single, displaced eyes. Post claims credit for the final look, inspired by a picture in *Gray's Anatomy* and the idea that nuclear fallout might have stripped the humans of their outer skin and hair, leaving flesh and veins exposed. Chambers was able to draw on painful memories of his experiences working with disfigured soldiers to realize the director's vision.

Jack Hirshberg seemed as keen as Jacobs on making up lists: he came up with no fewer than ten alternative titles to *Planet of the Apes Revisited*: *Grotto of the Bomb*, *Sign of the Bomb*, *The Inquisitors*, *The Thought Projectors*, *Bend of Time*, *70 Floors Lower*, *The Holy Fall Out*, *Blessed Be the Bomb*, *The Devil's Instrument* and *Vaguely Kept in Mind*.

He was worried a title that included the word 'Apes' might confuse people into thinking they had already seen the film. Jacobs and Zanuck decided against *Vaguely Kept in Mind*, perhaps because it was too vague to keep it in mind, though shooting had begun before the title was officially confirmed as *Beneath the Planet of the Apes*.

Heston recorded in his journals that he was 'slaving away on my promised chore in the *Apes* sequel' and that he regretted having agreed to it. 'This is the first film, first acting, I've ever done in my life for which I have no enthusiasm.' In a later entry he complained he had had to reshoot a scene with 'the girl', i.e. co-star Linda Harrison. 'She couldn't lie dead without blinking,' he notes, though Post enthuses about Harrison. 'She was a lovely, lovely person,' he says. 'They [Dehn and Abrahams] did nothing but have her just look and say nothing and feel nothing ... so we had to find an action for her, an intention in every scene, struggling to understand what was happening ... She gave the role a dimension it didn't have in the writing.' Working with Harrison was one of the few positive aspects of the film for Post. 'It was a very unhappy experience,' he says. 'I remember Richard Zanuck was in trouble because his regime was in the red ... and everybody seemed to be insecure in their feelings about what to do with this film.' Financial restrictions continued through post-production when it was decided Jerry Goldsmith, who composed the music for the first film, would be too expensive. Goldsmith had been nominated for an Oscar, but Jacobs could not imagine anyone wanting to play his atmospheric, avant-garde soundtrack at home, and was hoping for something more melodic this time, something that might make an impact in record shops as well as cinemas. Anthony Newley, with whom he worked on *Doctor Dolittle*, one of the most melodramatic and over-the-top singers in the history of popular music, offered to compose and sing a theme song. Unfortunately for Newley, and curious posterity, the gig went to Leonard Rosenman, who had composed music for *East of Eden*, *Rebel Without a Cause* and *Fantastic Voyage*.

*Beneath the Planet of the Apes* begins where the first film ended, or rather just before it ended, with Heston's farewell to Zira, Cornelius and Zaius and his discovery of the Statue of Liberty buried in the sand. The credits continue as he and Nova ride across the desert, before the film cuts to another crashed space-ship where Brent (Franciscus) tends his injured commander. 'We are following Taylor's trajectory, so whatever happened to us must have happened to him,' Brent tells his superior, as if he would not already know. He seems surprised to learn it is the year 3955, though in the first film Taylor knew all about the effect of speed on time. When the commander realizes his wife, daughters and friends are all dead, he seems to lose the will to live. No sooner has Brent buried him than Nova rides into view, alone. Brent realizes she is wearing Taylor's dog tags and attempts to ask her about him. The film flashes back to Taylor's unsuccessful attempts to teach her to speak. 'Why don't we just settle down and found a colony?' he suggests instead. But before they can do so, they encounter a wall of flame, lightning and an earthquake and Taylor vanishes into thin air. It is a messy beginning, mixing footage from the first film, a new hero and then a flashback.

Nova guides Brent to the ape city, where an open-air assembly is in progress, with Ursus about to launch himself into a big, rabble-rousing speech. 'I don't say all humans are evil, simply because their skin is white,' he tells the assembly, and for the first time the series specifically articulates the difference between its species in terms of skin colour. 'But our Lawgiver tells us that never, never, will the human have the divine faculty for being able to distinguish between evil and good,' he continues. And he adapts General Sheridan's infamous comment about Indians to conclude that 'the only good human is a dead human'. He mentions new evidence that the Forbidden Zone is inhabited and talks of a 'holy duty' to invade it, much to the delight of the excitable gorillas in the assembly, though Zaius clearly has reservations and Zira dismisses the idea as 'a senseless military adventure'. She will subsequently dismiss gorillas as 'stupid – all brawn and no brain'. In a curiously misjudged nude bathhouse scene, we learn from Zaius and Ursus that eleven army scouts have disappeared in the Forbidden Zone and a twelfth returned with strange tales of fires and earthquakes. Maurice Evans and James Gregory did not want to do the scene in the nude – ape nude, that is – and for once they look like what they are – men in monkey suits – because in other scenes clothes serve to disguise the shape of the human body. Nova guides Brent to the house of Zira and

Cornelius, though how she knows where they live, and just how much time has passed since the first film is unclear. The impression given at the beginning of the film was that Brent's arrival came hot on the heels of the first film's conclusion, but it now transpires Zira and Cornelius are married; that Cornelius, formerly an archaeologist, is now a psychologist; and that a reconciliation has been affected with Zaius. Zaius is to accompany Ursus's army, but entrusts the interests of science to Zira and Cornelius in his absence. 'I'm relying on you both,' he tells them. 'And we're counting on you too, doctor,' replies Zira. Clearly some dramatic shifts in power and allegiance have taken place since the first film.

Brent and Nova are captured, but Zira helps them escape, renewing the cycle of capture and escape that was established in the original. Pursued by gorillas, Brent and Nova enter a cave that leads to an underground world. At this point they are in the Forbidden Zone, though in the original film it was several days' ride from the ape city, and in the book a flight was needed to reach the site of the all-important archaeological dig. There was a certain sense of dislocation in the original, in that we never knew whether the ape city was the centre of a wider civilization or that was all there was. But in *Beneath the Planet of the Apes* the principals bump into each other as if they inhabited nothing more than a village, and the Forbidden Zone seems to be just a hop, skip and canter away. Brent has his Statue of Liberty moment when he discovers that he is in Queensboro Plaza subway station, though the site of the station sign hardly has the same worldwide visual punch as the Statue of Liberty. Just to reinforce the message he finds an old poster for a New York festival. 'What could have happened?' he wonders. 'My God, did we finally do it?' he asks, as if he had been handed the closing scenes from the original film and asked to vary the wording a little.

Meanwhile an orang-utan minister asks for divine blessing for the gorilla army on the eve of their 'holy war' and the film enjoys one of its strongest visual sequences as the gorilla troops march off, rifles on their shoulders. Their path is blocked by chimpanzee anti-war protesters carrying placards and shouting 'Stop the war' and 'Peace and freedom'. They are carried off by the gorillas. It is one of the most obvious allegories in the entire series, but none the less effective for that, reinforcing the message that the films are really dramas about human society, dressed up in apes' clothing. Abrahams says he did not set out to comment on the Vietnam war and the student protests, but that as he and Dehn developed the story they were certainly affected by the news coverage. Not everyone saw the parallels, however. 'Perhaps I'm a little naive,' says James Gregory, 'but never in my life, then or now, until you mentioned it, have I had any such perception.'

Brent discovers the ruins of New York City underground. Cheaply recreated in the form of photographs and artwork, they are much less effective and dramatic than the Statue of Liberty. Clearly acting under the influence of some sort of mind control, Brent attempts to drown Nova. In the ruins of a cathedral (we know it is St Patrick's because it is on 51st Street), he finds a man worshiping a bomb that looks like a huge, shiny, gold bullet. The man is part of an advanced race of humans, who dress in robes and what look like old-fashioned bathing caps, and who can communicate by thought, although the process is accompanied by a little nod and a sound that can vary from the Tinkerbell tinkle to the tooting of a distant car horn. Brent is interrogated by a number of these characters and informed they are 'the keepers of the Divine Bomb' and that it is 'a holy weapon of peace'.

The ape army freaks out when confronted by a wall of fire and the sight of gorillas crucified upside down has them jumping around like agitated monkeys. But when a statue of the Lawgiver is seen to bleed, Zaius realizes it is a hallucination and rides into the flames, destroying the illusions. The visual effects originally conceived by Dehn and Abrahams as one of the principal foundations of the film serve their dramatic purpose well. The humans gather to worship the Bomb and, with the words 'I reveal my inmost self unto my god,' peel off their faces to reveal the hideous, hairless, heavily veined and scarred reality behind the masks. Brent is thrown into a cell with Taylor, who has identified the bomb as the 'doomsday bomb' with the capacity to destroy the entire world. One of the mutants uses mind control to get them to fight each other to the death, but their jailer's train of thought is derailed by the appearance of Nova and her shout of 'Taylor', her first word. Brent and Taylor kill the mutant, but the apes are now in the city. There follows a wholesale slaughter, with Brent shooting Ursus and apes shooting Taylor, Brent, Nova and the mutants, who have primed their bomb ready for launching at the ape city. A mortally wounded Taylor appeals to Zaius to help him, but the orang-utan seems to be his old misanthropic self again and refuses. 'Man is evil, capable of nothing but destruction,' Zaius says. And, as if to prove him right, Taylor, as he collapses, deliberately reaches out a hand to the red plunger and pushes it downwards. A rumbling appears on the soundtrack, the screen fades to white and a voice announces: 'In one of the countless billions of galaxies in the universe lies a medium-sized star. And one of its satellites, a green and insignificant planet, is now dead.'

It is an effectively abrupt finish, though one that Dehn disliked and Post fought against all the way. 'I got angry, I really felt that it wasn't the right thing to do,' he says. 'Human beings should cling to at least a little bit of hope.' The arguments went all the way to the top, before Zanuck ordered Post to blow up the world, though even then Post did not have time to shoot it the way he wanted, because Heston wanted to get off-set as quickly as possible. Fox felt the ending was so powerful, and so final, that they wanted to dispense with the closing credits. Kubrick's *Dr Strangelove* had done exactly that in similar circumstances, but the Screen Actors' Guild insisted on the usual namechecks, pointing out that *Strangelove* was an overseas production. Critics can, legitimately, see the ending as a reflection of the fear and pessimism of the times, though there is a much more prosaic explanation. 'I discovered not too long ago that Chuck was the one who wanted to detonate the world,' says Post. 'He didn't want to be called back ever again.'

Despite his reservations, Post believed the film had a strong political message. During production he wrote a sort of mission statement to articulate his views. 'The world seems ready to destroy itself and *Beneath the Planet of the Apes* asks you not to contribute to that destruction. Our days on this planet at this moment are numbered and the reason for our finite, unrosy future is that we are corrupting ourselves out of existence – with our double standards, hypocrisy, injustice, anarchy, shortsightedness, very shallow forms of self-delusion, profound national disarray, sickness, a cold war that does not end, a hot war that does not end, a draft that does not end, and a poisonous race conflict that does not end. What this film is attempting to say satirically is that it is possible we as a society have been playing the wrong game in the wrong ball park ... Atom bombs for peace is a lethal contra-diction. We must forge new links between the spiritual values of human self-fulfilment and the material society in which we live. We have to choose a life which affirms the infinite worth of every human being. The idea that lurks behind the film transcends the adventurous misfortunes of the hero.'

The film is divided into two distinct halves. The first returns to characters and set-pieces from the original film, while search-ing desperately for some spark of originality or imagination. The film seems determined to get its money's worth out of Heston, but unsure how best to use the very limited time he had deigned to give it. There is a certain sloppiness about the first half and indeed there was good reason to be surprised by the astronauts' arrival in the year 3955, if they were following Taylor's journey exactly. Brent meets up with Taylor on the planet of the apes – twenty-three years before Taylor arrived there, for we saw quite clearly in the first film that Taylor does not arrive there till 3978. On the other hand, one or both sets of instruments could be wrong. And, to be fair, I noticed this anomaly only when I played the films repeatedly on video while taking notes at the same time. I offer the information as an amusing titbit, nothing more.

*Beneath the Planet of the Apes* gathers some momentum in the second half, which rather offhandedly dispenses with Zira and Cornelius without further ado (though this is made to make sense by their reappearance as the stars of the third film, *Escape from the Planet of the Apes*). The second half sets up a new story in the Forbidden Zone, dividing its time between the invading gorilla army and the human mutants, presenting the audience with two sets of villains and no heroes, other than Taylor and Brent – Heston and Mini-Heston. Heston, who traditionally had led the world to a better tomorrow, is faced with a nightmare vision of how the world will turn out. And it is Heston, Taylor, the man who despaired of man's accumulation of nuclear weapons, who finally presses the button and deliberately destroys the Earth.

Post felt his film compared poorly with the original. Mort Abrahams says: 'It was essentially my idea, but in the final analysis I'm not too sure it was a great idea.' It is difficult enough working up a story from a blank page and perhaps the film-makers gave themselves an impossible task, having to accommodate the scenario of the original film, and use its lead character, but only for a few days. A third of a preview audience in Phoenix in early 1970 rated it as poor, a quarter as fair. But the film was shrewdly marketed by Fox, posing the question: 'Can a planet long endure half human and half ape?' and declaring the answer 'terrifying'. It went on to become a hit, making $8.5 million in rentals on its initial North American release. Eric Greene points out, in *Planet of the Apes as American Myth: Race, Politics, and Popular Culture,* the similarity of the tag line to Abraham Lincoln's comment that 'this government cannot endure permanently half-slave and half-free'. But *Beneath* is one of the less political instalments in the series and children were attracted not by political allegory, but by the exotica of the apes and mutants and the promise of warfare with new combatants and new weaponry. 'The gorilla war machine is on the march,' screamed the trailer. 'Human mutants strike back with new frightening weapons of the mind.'

It is perhaps surprising how many people became fans of *Planet of the Apes* after watching one of the sequels or the television series, rather than the original, and *Beneath* figures prominently in recollections. 'I saw *Beneath the Planet of the Apes* at our local picture house in Jersey way back in 1970,' says Channel Islands banker Dean Preston. 'I was ten years old at the time ... Hooked ever since.' On the other side of the Atlantic, Cuban-born shop worker Alexander Ruiz saw it on television in Miami at the age of seven or eight and the trailer alone had him jumping up and down like an ape. *Beneath the Planet of the Apes* is a mess, and yet it is, at times, undeniably exciting and visually arresting. James Franciscus seems like a pale imitation of Heston, but James Gregory, as Ursus, delivers a thumping performance, sounding just a little like John Wayne; and the film has many memorable images – the ape army on the march, the chimpanzee protesters, the crucified apes, the mutants removing their masks and worshipping the bomb. And the chilling nothingness of the ending. '*Golden Voyage of Sinbad* never came close,' says Ruiz. '*Apes* was the best I've seen by far.' He now knows all five films word for word.

# CHAPTER ELEVEN

# LIFE AFTER DEATH

When *Planet of the Apes* was shot there was never any suggestion of a sequel. But if it was difficult to pick up the pieces and resume the story after Taylor's discovery of the Statue of Liberty, it seemed almost impossible after *Beneath the Planet of the Apes,* the ending of which, at least in the mind of Charlton Heston, specifically precluded any possibility of continuing the story. 'Fox said there would be no further sequels after this, kindly destroy the entire world,' writer Paul Dehn recalled a few years later. But before *Beneath* came out, Jacobs was so convinced it would be a hit and Fox would change their mind that he asked Dehn to try to think of ideas for a third instalment, though he could offer little in the way of suggestion. 'I don't know how to solve this,' said Jacobs. 'We did kill absolutely everyone, and I would assume this includes Cornelius and Zira, since we destroyed the planet.' Dehn seemed to be faced with an insurmountable problem, yet within days he had come up with a solution. Taylor, Nova, Brent, Zaius and Ursus all died on screen, but the audience never saw Cornelius and Zira die. On the other hand, given that Earth was blown up, their prospects of survival seemed slim. Then Dehn remembered Taylor's spaceship at the bottom of a lake somewhere in the Forbidden Zone.

*Escape from the Planet of the Apes* begins by the sea, just as the second film had begun and the original had ended, with a familiar US spaceship bobbing up and down on the waves. Three astronauts emerge in white spacesuits, their features hidden by their helmets. They are met by military top brass, who snap to attention and salute, but the general's 'Welcome gentlemen to the United ...' is suddenly cut short, as the camera cuts to the astronauts removing their helmets to reveal that they are chimpanzees, their noses sniffing the air, their eyes darting around their new surroundings. It is a brilliant opening, though fans must have known or suspected what was about to happen, even when the film was screened for the first time. But it plays like a classic sketch from *Fawlty Towers* – the fact the viewer may know what is coming only heightens the sense of anticipation and the delight in the stunned reactions of the welcome party. Zira and Cornelius are accompanied by a chimpanzee scientist called Milo, played by Sal Mineo, who was James Dean's ill-fated buddy Plato in *Rebel Without a Cause*. We subsequently learn that Milo salvaged Taylor's spaceship and that the chimps travelled through 'a backward disturbance in time' to their own planet almost 2,000 years earlier.

Despite having to accommodate a storyline that begins with the destruction of the world and work on a budget of just $2 million, *Escape* was to prove the easiest film in the series to guide from typewriter to cinema screen. Dehn did discuss the possibility of Zira and Cornelius going to another planet, but budgetary restrictions determined their destination as contemporary Los Angeles. Dehn doubted whether the apes could pilot the spaceship and suggested, if not a trip to Mars, then the involvement of 'benevolent Martians' in guiding their craft, though that option was never developed. Dehn worked on an outline, entitled *Apes, Go Home!*, tracing 'the adventures (comic, tragic, satirical and often touching) of these simian strangers'. It subsequently became *The Secret of the Planet of the Apes* before arriving at its final title, which Dehn styled as *EscAPE*. Dehn later cited it as his favourite instalment. 'The *Apes* films I think you can take seriously because one can make so many comments about present-day life. I suppose *Beneath the Planet of the Apes* was a little bit too much science-fictiony, but my own favourite was undoubtedly *Escape from the Planet of the Apes*, which was a science-fiction story, but it was about two characters, played marvellously by Kim and Roddy, and because it was a love story as well as being a comedy ... *Apes 3* was shot and directed almost exactly as I wrote it, and my relationship with the director, Don Taylor, who guided me brilliantly through the second and third drafts, was the best I have ever experienced.'

The dancer Gene Kelly had branched out into directing and Dick Zanuck and Stan Hough wanted him to do *Escape*, but the job went to another former actor, Don Taylor, who had appeared in the film *The Naked City*, *Father of the Bride* (with his namesake Elizabeth) and *Stalag 17* in the forties and fifties. He had directed a handful of films and several hundred television shows, including *Zane Grey Theatre* and *Dr Kildare*. Mort Abrahams had left Apjac to work with producer Ray Stark and his place as associate producer was taken by Frank Capra Jr, the son of the director of *It's a Wonderful Life*. Roddy McDowall was available again, though initially there was a slight question mark over Kim Hunter's continued involvement. She needed a lot of persuasion to go through the torture of the make-up process again for the second film and she now had a baby to look after as well. 'When it came to the third one they didn't have to talk me into it,' she says. 'In the second one I didn't really have anything to do, I didn't have any scenes that really turned me on particularly, but the third one was a whole different thing. I fell in love with the script.' Natalie Trundy got her biggest role as Stephanie Branton, one of the two animal psychiatrists who examine and befriend the apes. Leslie Nielsen, who later starred in a string of spoofs, including *Airplane* and *The Naked Gun*, was proposed as the American president, though the part finally went to William Windom. Filming began at the end of November 1970, with scenes at Los Angeles's natural history museum and then the city's zoo. Don Taylor described the experience as a joy. 'I never had to worry about the script … and didn't have to rewrite on the set. Every scene just worked beautifully.' One day's filming had to be repeated because of camera problems, otherwise it went, in Taylor's words, 'like clockwork'.

If only things had been running as smoothly in the executive suites at Fox. Dick Zanuck and Linda Harrison had married since the completion of *Beneath the Planet of the Apes* (they would later divorce), but Zanuck's relationship with his father was feeling the strain of a some major flops. On the back of *The Sound of Music*, Fox backed a string of expensive musicals, including *Doctor Dolittle*, but they failed to repeat the success of the singing nun. Four big prestigious productions – *Doctor Dolittle*, *Star!*, *Hello, Dolly!* and the war film *Tora! Tora! Tora!* – made a collective loss of more than $40 million. Two days before Christmas the *Los Angeles Times* broke the news: 'Zanuck to oust his son at Twentieth.' When push came to shove Darryl Zanuck showed no sign of nepotism – and push had very definitely come to shove. *Variety* subsequently reported that Zanuck junior had been ordered to be off the lot by noon.

*Escape from the Planet of the Apes* finished shooting in January 1971 and at the traditional Phoenix preview 90 per cent of the audience rated it good or excellent. Jerry Goldsmith, who was composer on the original film, was back and he produced a very different score this time: the convoy carrying the apes to an air base is accompanied by a flamboyant mix of strings, brass and percussion that is instantly familiar as a product of the late sixties or early seventies here on Earth. There is very little action in this particular instalment in the series, but the humour is established very early, first on the beach and then more definitely as the credits finish and the general and his aide discuss arrangements for the newcomers. The familiar character actor M. Emmet Walsh, bespectacled and looking not unlike Phil Silvers, tells the general that they are in luck, that the sick bay at the local zoo has room for the chimps alongside 'a mauled fox cub, a deer with pneumonia and a depressed gorilla'. Zira seems momentarily embarrassed when the general walks in while she is changing into her familiar green chimpanzee dress. 'They are pretending to dress, sir,' says the aide. 'What do you mean, pretending? They are dressing,' says the general. This is delightful stuff, much more promising and assured than the messy scenes that opened *Beneath the Planet of the Apes*.

Milo advises caution and suggests they do not reveal that they can talk. But Zira, show-off that she is, cannot resist her big moment. She easily assembles the building blocks to reach a banana hung from the ceiling – an idea lifted from the novel, where Ulysse was faced with much the same task. She climbs to the top of the blocks, where she simply sits and looks at the fruit. 'Why doesn't she take it?' asks animal psychiatrist Dr Stephanie Branton. 'Because I loathe bananas,' says Zira emphatically. Zira is impetuous and flirtatious, fluttering her eyelashes at Branton's colleague, Lewis Dixon, and announcing that she likes him, with all the seductive charm of Dick Emery in drag. Having served his purpose, Milo is killed by the depressed gorilla in the next cage, a gorilla, which – presumably to differentiate it from the intelligent gorillas on the planet of the apes – looks surprisingly like a man in a traditional Hollywood B-movie gorilla outfit. This leaves Cornelius and Zira to take centre stage for the rest of the film, beginning with an appearance at a presidential commission of inquiry.

Dixon tells Zira just to be herself, though Cornelius suggests she should be her 'better self'. Dixon reveals to an incredulous panel that the apes can talk. Zira tells them her name, but they are not convinced that her response constitutes intelligent language.

Dixon is asked if the other one speaks too, giving Cornelius one of his best moments, when he indicates Zira and replies: 'Only when she lets me.' Zira claims they have come from Earth's future. Cornelius explains that in this future apes talk and humans are dumb and admits the gorillas waged a terrible war. Zira dismisses them as 'militaristic nincompoops'. We are told chimps, on the other hand, are intellectuals and pacifists. Zira and Cornelius seem to delight everyone, except for a church minister, who is outraged at their claim to be married, and the famous Dr Hasslein, whose theory of time and space travel was quoted by Taylor in the pre-credit sequence of the original film. Hasslein, who is the President's senior science adviser, spots Zira's discomfort and hesitation when she begins to say she has 'dissec...' and changes her mind, saying instead she has 'examined' many humans. The chimps become instant celebrities; they are transferred from the zoo to the Beverly Wilshire Hotel and travel by limousine. Cornelius is kitted out in a grey business suit, shirt and tie, while Zira enjoys a bubble bath and acquires a taste for champagne – 'grape juice plus', as she calls it. Cornelius is disgusted by a boxing match, while Zira is fêted as guest speaker at a women's club, when the series finally tackles the issue of women's lib. 'A marriage bed is made for two, but every damn morning it's the woman who has to make it,' she tells her audience. 'We've heads as well as hands. I call upon men to let us use them.' Women's lib was one of the few big contemporary issue the series had avoided, though Zira's qualifications as a spokeswoman for the females of a different species and a different time are not entirely clear. Never mind, it is amusing anyway.

Hasslein learns Zira is pregnant and when he gets her drunk she admits she saw the Earth blown up from the spaceship. Hasslein warns the President: 'One day talking apes will dominate this Earth and eventually destroy it.' The President asks if Hasslein is suggesting they kill Zira, Cornelius and the baby. 'Herod tried that, and Christ survived,' he says. 'Herod lacked our facilities,' Hasslein chillingly replies. There was a growing suspicion of government in the US at this time and President Nixon would be forced to resign from office just three years after *Escape from the Planet of the Apes* was released. But the film's nameless president is portrayed as an intelligent, decent and entirely honourable man, questioning whether it is right to alter the future, even if we have the power to do so. Hasslein wonders if killing the apes would be any different from assassinating Hitler if it were for the benefit of mankind. 'Yes,' says the President, 'but would we have approved killing him in babyhood when he was still innocent, or killing his mother when she was still in her womb, or slaughtering his remote ancestors?'

Subjected to further questioning, Zira blames the gorillas and orang-utans for the war. 'What's the difference? You're all monkeys,' says one of her interrogators. 'Please do not use the word monkey,' says Cornelius. 'It is offensive to us.' He is an archaeologist again, after a brief flirtation with psychology in *Beneath the Planet of the Apes*, though Zira is now introducing herself as a psychiatrist, rather than a psychologist. 'As an archaeologist, I had access to history scrolls which were kept secret from the masses and I suspect that the weapon which destroyed Earth was man's own invention,' says Cornelius. He blames human wars for the downfall of *Homo sapiens* and goes on to detail the rise of the apes, beginning with their adoption as pets, following a plague that wiped out cats and dogs. They proved so intelligent that within two centuries they were cooking, cleaning and shopping. But they grew to resent their position as a new slave class and the Sacred Scrolls record that one day an ape called Aldo uttered the species's first word, and it was 'no'. Cornelius certainly seems to have undertaken an incredible crash course in history since the first film, which hinted that Zaius knew more about man than he let on, without suggesting anyone was in possession of such a detailed knowledge of the transfer of power between the species. Under the influence of a truth drug, Zira admits she dissected human brains and experimented on live humans.

While accepting that 'what apes will do to humans is no more than what humans are now doing to beasts', the presidential commission rules that Zira's pregnancy should be terminated and the parents sterilized. Cornelius and Zira escape from the interrogation centre, and are helped by Dixon and Branton, who fulfil the roles played by Zira and Cornelius in the earlier films, that of the sympathetic, humane face of science and learning, while Hasslein takes over the role previously played by Zaius – the heavy hand of official science and authority. Dixon arranges for Zira and Cornelius to hide in a circus, where he recently supervised the birth of another chimp. Zira gives birth and the circus owner gives her baby a little medallion showing St Francis of Assisi, patron saint of animals. But they have to move again when Hasslein orders a check on circuses and zoos. They take refuge in a derelict tanker in a deserted harbour on the outskirts of LA. Hasslein tracks them down and, in a shoot-out, Hasslein, Zira, Cornelius and the baby are all killed. Zira's final act is to crawl over to her husband's body and embrace it. But the final scene of the film is one of a baby chimp, at the circus, wearing a St Francis medallion, and calling out: 'Mama ... Mama ...,' a plaintive cry that continues even after the screen has turned black. It is another superb twist – even if we might have suspected the switch. The fact the viewer may know what is coming only heightens the sense of anticipation.

And for once this ending is very definitely not the end. The film got some impressive reviews, though Arthur Jacobs was dismayed by the number of publications which simply ignored it and by the lack of promotional backing from Fox. Nevertheless, it would become the studio's second biggest hit of the year, behind *The French Connection*, bringing in $5.5 million in rentals. All the original characters were now dead – definitely, and Abrahams and Zanuck had moved on, but life on the Planet of the Apes would go on and on.

# CHAPTER TWELVE

# THE LAST PICTURE SHOWS

After the social comedy of *Escape from the Planet of the Apes*, Twentieth Century Fox demanded more apes and more action. With *Conquest of the Planet of the Apes*, they got more of both ... more than they bargained for, and more than they could handle. For this fourth instalment, the film-makers consciously turned for their story to the historical plight of black Americans. In the end the apes revolt against their human oppressors, shoot the police and set the city on fire. And writer Paul Dehn and director J. Lee Thompson quite specifically drew visual and thematic inspiration from the race riots that had exploded in 1965 on the streets of the black Los Angeles neighbourhood of Watts, just down the road from the Fox studio. The violence and politics brought Apjac into conflict with Fox and the American censors. In the new role of Caesar, the son of Zira and Cornelius, Roddy McDowall originally finished the film with a call for revolution. He was recalled by Apjac to record a new, placatory ending, designed to dampen down any incendiary emotions he might have aroused in audiences, particularly the black audiences with whom the films were proving especially popular.

Now, just when it seems like he has finished his final speech, he starts off again, like the traditional, even-handed broadsheet leader column, beginning with that old chestnut 'but', before running through all the counter arguments. The release schedule was so tight, however, that there was no time to shoot any new footage, just to record a little extra dialogue, which is why the final scene consists mainly of reaction shots. And when the audience does see McDowall's eyes, which he relied upon heavily to convey his feelings because of the heavy ape make-up, they still seem fired up with anger, even though the message is one of reconciliation. Nevertheless, *Conquest of the Planet of the Apes* went on to become Fox's biggest hit of 1972. Fox, Apjac, Dehn and Thompson settled their differences and teamed up again for a fifth and final

142

instalment, completing a saga that would stand unchallenged in science-fiction cinema, in scope and historical richness, until the arrival of the *Star Wars, Star Trek* and *Aliens* series.

The ending of *Escape from the Planet of the Apes*, with the baby chimp calling for his mama, was clearly designed to leave open the possibility of another sequel, though nobody seemed to think very far ahead in terms of where the story was going in future episodes, or could go; unlike George Lucas, who had the *Star Wars* series planned out in advance. Lucas waited twenty years to shoot *The Phantom Menace* and then spent several years making it, whereas Apjac was taking its *Apes* films from conception, through writing and filming, and getting them into cinemas, in little over a year. While Lucas mapped out a careful history for his galaxy far, far away, the *Apes* world history, like real-life history, was unplanned, a much more accidental sequence of events. These seemingly haphazard events did have the effect of boxing the film-makers in on future projects – whatever they came up with next had to fit in with the history as established in previous episodes. By the time they made *Escape* Apjac had wised up to the possibility that Fox might want another instalment, without knowing for sure, or thinking the series through to any logical conclusion. By now a pattern was developing – the latest *Apes* film would be a hit and Fox would say: 'Can we have another please?' Associate producer Frank Capra Jr recalls what happened then. 'Each time we would have to get Paul [writer Paul Dehn] and say: "Now, how are we going to get ourselves out of this one?"' And Dehn, in consultation with Capra and Arthur Jacobs, would work out how. And unlike the monumentally empty *Star Wars* films, the *Apes* movies managed to combine sci-fi exotica with serious themes. And they did not take place in a galaxy far, far away. They took place on Earth and reflected the world in which they were made.

*Escape from the Planet of the Apes* had been a hit, but for the next instalment Fox's marketing people wanted a return to the action and adventure of the first two films, while also cutting the budget to reflect the fall in takings of the third film compared with the first two – *Escape* cost $2 million, whereas No. 4 was to cost just $1.6 million. Jacobs hired J. Lee Thompson, a highly experienced English director who would have directed the original *Planet of the Apes*, had the process of getting it off the ground not proved so tortuous, and who had worked with Jacobs on other films too. Jacobs knew Thompson could work quickly and within budget. But more than that, he had a proven track record in the action genre, having directed the big 1961 Second World War hit *The Guns of Navarone*. Born in Bristol in 1914, to a Welsh father and Scottish mother, he started off as an actor in English rep in his teens, wrote his own plays and had had the first of them staged before he was twenty. He acted in films too, before switching to writing and then directing. In the 1998 documentary *Behind the Planet of the Apes*, host Roddy McDowall describes him as 'a prolific craftsman'. But he was more than a busy craftsman, with a strong visual sense. Although Thompson had directed in a number of mainstream genres, including action and comedy, some of his films had a very dark edge to them and had been controversial at the time of release, including the original 1962 version of *Cape Fear*, with Robert Mitchum as the deranged, southern ex-con who blames lawyer Gregory Peck for his imprisonment and plans a horrible revenge on his family, and the evocatively titled *Yield to the Night* (aka the equally evocative *Blonde Sinner*), a 1956 English film in which Diana Dors was a condemned killer reflecting on her past while awaiting the hangman's noose.

Thompson had been fascinated by the explosion of black anger in the Watts riots, which left twenty-eight dead and hundreds wounded, and he was certainly not alone in believing at the time that they might even be the beginning of a race war. California Governor Pat Brown described the riots as a 'war' and the LA police chief compared the rioters to 'monkeys in a zoo'. As recently as 1991, Capra maintained that *Conquest* 'didn't intentionally try to draw off the Watts riots or any other riots' and that any influence was subliminal. Now, however, he acknowledges the film was directly influenced by 'the way the winds were blowing' through US society. 'Of course the Watts riots stuff had an effect on the imagery,' he says, 'and I think Lee felt strongly that he wanted to make some political statement out of it.' The US Civil Rights Act of 1964 abolished discrimination and segregation in public life and a second act the following year reinforced black voting rights in the deeply conservative southern states. Many blacks believed the new measures did not go far enough; many whites believed they went too far. While Martin Luther King advocated peaceful protest and

progress, Malcolm X predicted increasing violence at the beginning of 1965. He was right, though he did not live to see it. Watts
was just one of a series of riots in US cities over the next few years.
No one was entirely sure what caused the Watts riots, which lasted
six days and involved thousands of national guardsmen and as
many as 50,000 rioters. Some blamed police brutality and others
the hot weather. Many black activists became increasingly militant
and white liberals became more and more uncomfortable at the
volatility of the situation. Stokely Carmichael advocated 'killing the
honkies' and predicted Black Power would 'smash' Western civilization. The riots did not flare into a race war, however, and by the
time Apjac came to consider a fourth *Apes* film they were in the
past; but it was the very recent past and racial tensions continued to
divide the nation. There would have been little question of a
Hollywood studio making a feature film with one of the riot leaders as its hero, but Thompson believed they could mirror the riots
in the new *Apes* film and suggested it to Dehn, who produced a plot
outline in March 1971, a couple of months before *Escape* opened,
though he did not get down to the serious work of writing the script
till *Escape* had shown that audiences had still not had their fill of
apes. 'I always looked upon it as a political film,' says Thompson,
'and I enjoyed making it very much because of that. I thought it
had something serious to say. I did have some trouble with it.'

*Conquest of the Planet of the Apes* does its utmost to compensate
for the shortage of apes in *Escape* by beginning with the impressive sight of hundreds of chimps and gorillas, swarming down
stairs and seeming to emerge from underground, to fill a slightly
futuristic environment, an unwelcoming landscape of sharp
angles and cold concrete, captioned as North America in 1991.
The film was shot in Century City, a new residential and commercial development, on land formerly occupied by part of Fox's
extensive backlot, and on the University of California's Irvine
campus to the south of LA. The apes are herded by human over-
seers, chimps in green overalls, gorillas in red – possibly the
origin of the idea of colour-coding each species in ape society, as
presented in the original film. Instructors teach them menial
tasks such as mopping floors and shining shoes. While the jazzy
soundtrack is hip and modern, in a seventies sort of way, it also
contains distant echoes of Africa. Circus owner Armando arrives

on the scene with the chimpanzee Caesar, the son of Zira and Cornelius. Armando explains to Caesar that, during the years he has sheltered him, a plague wiped out cats and dogs, humans adopted apes as pets and subsequently trained them to do basic work. But it is quickly apparent that all is not well in this brave new world, with humans demonstrating against apes taking their jobs, a 'rising tide of disobedience' among ape servants, and police – dressed in fascist black like Nazi stormtroopers – forcibly dispersing apes wherever they congregate. When Caesar sees police abusing an ape he cannot control himself and curses them as 'lousy human bastards' – he clearly takes after his mum, rather than his more cautious father.

Armando insists it was he who called out, and that he called the police 'lousy inhuman bastards'. He reports to a police station for questioning and advises Caesar that, if he does not return, Caesar should mix in with new shipments of apes from abroad. The authorities check on Armando's records and immediately suspect his chimp may be Zira and Cornelius's offspring, and therefore a risk to humanity. Caesar duly joins a batch of orang-utans from Borneo and undergoes instruction in the Ape Management centre, where he shines in the company of other apes who are shown how to wash and dry their hands, but manage to get the two tasks the wrong way round – drying their hands before washing them. He is bought at auction by Governor Breck, but when Caesar sprays himself with soda he is deemed unfit for the post of the governor's bartender and relegated to work in the 'Command Post'. 'It seems the little fellow is not quite so bright after all,' says Breck. 'No,' says his liberal aide, MacDonald, who is black, 'but brightness has never been encouraged amongst slaves.' Never mind slavery ... if this is the way future man will prioritize public positions, is it any wonder he is headed for a fall? While working in the Command Post, Caesar is dismayed to hear of Armando's death during interrogation and organizes apes in minor acts of revolt, such as emptying litter bins on the pavement and putting shoe polish on a customer's white socks. He also has them collect knives and other possible weapons, with one ape handing in a small tea-strainer.

Faced with mounting disobedience among the apes, Breck announces that he intends to crush the ringleaders. He is told that Ape Management's computers have spotted that a shipment from Borneo comprised three orang-utans and one chimp. 'So?' asks the bemused governor. 'There are no chimpanzees in Borneo,' says his security chief, Inspector Kolp. The fact that it has taken a lengthy computer operation to spot this anomaly might be regarded as further evidence of a species fast in decline. The mystery chimp is identified from records as the one Breck bought at auction. The governor phones MacDonald in the Command Post and orders him to hand Caesar over to Kolp. But MacDonald is sympathetic to the ape cause and pretends Caesar is out on an errand. Caesar reveals to MacDonald that he can speak and explains he intends to organize a revolt. 'You above everyone else should understand,' says Caesar. Inevitably Caesar is captured, and he is tortured with electric shocks to force him to talk and confirm Breck's suspicions that he is the ape for whom they are looking. Caesar is to be given one final, fatal electric shock, but MacDonald surreptitiously switches off the power and Caesar merely pretends to die an agonizing death when the switch is thrown.

He fulfils his destiny by leading the apes in a mass uprising, in which he uses his ingenuity to defeat an enemy armed with superior firepower. Breck warns that if mankind loses the battle it 'will be the end of human civilization and the world will belong to a planet of apes'. Ultimately the apes overrun the Command Post and take Breck prisoner. He is about to be killed when MacDonald appeals for mercy and humanity. 'Violence prolongs hate, hate prolongs violence,' he says. Caesar argues that it is the slave's right to punish his persecutors. MacDonald points out that he is 'a descendant of slaves' and asks if Caesar thinks he can free his kind by rioting. Caesar forecasts that the revolt will quickly spread across five continents. *Conquest* has compressed the history previously outlined by Zira and Cornelius in *Escape*. But it cannot ignore the climax of the original *Planet of the Apes* film and Charlton Heston's encounter with the Statue of Liberty – of course, the apes cannot take over the world quite yet, because we know Earth will be devastated by a nuclear war, caused by humans. Caesar – and the film – do their best to get round this when Caesar declares the apes will conspire, plot and plan for 'the inevitable day of man's downfall, the day when he finally and self-destructively turns his weapons against his own kind'. In his outline Dehn had followed the ape uprising by having China drop the bomb on America, but that was considered overkill.

Of all the *Apes* films *Conquest* is the one that most openly tackles the subject of race, and uses the apes to represent black Americans, drawing on historic white fears of slave revolts and the continuing concern about Black Power. In Dehn's original story outline Caesar is forced to flee the circus, is captured (inevitably), sold into slavery and 'whipped as the Negro slaves were', before being helped by the astronaut who brought back the virus that killed the cats and dogs, and going on to lead the revolt. And later the script included a scene in which Breck was strung up by the apes and whipped senseless, a very literal depiction of the transfer of power (and oppression). Although the final version is heavily political, it never gets bogged down by its politics, and works very well as a simple, linear action-adventure story, thanks in large part to the sure-footed work of J. Lee Thompson and his team. The final third of the film is devoted to the ape revolt, and, despite the limited budget, *Conquest* contains the best action sequences since the original, with the awesome sight of an ape army swarming into the attack. With fires rising behind him, Caesar announces: 'I will lead my people from their captivity and we shall build our own cities in which there will be no place for humans, except to serve our ends. And we shall found our own armies, our own religion, our own dynasty. And that day is upon you now.'

'We had a test screening somewhere in Los Angeles, and it was a largely black audience, and they screamed with pleasure,' says Thompson. He describes the screening as 'riotous', an interesting choice of adjective in the circumstances. But a second test screening to a white audience in Phoenix was disrupted by distraught parents wrestling their children from the cinema. 'The one in Phoenix got a lot of criticism and it was after that test screening that we made the alterations,' says Thompson. Capra says: 'The ending where he [Caesar] orders them to kill and to create a revolution was too rough and the censors didn't like it and Fox's marketing people didn't like it. Kids liked the pictures and I think Fox didn't want to turn away the younger audience ... I look back on it now and I think there really was a little too much violence in it, and that really was Lee.' Thompson believes it was the mixture of violence and politics that caused most concern. 'There was a lot of resistance to the fact that it was so obviously about the Watts riots, at that time ... today an audience I don't think would think of that. So there was a resistance against the film from the censors and from other quarters.'

The violence was toned down, but Fox did not feel that was enough, and McDowall, as Caesar, was required to add to his speech, making it clear that he finally accepts MacDonald's arguments. The film started shooting at the end of January 1972, wrapped in March and was to be in cinemas three months later – an incredibly tight schedule even without the changes to the ending. As the apes raise their weapons to kill Breck, Caesar resumes his speech. 'But,' he says, with almost comic timing, given what has gone before, 'now, we will put away our hatred. Now we will put down our weapons. We have passed through the night of the fires.' 'I didn't like that,' says Thompson. 'I wanted the more gritty ending.' Thompson maintains he did not intend the film as a call to America's black population to rise up in revolt, but as an attempt to understand why they had already done so and he feels there was already a balance between the views of Caesar, embittered by experience, and those of MacDonald. But, ironically, while the black character MacDonald was representing the views of white, liberal America, blacks identified most readily with the revolutionary ape. However, there is a slight sting in the tail of Caesar's speech when he adds: 'Those that were our masters are now our servants, and we who are not human can afford to be humane ... Cast out your vengeance. Tonight we have seen the birth of the planet of the apes.' The final comment is not only dramatic, but also provides an ironic echo to D.W. Griffith's silent film *The Birth of a Nation*, with its heroic vision of the Ku Klux Klan and its demeaning portrait of black Americans. We can only speculate how different the first *Planet of the Apes* film might have been with Thompson, rather than Schaffner, in the director's chair. *Conquest* took $4.5 million in rentals in North America and Fox ordered a fifth instalment for the following year.

Paul Dehn decided the time had come to show apes could be every bit as nasty as humans. In his story outline for the fifth film, *Battle for the Planet of the Apes*, Caesar has enslaved the humans and rules as emperor, with MacDonald as his personal assistant.

But other humans still occupy what is effectively a neighbouring state and demand that the apes free their slaves – a curious spin on the series's previous allegories, with the humans now cast in the role of Abraham Lincoln and the apes playing the Confederacy. War breaks out between the two sides and the humans bomb the ape city. Caesar sees the error of his ways, but both he and MacDonald are killed by the gorilla general Aldo. The humans fire a 'genocide bomb' that will supposedly emit a gas to make the apes sterile. It turns out the missile was empty, but the apes do not know that, and they retreat and designate the area 'The Forbidden Zone'. But Dehn's vision was an expensive one. *Apes 5* would be the first time the budget had not been cut; nevertheless, it was to cost only marginally more than *Apes 4*. And although Fox wanted action, they did not want the sort of violence and political under-tones that informed *Conquest*. 'The first script was again too violent,' says Thompson, 'and so we had a different angle on it.' Dehn was on the point of collapse, suffering from respiratory problems and what his doctor called 'a tension state'. Apjac hired John William Corrington and Joyce Hooper Corrington, who had written *The Omega Man*, a recent sci-fi film in which Charlton Heston battles with mutants after a terrible war has all but wiped out mankind. The husband-and-wife team reworked Dehn's mate-rial, retaining the central ideas, of apes showing themselves to be as imperfect as humans and of a war between apes and humans, while also downsizing the scale of the project. The Corringtons got on-screen credit for the screenplay, while Dehn got a credit for the story, and was absolutely furious. His involvement had not ended when the Corringtons came on board. He had returned to the project when his health improved and had in turn rewritten the Corringtons' work. It is standard practice in cases where a number of writers have contributed to a script for the Writers' Guild of America to decide who gets what credit. Arthur Jacobs confirmed Dehn wrote 'almost 100 per cent of the dialogue', but to no avail, and Dehn had to settle for the story credit. He was especially bitter because it was not his first run-in with the WGA, who had forced him to share screenplay credit with Guy Trosper, on the 1965 adap-tation of John Le Carré's *The Spy Who Came in From the Cold*, though Trosper died long before the film was made and Dehn claimed never even to have seen the Trosper version of the script. As far as

Thompson was concerned, however, *Battle* was hardly worth arguing over. 'I thought it didn't have any very serious content, it wasn't anything like *Conquest*, and it should be directed towards kids,' he says. 'And it was very successful and the kids liked it.'

A caption announces that *Battle for the Planet of the Apes* is set in North America in 2670 and the familiar, hugely authoritative voice of John Huston, the veteran actor and director, declares: 'In the beginning, God created beast and man, so that both might live in friendship and share dominion over a world at peace.' However, evil men 'betrayed God's trust' and waged wars against one another and reduced apes to slavery. The language was biblical and the choice of Huston no accident. He had played Noah, and narrated and directed Twentieth Century Fox's 1966 epic *The Bible*. He brought more than ordinary terrestrial authority to the role. The obvious choice might have been Charlton Heston, but he had been so difficult on *Beneath the Planet of the Apes* no one dared asked him to make a comeback in a different role. Joyce Hooper Corrington has said that her portrait of the gorillas was inspired by negative perceptions of Black Power and the notion of reverse racism, but that the main inspirations were religious, and the murder of Caesar's only son manages to evoke both Christ's death and the story of Cain and Abel.

The camera pans from a forest to the narrator, who is revealed to be an orang-utan, dressed in the familiar tan-coloured outfit of the species. Huston recounts the story of the apes' 'saviour', beginning with flashbacks to his birth in *Escape from the Planet of the Apes* and the ape rebellion in *Conquest of the Planet of the Apes*. 'Yet in the aftermath of his victory, the surface of the world was ravaged by the vilest war in human history. The great cities of the world split asunder and were flattened. And out of one such city our saviour led a remnant of those who survived, in search of greener pastures, where ape and human might for ever live in friendship ... This is his story in those far-off days.' The opening scenes feature a green landscape, horses and carts and an almost medieval village, complete with tree houses, an environment that bears more resemblance to the world of Robin Hood than to the previous *Apes* film, *Conquest*, except it is populated by apes. The apes have very quickly acquired the power of speech and share their Ape Eden with sympathetic humans, though the humans have been reduced, if not quite to the level of slaves, then to an underclass of servants, without representation on the village council. The council seems to have merely an advisory role anyway, with real power resting in the benevolent dictatorship of Caesar. Nevertheless, one of the humans is entrusted with the role of teacher, instructing his pupils, who include General Aldo and other adult gorillas, how to write the most important of the ape commandments: 'Ape shall never kill ape.'

Among Caesar's human allies is the brother of the MacDonald who helped him in *Conquest*. The reason why it is MacDonald's brother and not MacDonald is simple – actor Hari Rhodes, who played MacDonald No. 1, was unavailable, though why Apjac could not simply have cast replacement Austin Stoker as the original character, rather than his brother, is unclear: after all the James Bond producers managed to replace Sean Connery with a succession of actors without having to present them as James's brothers, children and grandchildren.

Caesar and MacDonald plan to visit the ruins of Governor Breck's city, with the intention of locating the bomb-proof, underground archives that housed film showing the questioning of Caesar's parents. Caesar is anxious to see what his parents looked like and also to learn exactly what they said about Earth's future and its possible demise. They fear some humans may still be living in the 'Forbidden City' and withdraw firearms from an arsenal which is supervised by an orang-utan called Mandemus. Although Caesar rules his small domain, he must persuade Mandemus he has a valid reason to withdraw weapons, having appointed him to act as his 'conscience'. Caesar and MacDonald are accompanied by another orang-utan, Virgil, who 'knows everything about everything'. Never previously have the differences between the ape species been so clearly delineated, with the orang-utans presented as brilliant intellectuals, in contrast to Zira's description of them as 'a bunch of pseudo-scientific geese' in *Escape*, though the gorillas live up to her dismissal of them as 'militaristic nincompoops'.

The city is populated by radiation-scarred humans and is governed by Breck's former security man, Kolp. He recognizes Caesar and MacDonald on closed-circuit television and orders their apprehension. When reminded that there has been twelve years of peace, he replies: 'Yes, it has been rather boring.' Caesar's party

*Above: Charlton Heston had been Ben-Hur, John the Baptist and Moses, in* The Ten Commandments *(pictured). He was God's right-hand man and he symbolised thousands of years of western civilisation. No other actor could have provided such a complete sense of downfall and humiliation at the hands of those 'damn dirty apes', though the film-makers never discussed the real meaning of the film with its conservative star (picture courtesy of the Kobal Collection, © Twentieth Century Fox).*

*Above: Taylor and Zira say an emotional goodbye on the beach, though Boulle had gone much further in the original novel in suggesting a sexual chemistry between the two (picture courtesy of the Kobal Collection, © Twentieth Century Fox).*

*Above: Charlton Heston agreed to only a brief appearance in* Beneath the Planet of the Apes *and the script was rewritten to accommodate a new astronaut, James Franciscus. Linda Harrison and Kim Hunter reprised the roles of Nova and Zira (picture courtesy of the Kobal Collection, © Twentieth Century Fox).*

*Opposite: Former child star Roddy McDowall was to become a mainstay of the film and television series, originally as the chimpanzee intellectual Cornelius (pictured) and later as Caesar and Galen (picture courtesy of the Kobal Collection, © Twentieth Century Fox).*

Above: Cast and crew collapsed from heat exhaustion on
the bleached desert landscape on the Utah-Arizona border, but
Charlton Heston proved his manliness with a daily two-mile run
during the lunch break (picture courtesy of the Academy of
Motion Picture Arts and Sciences, © Twentieth Century Fox).

*Above: Scenes shot in the desert include one in which Zira discovers Nova is going to have a baby ... except she never did become a mum. The scene was cut from the final film, prompting allegations of censorship against Twentieth Century Fox (picture courtesy of the Academy of Motion Picture Arts and Sciences, © Twentieth Century Fox).*

**HOW TO WIN AN OSCAR**

*Make-Up Artist*

MAGAZINE

GHOSTS OF MISSISSIPPI
MATTHEW MUNGLE

BOBBI BROWN
EXCLUSIVE
INTERVIEW

A TRIBUTE TO
JOHN CHAMBERS

0 74470 90399 4

02>

*Above: Walter Matthau shared presentation duties with a
chimpanzee when it came to handing over the Oscar to John
Chambers for his remarkable make-up. Chambers looks delighted,
Matthau looks wary, possibly with good reason, for the chimp
peed on him at the rehearsal – just one more humiliation
inflicted on the Hollywood star system by the apes
(picture courtesy of* Make-Up Artist Magazine*).*

*Above: Roddy McDowall, Kim Hunter and Charlton Heston got back together for an anniversary party in August 1998, where they met members of the Apemania tribute group. McDowall died a few weeks later (picture courtesy of Apemania).*

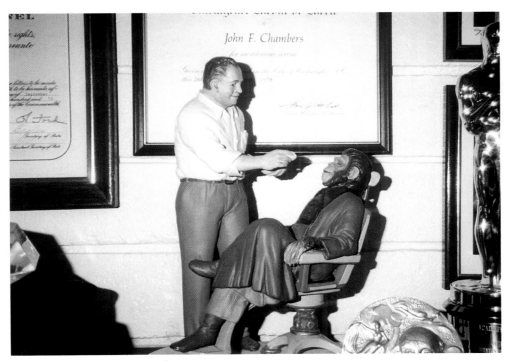

*Above: John Chambers inspired Apemania founder Brian Penikas to become a make-up artist and won the appreciation of thousands of fans. One crafted a model of Chambers making up Kim Hunter as Zira and sent it to him as a present. It takes pride of place alongside the Oscar (picture courtesy of Brian Pendreigh).*

*Above: The apes found new life on television, with Ron Harper as astronaut Alan Virdon facing up to the menace of General Urko (Mark Lenard) and a new Dr Zaius (Booth Colman). (Picture courtesy of the Kobal Collection, © Twentieth Century Fox).*

*Above: The posters reflect their times, a fashion for original artwork and the colour and excitement of a planet turned upside down, where men are hunted for sport and apes are the dominant species (pictures courtesy of the Kobal Collection, © Twentieth Century Fox).*

escapes, but Kolp's scouts follow them and locate 'Ape City'. The Corringtons called their version of the story *Epic of the Planet of the Apes*, before it was decided to stick with Dehn's title, but the budget restrictions were really beginning to show and the fifth film might more properly have been called *Battle for the Village of the Apes*. It was not just in the scale of the encampment that budget restrictions were evident, but in the short cuts that were now being taken with ape make-up. On the final two films an increasing number of actors were wearing ape masks, rather than having their make-up applied layer by layer. The film-makers were well aware that the masks hardly measured up to John Chambers's original concept, but felt they had no choice when faced with the options of a pull-on mask or hours and hours in make-up, with huge bills for overtime for both actors and make-up artists. The films were beginning to look like television. The schedule on the final film was also incredibly tight. It began shooting in January 1973 and was in cinemas six months later. 'That's never a good thing,' says Thompson. 'You want time really to study the editing. The editing of a film is so important and can turn a comparatively bad first cut into a very good film ... We had, frankly, no time to really study it. I remember we worked all round the clock and we had to rush it.'

Caesar's wife Lisa (Natalie Trundy again) argues the humans in the Forbidden City may have opened fire on Caesar simply because they felt threatened. Kolp does indeed fear the apes may return to attack him. But he also wants to plunder their orchards and vineyards, and prepares his own forces for an attack. Scenes were shot in which Kolp orders one of his assistants to fire their nuclear missile at Ape City if they lose the battle. She is, however, dissuaded by another aide, who says: 'It must never be exploded. It must be respected, even venerated, for one of its ancestors made us what we are.' The scenes were cut from release prints of the film, but are included in an alternative television version, and provide a back-story for the religious cult in *Beneath the Planet of the Apes*.

Aldo also anticipates war, and plans his own rebellion to overthrow Caesar. When Aldo discovers he has been overheard by Caesar's son, Cornelius, he chops through the branch on which Cornelius has taken refuge, and the young chimp plunges to the ground. It is MacDonald who later spots the evidence of the cut branch and tells Virgil. The film neatly sets up simple, overlapping storylines, in the manner of modern television drama, with Caesar tending his desperately ill son, the humans marching on the ape encampment and Aldo taking the opportunity to seize power and lock up the village's humans. Aldo, however, is a very one-dimensional and rather thick villain, with none of the complexity of Zaius or Hasslein. Cornelius dies, the humans attack in a variety of vehicles, including a familiar yellow school bus, and again Caesar uses his intelligence to defeat them, lulling them into a false sense of security by pretending the apes are defeated. He orders that the prisoners should not be killed, though Aldo's troops massacre those who try to escape, including Kolp.

Aldo orders the execution of all the humans in the village, but Virgil confronts him with the death of Cornelius. Realizing Aldo has broken their most sacred rule, the apes turn against Aldo, chanting: 'Ape has killed ape.' Aldo retreats into a tree, where he wrestles briefly with Caesar, before falling to his death. It is a silly scene, and there is no reason to believe a chimp could get the better of a gorilla, particularly a gorilla warrior. MacDonald suggests to Caesar that perhaps they can change the future and avoid the scheduled apocalypse. Back in 2670, Huston's character, who is revealed as the Lawgiver, tells his audience of young apes and humans: 'We still wait my children, but as I look at apes and humans living in friendship, harmony and at peace, now some 600 years after Caesar's death, at least we wait with hope for the future.' Asked who knows what the future holds, the Lawgiver suggests that perhaps only the dead know. And the camera pans, for the final shot of the whole series of films, to a statue of Caesar, which is seen to be weeping. Although audiences could hardly have been expected to spot the significance of the year 2670, at that very moment Taylor must have been doing his captain's log bit at the beginning of the original *Planet of the Apes* film. The series had come full circle.

# CHAPTER THIRTEEN

# BOOMERANGUTANG

*The Apes Just Keep Coming Back*

It is popularly believed film merchandising took off with George Lucas and *Star Wars*, but the United States went ape over *Planet of the Apes* toys, clothes and other tie-ins three years earlier in 1974 – the year after the last film was released. Every *Apes* film made a profit, but revenue fell with each instalment. A sixth film was discussed, but it was decided *Battle for the Planet of the Apes* should be the last. Arthur P. Jacobs, who had been troubled with heart problems for years, died soon after *Battle* was released. Love him or loathe him, Jacobs was undoubtedly the driving force behind the films. But, far from his death marking the end of the road for talking chimps, gorillas and orang-utans, they were to get a whole new lease of life with the release of the films in a marathon 'Go Ape!' quintuple bill, a television spin-off series and a belated marketing blitz, which introduced thousands, possibly millions, of young fans to *Planet of the Apes*, and which, for better or worse, would redefine the relationship between, on the one hand, cinema and television, and, on the other, toys and other consumer goods, leading to the current situation in which it is now more difficult to buy a burger without a plastic toy than it is to buy one without ketchup.

It might have happened earlier, because Arthur Jacobs firmly believed there was a huge untapped market for movies and movie characters outside the cinema itself. Disney successfully produced a range of toys and other products, inspired by the enduring popularity of their films, and, most ambitious of all, had provided the public with a prototype interactive experience at Disneyland theme park. Disney was regarded very much as a special case, but James Bond proved the spin-off market was not exclusive to a single company, with 007 toy guns, models, games and, of course, the Aston Martin car, with its famous ejector seat, fondly remembered by a generation of schoolboys. Jacobs wanted a slice of the cake ... but he chose the wrong film on which to pin his hopes. There were *Doctor Dolittle* T-shirts, toys – including a vet kit, even pet food tie-ins, and the initial pressing of the soundtrack album ran to 500,000 copies – the biggest in history. They proved about as popular as veal at a vegetarian dinner party. But in the long run Jacobs was right, the market was there for film tie-ins, just not for *Doctor Dolittle* tie-ins. Terry Hoknes, organizer of the International Planet of the Apes Fan Club, compiled a database of memorabilia for his fanzine *Ape Chronicles* in 1995, listing almost a thousand items. As well as the usual model figures, toy weapons, clothing, posters and film stills, it included masks, trading cards, confectionery, belt buckles, key chains, mugs, magnets, pillows, inflatable rubber rings for swimming, beanbag chairs, sleeping bags, rubbish bins, kites, light-switch plates, frisbees, torches, bagatelle, beach balls, soap, toy periscopes and even a 'boomerangutang'. By 1975, the year in which *Planet of the Apes* became a cartoon series, it was reported that the merchandising boom was approaching $100 million.

Arthur Jacobs had been desperate to widen his scope beyond talking animals and teamed up with Woody Allen on *Play It Again, Sam*, which brought a trench-coated Humphrey Bogart back from the dead as Allen's mentor and indulged Jacobs's passion for classic cinema. He subsequently turned his attention from Woody and Bogie to an earlier American cultural lion, Mark Twain, and musical adaptations of Twain's classic tales of Americana *Tom Sawyer* and *Huckleberry Finn*. But Jacobs's relationship with Frank Capra Jr was beginning to come under strain. 'Arthur and I parted company a little bit unpleasantly,' says Capra, who, like Abrahams before him, wanted producer credit rather than that of associate producer. It was Capra who set up *Tom Sawyer*, with director Don Taylor and a cast that included Warren Oates and Jodie Foster, and it was Capra who was on the set every day dealing with the logistics of film production. Jacobs promised he would consider crediting him, on screen, as the film's producer when it was finished, depending on whether he thought he had done a good enough job. 'I showed it to him,' says Capra, 'and he said to me: "Well, this is way too good. I can't take my name off as producer."' Capra walked out and subsequently became president of Screen Gem Studios in North Carolina, home of the popular television teen drama series *Dawson's Creek.* Jacobs was a master of intrigue and duplicity, who knew the value of publicity, the half-truth and the total fabrication, who would use others to advance his ambitions and then ruthlessly cut them adrift, no matter how big a name they might be. In short he was the very model of a successful Hollywood producer. He also had vision, ambition and drive. If he had lacked any of those attributes, he might never have managed to defy the odds and turn *Planet of the Apes* from a French satirical novel into a hugely popular Hollywood movie. 'He came from the world of public relations and he had great ideas,' says Capra. 'And he had great contacts throughout the industry. And he was very well liked.' Despite all the wheeling and dealing, many colleagues could not help but admire him. And more than that, unlike many producers today, Arthur P. Jacobs loved cinema.

His apes would outlive him on the small screen, where Fox needed a science-fiction series to replace those of the legendary Irwin Allen. Between 1964 and 1970 Allen produced, wrote and directed a string of TV series, including *Voyage to the Bottom of the Sea*, *Lost in Space*, *The Time Tunnel* and *Land of the Giants*, but he had recently returned to film production and Fox wanted some-thing new to plug the gap. Or at least new to television. The idea of a television series based on a hit film was hardly revolutionary. Hollywood studio bosses blamed TV for the drop in cinema attendance after the Second World War. Jack Warner banned his stars from appearing on television, and banned television sets from appearing in his movies. But before long even Warner was working with the new medium, with series based on *Cheyenne*, *Kings Row* and *Casablanca*. The studios had an increasing stake in television and their old movies provided a ready and cheap source of characters and storylines. *The Thin Man, Father of the Bride* and *National Velvet* were all adapted for the small screen in the fifties and early sixties in the US, and British television brought *The Third Man* and *Dixon of Dock Green* back from the dead. By the end of the sixties television had begun to produce its own heroes (who would be hijacked by cinema in later decades) and the flow of ideas from cinema to TV had slowed to a trickle. But in 1972 Fox successfully transferred *M\*A\*S\*H* from the big screen to the small, where it would last several times longer than the war during which it was set. Stan Hough was the Fox executive who first proposed a sequel to *Planet of the Apes* and he took personal charge of the TV version of *Planet of the Apes*, a series of fourteen hour-long episodes, first screened in 1974 on CBS in the US and ITV in the UK.

Three American astronauts leave Earth in 1980 and crash on an unknown planet in 3085 – 900 years before the events of the original film and 400 years after John Huston's spiel at the end of *Battle for the Planet of the Apes*. The credit sequence introduces us to chimpanzee Galen (Roddy McDowall) and American astronauts Alan Virdon (Ron Harper, star of the TV *Dirty Dozen* imitation ironically entitled *Garrison's Gorillas*) and Pete Burke (James Naughton from the private eye series *Faraday and Company*). They are seen running from gorillas, who are on horseback and dramatically silhouetted against the sun – motifs which go a long way towards summing up a show that projected the intermittent sense of motion of *The Fugitive*, *Alias Smith and Jones* and *Wagon Train* on to a *Planet of the Apes* template. The cycle of pursuit, capture and escape, which was established in the original film and was probably its biggest weakness, is taken to surreal extremes here. One or other of the principals is incarcerated almost every week, only to escape from under the nose of the gorilla general Urko, usually by nothing more devious than jumping through a window or biffing a sentry when he comes through the door. We know that our heroes are not about to be executed in episode two and the series suffers from an increasing lack of menace. In one episode Virdon even takes part in a horse race Urko is watching, having covered himself in mud to avoid recognition.

The series opens promisingly with a scene in which an old man takes refuge in a tree from a young chimp (Bobby Porter, who played Caesar's son in *Battle*) and his dog, even though we were told in the films that dogs had been wiped out by plague. It immediately calls to mind images of Uncle Tom and fugitive slaves. 'That's enough … It's only a human,' says Porter's character, before his attention is distracted by the crash of the spaceship – indicated by a loud noise and the wind machine. At least Charlton Heston got his own spaceship – Harper and Naughton had to make do with Chuck's old one. No wonder it crashed – it was second-hand. There were originally three astronauts, but the third was dead on arrival. 'We could have landed in a worse place,' says Burke, a comment which prompts a volley of gunfire. Virdon and Burke escape, discover an old book containing pictures of New York, and realize they are on Earth. Meanwhile orang-utan leader Zaius is about to appoint the young chimp Galen as his assistant when he hears news of the spaceship. These characters presumably cannot be the Zaius and Galen from the original film, unless apes have not only evolved spectacularly quickly, but have also extended their lifespan by a millennium or so. Zaius reveals that another spaceship preceded this one, more than ten years earlier. The ape leaders know something of man's past and fear the effect of intelligent humans on the local human population. When the astronauts are captured, Urko wants to kill them at once, Zaius wants to question them first and the inquisitive Galen thirsts after the truth. Urko engineers their escape to provide a justification for killing them. Galen tries to warn them and a guard is killed in the struggle, forcing Galen (ultimately) to flee with the two astronauts. And so begins their life on the run.

The humans look and dress as if they have just wandered off the set of *Robin Hood* and they can talk, a gift considered essential for securing guest stars of the calibre of John Ireland. Ape society revolves around Central City, though, fortunately for the fugitives, there are many outlying communities and farms, where they can pass unrecognized. Some humans are slaves, while others live in their own villages; sometimes, though not always, governed by an ape prefect and overseen by an ape garrison. In the second episode Virdon and Burke are captured and Burke is forced to fight in a gladiatorial contest against another human, providing a lesson in humanity when he spares his opponent's life. In the third instalment, *The Trap*, Burke and Urko are trapped in the ruins of the San Francisco area subway and forced to co-operate to save themselves. '*The Trap* is the *Apes* television show's most heartfelt symbolic address of American race relations,' says Eric Greene in *Planet of the Apes as American Myth: Race, Politics, and Popular Culture*. '*The Trap* makes the point that the races are bound together in conflict, bound together in a painful history, and bound together in the need to learn from that history and cooperate if they are to free themselves from it.' But he stretches his argument beyond breaking point when he adds: 'Burke and

Urko must pass through the subway station to freedom just as enslaved Africans in the United States also used an "underground railroad" to liberate themselves.'

In the fourth episode Virdon draws on his farming background to win over a family of peasant chimps, including the distrustful and scheming elder son, who had feared the humans had put a curse on his cow. However, the series subsequently becomes formulaic, with the three fugitives going from place to place, teaching the local apes and humans one lesson after another: about the use of quinine against malaria; the principles of flight (through the air – not running away, though they get lots of practice at that); and the advantages of fishing nets, in an episode that combines underwater footage of real sharks with the slowest-moving, jerkiest, least-convincing fins since Adam West took off his bat-tights. The element of the original film that satirized man's arrogance has been lost completely. Greene is right when he says: 'The image that was repeated week after week was one of white Western men going to "native" villages and using their superior knowledge, technology, and talents to solve the locals' problems ... Whereas the United States may have lost the hearts and minds of the peasants of Vietnam, it at least won the hearts and minds of the peasants on the planet of the apes.'

Each episode had a different writer and took only seven days to shoot, mainly at the Fox studios and the ranch. The standard was variable and was at its best when it departed from the 'hearts and minds' formula. The format, and cumulative running time, allowed for a greater development and delineation of the ape characters: a chimp mask was no longer shorthand for intellectual liberalism and gorilla make-up no longer meant mindless thuggery, well, not among the guest stars anyway. The bespectacled Wanda may look like a chimp version of your favourite aunt, but her experiments at brainwashing Burke are reminiscent of the Nazis (and a number of sixties Cold War thrillers). This episode, *The Interrogation*, also features Galen in drag, a visit to his mum and dad's house and political arguments that reflected the generation gap in Western society. Even the belligerent Urko is shown to be a warm and amusing companion among his kin folk, with his own sense of decency and principles. The best episode is *The Deception*. Some might argue for *The Liberator*, but the apes have only walk-on roles in it. *The Liberator* is set around a human village where those who transgress local laws must enter the temple for judgement by the gods and the sentence is always death. We subsequently learn there is poison gas there. Virdon and Burke encourage the villagers to resist the apes' recurring demands for slaves, but are horrified to discover the village leader has a secret gas-bomb factory and is intent on genocide. The message is: it's right to fight, but keep it clean. The oppressors in *The Liberator* did not have to be apes, they could have been Eli Wallach's Mexican bandits from *The Magnificent Seven*. It was the nature of American television drama at the time that stories could be readily adapted to suit just about any series, particularly those series in which the principals faced a new adventure or tackled a new social issue, in a new setting every week, such as *Wagon Train* and *Star Trek*.

In *The Deception* Burke and Virdon are forced to pretend they are apes when they meet a blind female chimp, Fauna, who is grieving for a father murdered by humans. Burke discovers from her father's diaries that he supported human rights, Fauna falls in love with Burke's voice and his stories, while Galen infiltrates the Dragoons, a secret society of racist, hooded terrorists. 'We've seen this kind of thing before,' says Virdon, 'another time, another place.' Fauna's uncle, Sestus, is a member, and the writers strive to explain not simply the injustice of such mob violence, but also the causes. Local gorilla policeman Perdix is determined to smash the Dragoons, and it transpires Fauna's father was not killed by humans at all. Even the most naive viewer could not have missed the fact that there was more to the television series than simple entertainment. Producer Stan Hough said at the time: 'We have so much latitude in what we can say, dressed up in monkey suits. We are enjoying the freedom, the fun, of creating a whole culture and society from the ground up. We can reveal truths and show things we could never otherwise get away with, make social statements about the violent side of human nature, about the horrors of the police state, about the blindness of prejudice.' Issues and storyline are perfectly interwoven in *The Deception*, Jane Actman is outstanding in the role of Fauna, and although it might seem heavy on the political message, this episode boasts stronger, richer characters than any other.

Despite the success of the merchandising blitz, the television series lasted only one season. It was succeeded the following year by *Return to the Planet of the Apes*, a cartoon series of thirteen half-hour episodes, with a wonderful credit sequence that includes apes crucified upside down, a gorilla blowing a horn and dark ranks of gorilla soldiers. Three American astronauts travel through space from 1976 to 2081, concluding that 'Dr Stanton's theory of time thrust' is correct. The trio of astronauts here include a woman, Judy, and a black man, Jeff, though the commander, Bill, is a white male. Suddenly the clock goes haywire and they career forward to 3979, coming to land in a lake, and setting off on a long trek that parallels that of the film. The sequence lasts several minutes, with hardly any dialogue, brave stuff for a cartoon. They eventually come across a sort of Mount Rushmore with ape faces, a variation on Don Peters's original idea that the astronauts in the film should come across an ape statue. Coincidentally the ape parliament has heard reports that humanoids have developed the power of speech. The gorilla general Urko argues for their extermination, the chimp Cornelius argues they should be studied and the orang-utans, who seem to wield the power, rule that they can be hunted but not systematically wiped out. Judy disappears through a crack in the earth and Bill and Jeff meet the local human, or rather 'humanoid', population of mute, hairy cavemen. Among them is Nova, who is wearing dog tags belonging to Brent, another astronaut from an earlier era, who will crop up later in the series.

In the cartoon version the ape society is a technologically advanced one, possessing cars and tanks and latterly aircraft. A few orang-utan elders know humans once ruled Earth, but destroyed it in a war. Writings prophesy that if ever they regain language they will take over the world and destroy it once more. Faced with the prospect of brain surgery, however, Bill reveals to Cornelius and Zira that he can speak and they help him escape. Meanwhile Judy has ended up with the Underdwellers. A variation on the mutant humans in *Beneath the Planet of the Apes*, they live in the ruins of New York City and cover their heads with hoods – the disfigured features of the prototypes having been deemed too scary for small children. One of the most imaginative ideas of the series is that Judy has come to fulfil a prophecy and help the Underdwellers return to the green world, a prophecy based on their possession of a statue of Judy, presumably built centuries ago when she failed to return to Earth. They call her USA, pronounced 'Oosa', after the inscription on the statue. In a later episode the Underdwellers free her after Bill and Jeff use their laser to divert lava away from their underground sanctuary. One of the best episodes, *Terror on Ice Mountain*, follows Cornelius's discovery, at an archaeological dig, of a human book, *A Day at the Zoo*, and of plans for a hot-air balloon. He constructs the balloon and he and Bill set off over the mountains, landing in a storm on a mountainside, which is home to a mystical order of orang-utans, who believe 'all creatures with loving hearts are equal', and who worship a huge gorilla, who breaks free from the ice only when they need him – *Lost Horizon* meets *King Kong*. Bill and Cornelius leave their book with the mountain apes for safe keeping.

In *Trail to the Unknown* Bill, Jeff and Judy lead the humanoids across desert and river to a new homeland called the New Valley, where they build fortifications against the ape army. 'The US forces decide to interpose themselves by acting as advisers in what could be seen as a "foreign civil war" and by relocating the "natives" to more secure positions, just as the United States moved many South Vietnamese into strategic hamlets,' writes Greene. Doug Wildey, the supervising director and associate producer, whose other work included the legendary *Jonny Quest*, maintained he did not intend the series as an allegory on Vietnam, but Greene is undeterred: 'He need not have intended to make the series a forum for responding to the war in order for it to serve as such.' There is no doubt Vietnam continues to cast a shadow, albeit a subconscious shadow across the Planet of the Apes, as it did across so much of American society and American thinking in the mid-seventies. So too does Watergate. Urko is no longer the principled warlord of the live-action series, but a paranoid militarist, intent on personal power. He even stages a break-in, stealing art treasures and blaming the theft on the Underdwellers, to advance his own personal agenda. The most obvious parallel, however, is not Vietnam and Nixon; it is the fact that the human hero, the whipping boy of the original film, has recovered his status as Moses, leading his people to the promised land. Either way the cartoon series serves as an escape from reality – which is what entertainment is primarily about.

With Urko discredited, Cornelius and Bill retrieve *A Day at the Zoo* from the order of holy orang-utans, with the intention of presenting the book to the ape rulers as proof of man's intelligence. 'It's the one piece of solid evidence that could convince the senate to grant your people full rights,' says Cornelius. A-a-h, nice happy ending. Or is it? The senate are fully aware of man's past intellectual 'achievements' and have made it clear that if ever he regains language he will be exterminated. The ending with Bill and Cornelius flying off towards the prospect of a bright, new, emancipated tomorrow is either an unbelievably incompetent piece of storytelling; or, following the story through logically from its outset to its logical conclusion, it is the most deliciously black moment in the entire *Apes* saga.

# CHAPTER FOURTEEN
# -273 DEGREES OF COOL

*The Legend Grows*

It was Benjamin Disraeli who supposedly said: 'There are three kinds of lies – lies, damned lies and statistics.' Now there is a fourth – lies, damned lies, statistics and Hollywood accounting. You can make statistics mean anything you want. And yet, looking at the tables for the highest-earning films of the sixties and the seventies, it is clear something significant happened in those decades that changed the course of cinema history. There was not a single sci-fi film in the North American top ten for the 1960s. A decade down the road and no fewer than three of the top ten positions were occupied by sci-fi films. There was *Superman* and *Close Encounters of the Third Kind*, while *Star Wars* had established itself as the highest-grossing film of all time, a position it would hold until the release of *ET* a couple of years later. *Planet of the Apes* was an adaptation of a satirical novel; *Star Wars* was an attempt to recreate the joys of Saturday-morning serials with big-budget special effects. It would seem foolhardy to suggest that any of these three seventies films was jumping on a bandwagon started by *Planet of the Apes*. But both *Planet of the Apes* and *2001* had shown there was a big mainstream market for science fiction while taking sci-fi in new and interesting directions. Many sci-fi films in the fifties were predicated on a fear of the unknown, with some, such as *The War of the Worlds*, suggesting it was better to shoot first and ask questions later. *2001* wallowed in the unknown, relished the awesome mysteries of the universe, while *Planet of the Apes* combined action and adventure with an element of political comment. *2001* had a more obvious influence on later films, but the most immediate effect of both films was to set up a climate at the studios where offbeat, off-world proposals were not simply dismissed out of hand.

'Fantasies set in outer space had long been a staple of the comic strips and Saturday-morning kiddie TV, but had been disdained by Hollywood,' Charlton Heston wrote in his autobiography, *In the Arena*. 'Later, Steven Spielberg and George Lucas were to explore space wonderfully, with far better technology, over a series of films, but *Apes* broke the ground.' It is significant that, when Lucas failed to get support for *Star Wars* at Universal, a studio for whom he had just made a small fortune with *American Graffiti*, it was Twentieth Century Fox that came to his assistance. Fox took the lead in science fiction in the seventies, backing not just *Star Wars*, but also *Alien*. Would we have had *Star Wars*, *ET* and *Alien* without *Planet of the Apes*? 'I never really thought about it in that way,' says Dick Zanuck. 'It could have had a great influence on all those films, but they're all so vastly different ... We never liked to think of it as purely a science-fiction movie.' Perhaps he hits the nail squarely on the head with that comment. Was *Star Wars* 'just science fiction', or was it folklore, fairy tale and a substitute for the great American art form, the western, for which Sam Peckinpah *et al* had by then written such powerful epitaphs? *Alien* bore more resemblance to *Rear Window* than it did to *Planet of the Apes* or *2001*, replacing Raymond Burr with a gigantic, slavering monster. It was a thriller set in outer space – though the hibernation capsules on the *Nostromo* are similar to those on Taylor's spaceship. *Blade Runner* was Philip Marlowe in the twenty-first century. It left its hero, and his new girlfriend, facing an uncertain future, in an unfamiliar landscape. One of the strengths of sci-fi, like the western before it, was its flexibility. Heston went on to make two science-fiction films in the first half of the seventies – *The Omega Man*, battling mutants after war has all but wiped out mankind, and *Soylent Green*, set in the horribly overcrowded New York of 2022, with Heston as a cop who uncovers the source of the artificial foodstuff 'Soylent Green' – human corpses.

*Planet of the Apes* was not the first film to use nuclear war as a starting point for its story, but it was one of the first to set its narrative firmly in a post-apocalyptic landscape, even if we do not realize the exact nature of that landscape till the end of the movie. The Statue of Liberty scenes were enormously effective at punching home the full horror of what man had done to his planet, turning it into a desert. *Beneath the Planet of the Apes* elaborated visually on the original's theme, with its subterranean ruins of New York City and its human mutants. At the end of the seventies an Australian doctor called George Miller made a cheap film in the countryside near his home in Melbourne, with an unknown actor called Gibson as a cop in a barren future world. Warner Brothers came on board for *Mad Max 2*, which fleshed out the back-story by opening with newsreel footage of a war that engulfed the planet. While some post-apocalyptic films, including *The Omega Man*, were set in the ruins of great cities, others, most notably the two *Mad Max* sequels, relished the emptiness of the desert.

*Planet of the Apes* not only prepared the ground for a new wave of sci-fi films, and post-apocalyptic tales in particular, it also rewrote the rules on sequels, although perhaps not as dramatically as it might have done. There is a fine dividing line between a film that serves as number two or three in a series and a film that is a sequel. Hollywood had been making film series, presenting the same actors, characters and often storylines, since the silent days of Broncho Billy and Fatty Arbuckle. Often these were westerns or comedies, and later detective stories, with the likes of the Thin Man, Charlie Chan and Sherlock Holmes. They were cheap to produce and had all the easy familiarity of television sitcoms. And it was television that effectively killed them off in the fifties. The essence of this familiarity had been the knowledge that nothing really changed from episode to episode. And, of course, things did change in *Planet of the Apes*. A series might normally involve an element of planning, whereas no one intended there should be a second batch of *Apes*, and there seemed no chance of a third after Chuck blew up the world at the end of *Beneath the Planet of the Apes*. But, as Macaulay Culkin said, when asked how his parents could leave him 'home alone' a second time: ''Cos the studio raked in 500 million bucks the first time.' Where there's a will there's a way. And in Hollywood you can substitute the word 'dollar' for the word 'will'. These days producers would have been discussing the possibility of a sequel before *Planet of the Apes* started shooting, but sequels were not on the agenda in the sixties. Fox neglected to secure sequel rights for *Star Wars* before they put up the money for the first one, though George Lucas planned it as a series from the outset. Most of the major sci-fi films of the period – *Alien, Star Trek, Mad Max*, even *2001* – would spawn sequels.

The success of the *Planet of the Apes* sequels helped ensure we would see sequels to everything from *Home Alone* through *Lethal Weapon* and *Die Hard* to *Rocky*, even when a sequel seemed entirely inappropriate. The *Rocky* sequels defied the logic and romance of the original film, in which the no-hoper does better than anyone could have imagined ... and *almost* wins. That is the point – he almost wins, and he goes away with his head held high. Why did they bring him back and turn him into the greatest boxer that ever lived, and in so doing undermine the integrity of the original? See Macaulay Culkin above. *Planet of the Apes* proved producers could return again and again to the same feature-film seam, and extract more gold from it. *Planet of the Apes* also established the law of diminishing returns – there was money in sequels, but each film would make less than the last. For many years it was accepted simply as part of the nature of sequels, rather than a reflection of the fact that Fox kept on cutting the budget on *Apes*. The *Terminator* and *Austin Powers* sequels showed the law was not immutable. These days producers would be looking at investing more to make more, and refusing to rush into production with something as half-baked as *Beneath the Planet of the Apes*. After blowing up the world in the second *Apes* film, the producers were forced into the development of the concept of the 'prequel' to continue the series. The word itself came into common usage only with *Butch and Sundance: The Early Days* at the end of the seventies, but Jacobs and Dehn preceded Butch and Sundance when they went back in time in the final three *Apes* films to tell the story of what happened before the first film.

*Escape from the Planet of the Apes* is the most ingenious *Apes* film, not only because here Paul Dehn found a way to continue the saga, but also because of the circle it created. Zira and Cornelius leave a planet ruled by apes and journey into the past to a time when *Homo sapiens* is king. Fearing for his future prospects, mankind kills the two intelligent chimps. But it is already too late – Zira and Cornelius have given birth to the baby who will grow up to lead the ape revolution. The storyline was appropriated by the original *Terminator* movie in 1984. *The Terminator* was written and directed by James Cameron, whose only previous film as director was *Piranha II*. In a post-apocalyptic future, machines have taken over the world and are exterminating humans. A terminator

(Arnold Schwarzenegger), part-man, part-machine, is sent back to 1984 to kill Sarah Connor, the mother of John Connor, who is destined to become the saviour of mankind. But the terminator is followed by a resistance fighter, Kyle Reese, dispatched to protect Sarah. Reese becomes Sarah's lover and the father of the child who will one day lead the human revolution. 'The audience walks out surprised and satisfied,' writes Sean French in his book *The Terminator.* 'This efficiency of construction, a cross between *Star Trek* and O. Henry, may seem a small thing, but it was a witty variation on the linear chase-and-kill structure of *Alien, Halloween* and even *Blade Runner.*' And never a mention of *Planet of the Apes.* That is not to detract from *The Terminator,* a brilliant film that pioneered techno noir. Films are always repackaging ideas from other films. Cameron was production designer and second-unit director on *Battle Beyond the Stars,* a sci-fi remake of *The Magnificent Seven,* which was in turn a remake of the Japanese film *Seven Samurai.* It is simply to pay credit where it is due.

It is stating the obvious to say people are more interested in apes than in most other animals. Magazines have reported increased sales with an ape on the cover, and the advances in ape make-up on *Planet of the Apes,* as well as the success of the film, made future ape films more likely. *Greystoke, Congo* (a sadly underrated piece of hokum), the remake of *Mighty Joe Young* and even *Gorillas in the Mist* all used humans in ape clothing. Rick Baker was designer on all except *Congo,* and would in due course work on Tim Burton's *Planet of the Apes* film too. One very specific effect *Planet of the Apes* had on other films concerns its use of the Statue of Liberty as the definitive symbol of the United States. King Kong had chosen the Empire State Building for his famous ascent, but it was new at the time and was subsequently superseded by several other buildings as the tallest in the world. The Statue of Liberty was a more enduring, internationally recognizable and dramatic monument. Following its devastating cameo in *Planet of the Apes,* it appeared in a series of sci-fi and superhero films, including *Batman Forever, Judge Dredd, Independence Day* and *Deep Impact,* before serving as the setting for the climactic battle in *X-Men.* The grand old lady is battered, drowned, decapitated and generally abused – a feminist version of Eric Greene could have a field day with that little lot.

In the 1987 comedy *Spaceballs* Mel Brooks provided an elaborate spin on *Planet of the Apes*'s Statue of Liberty scene, which depended on the audience's knowledge of the original for its success, almost twenty years after *Planet of the Apes* came out and more than ten years after the final sequel and the television series. And from there it seemed to be just one small step to John Glenn Internet jokes and all those *Planet of the Apes* references in *The Simpsons*. If Homer had seen the film – and (belatedly) worked out the meaning of the ending – then *Planet of the Apes* had truly become a part of Western culture. The original reviews had been good, but not brilliant, and *Planet of the Apes* did not figure alongside *The Godfather*s and the *Casablanca*s in critical lists of the all-time greats. It was not the critics who eventually turned *Planet of the Apes* into a cultural touchstone. It was the fans, many of whom had grown up with it, though certainly not all. Marvel's *Planet of the Apes* comics provided vivid, stylized comic-strip adaptations of the films in the seventies, incorporating some scenes that existed in script form but never made it to the screen. There were novelizations of the film sequels and the two television series. And Marvel continued the *Apes* saga with new stories, such as *Evolution's Nightmare*, in which one ape and one human survive a battle and must cooperate against common enemies. One cover shows an ape soldier wielding a sword against a big blue monster with huge jaws. 'Monster vs Ape! in a world gone mad,' it screams. The films remained popular on video and television long after the comics ran their course, and the international proliferation of channels provided new markets and new audiences for both the films and the TV series, episodes of which were combined and repackaged as TV movies. In the early nineties the American company Adventure Comics reissued some of the seventies comic strips and published new ones as well, in which Caesar's grandson Alexander featured prominently. There were new *Planet of the Apes* figures and models, the videos were reissued, a new fuller version of Jerry Goldsmith's soundtrack was released, and there was an assortment of books on various aspects of *Planet of the Apes*, from race to memorabilia. 'I have been asked on several occasions why people collect *Planet of the Apes* merchandise,' says Christopher Sausville, the American financial analyst who compiled *Planet of the Apes Collectibles – Unauthorized Guide with Trivia & Values* (1998).

'The best answer I can give is from my own experience. Probably the most important reason is the same reason anyone collects toys, it is rekindling fond memories of their childhood.' And, of course, there were reports and rumours throughout much of the decade about the possibility of a new movie.

John Russell Taylor completely ignored *Planet of the Apes* in his 1987 book *Great Movie Moments*, while John Brosnan dismissed it in a few paragraphs in *The Primal Screen: A History of Science Fiction Film* in 1991. Brosnan did acknowledge *Planet of the Apes* had been a huge hit, before adding that he had 'never been able to figure out why exactly'. Those less charitably inclined might venture that such lack of insight suggests Mr Brosnan would have been better suited to a career outside film criticism. In 1998 *Empire* film magazine included *Planet of the Apes* in its supplement on 'The 10 Definitive Science-Fiction Films of All Time'. 'If you grew up in the early 1970s, there were certain things you had, things that defined you,' wrote Bob McCabe. 'Slade or The Sweet? You had to be one or the other. Starsky or Hutch? Which Roller was yours? And then you had your favourite *Planet of the Apes* film – the second one if you liked cool-looking mutants; the third one if you were a bit soft; the fourth if you were old enough – it was after all a "double A" as they were then. And of course, the fifth one if you felt that John Huston's work as an actor was vastly under-appreciated in light of his more than established directorial prowess. Admittedly, not that many picked the fifth one. As with so many things, hindsight shows you just how crushingly wrong you were. The sequels – and, Bond aside, this was a time when sequels were the exception rather than the norm – weren't up to much. There was really only one *Planet of the Apes*. Released in 1968, *Planet of the Apes* was, very simply, unique. A Swiftian satire, a modern morality play, a wittily disguised allegory on contemporary human mores in the era of Vietnam, a bitingly cynical look at the progress of mankind mere months after the apogee that was retrospectively called the Summer of Love. And a chance to see Ben-Hur's arse. *Planet of the Apes* was all these things. And much more.'

By the turn of the century *Planet of the Apes* seemed to have acquired cult status. It is difficult to define a cult film. Many were critical and/or commercial disappointments at the time of release

– *The Rocky Horror Picture Show*, *The Blues Brothers*, *The Wicker Man*, even *Blade Runner*. There is often an element of rediscovery and reassessment involved. Initial failure is not, however, a prerequisite. It is difficult, but not impossible, for a mainstream hit to claim cult status, and *Star Wars* and *Star Trek* both boast huge cult followings. The essential element lies with the fans themselves, fans who are unlikely to be content simply with watching the film – they will often be prepared to spend a great deal of time and money getting together, buying and selling memorabilia and perhaps dressing up in costume. And their appreciation for the film will often differ from that of the general public, finding meanings that may elude the more casual observer, delighting in the minutiae of it all. By the early nineties *Planet of the Apes* had begun to acquire the trappings of cultdom, with the appearance of new fan clubs, fanzines and Internet sites. Terry Hoknes's publication *Ape Chronicles* first appeared in Canada in 1991, followed by several others, including *Ape Crazy* in the US and *Simian Scrolls* in the UK. They mixed news about memorabilia and fan conventions with personal assessments of the films and new *Apes* fiction written by fans. In 1996 Brian Penikas founded Apemania, a group of enthusiasts in California, who would dress up as apes and bring the film back to life at parties and functions. But this revival, or rather intensification, of interest was by no means confined to North America and Europe. Brazil had led the way with a fan club and fanzine, *Century City News*, in the mid-eighties, largely due to the commitment of one particular devotee, Luiz Saulo Adami – Adami of the Apes – who wrote the book *O Unico Humano Bom é Aquele que Está Morto!* (The Only Good Human is a Dead Human), which was published locally. In Japan *Planet of the Apes* shook off any suspicion of camp and became the very definition of cool in the nineties. Businessman Nigo was inspired by his passion for the film to create the trendy and very expensive A Bathing Ape brand of clothing, while Cornelius, one of the few Japanese pop stars to make any impact in the West, took his stage name from Roddy McDowall's character and 'sampled' *Planet of the Apes* at his concerts. *Planet of the Apes* was even honoured with its own commemorative postage stamp in the Central African Republic in 1995.

The foundations of the *Planet of the Apes* cult were often laid in childhood. Brian Penikas saw the original film on black and white television, in the seventies, when he was about ten. 'I remember being completely caught off guard by the end of the first film.' He and his school friends often dressed up as apes, heralding the formation of Apemania two decades later. Apemania started as a one-off idea to gatecrash a cocktail party and grew from there. Fox recruited the group to promote the *Apes* videos and computer game. They also made an appearance at the thirtieth-anniversary screening and cast reunion at the Academy of Motion Picture Arts and Sciences. *Planet of the Apes* not only inspired Penikas to found Apemania, but also to become a Hollywood make-up artist. His credits include *Stargate, Mars Attacks!, Galaxy Quest* and the Batman and Addams Family films. *Planet of the Apes* also inspired Robert Thorpe to pursue a career in the arts, designing sets and light shows, after he saw it on television in the mid-seventies, when he was thirteen. 'My most treasured memory was doing a show called *Do Not Go Gentle* back in '93,' he says. 'It starred Kim Hunter. She was wonderful to work with.' Thorpe collects magazines and toys and his most valuable item is an original Cornelius mask.

Terry Hoknes, editor of *Ape Chronicles*, first saw *Planet of the Apes* after school in 1977, when he was six. John Roche, editor of *Simian Scrolls*, saw the television series in 1975, aged about nine. 'The first time I saw a *Planet of the Apes* movie itself was probably in the late seventies when they were first transmitted on UK television,' says Roche, a solicitor, whose other passion is Swansea City Football Club. 'I can recall seeing the first movie and being in awe of its serious tone and just how well done it was. Whilst I enjoyed and loved the TV series, I found that, with the film, I had an abiding respect for all involved and it caused me to ponder far more deeply upon the messages which *Apes* contains at all levels.' Alan Maxwell of Fife was not even born until after the *Planet of the Apes* series ended. His introduction was *Battle for the Planet of the Apes* on TV in the eighties, when he was about ten. He subsequently collected posters, magazines and figures. 'Like all kids my age, I really loved the *Star Wars* films and bought the toys, but there was just something different about the *Apes* films. I found them totally spellbinding … I think it remains popular because it succeeds on every level. For children, it captures the imagination – not aliens, not Disney cartoon-style talking animals, something else entirely – and has enough action to keep them interested. Later on, you grow to appreciate some of the finer details of the film, not to mention the legendary endings. Then, as you grow older, you begin to see the philosophical and political themes running through it. It's one of those films that never seems dated, because as you grow up, the film grows up with you.'

Dave Ballard was introduced to *Planet of the Apes* by his elder brother, who collected the bubblegum cards, and saw *Beneath the Planet of the Apes* in a double bill with another James Franciscus film, *Valley of Gwangi*, at the Granada cinema in Tooting, London, when he was about ten. He has taken it upon himself to pass on the delights of the series to his son, breaking him in gently, though his wife Caroline has proved less appreciative. 'My wife is totally bemused by my affection for the *Apes*,' he says. 'She's never seen a movie or TV show and would almost certainly leave the room if I were to put one on, but then again she watches *Sabrina the Teenage Witch*. My son Christopher [who is seven] would rather watch Cartoon Network than *POTA*, but he has seen the cartoon show and *Escape*, which he rather enjoyed. I may show him *Battle* one day soon, but I think he's a little too young for the other movies right now.' Despite Caroline's reservations, Dave Ballard has found no shortage of admirers for *Planet of the Apes*. 'While it's easy to find a *Star Trek* fan who will rubbish *Babylon 5* and vice versa, or a *Buffy* fan who will put down *Farscape*, all these "cults" will agree that, while not their favourite subject, *Apes* is cool,' he says. 'If a great movie can be judged by the possession of a "magic moment" – the shower scene in *Psycho*, the goodbye scene in *Casablanca* – then *Apes* is jam-packed with them. The crash-landing. The hunt. "Get your stinking paws off me." And then, just when you think it's over … Bam! The Statue of Liberty!' The last two scenes he mentions both featured in April 2001 in *Empire* magazine's list of the 273 coolest movie moments ever: -273 degrees Celsius is the equivalent of absolute zero on the Kelvin scale.

*Planet of the Apes* is not just a cult, however. There is a hard core of devotees, predominantly male, many too young to remember when it first came out; but it also seems to have become increasingly popular with a more general public as well. William Creber, whose input was so important to the Statue of Liberty scene, told me a story about a party he once attended. He knew hardly anyone there, except the hosts. Someone suggested an impromptu parlour game and, in turn, everyone had to nominate a single scene from a single film as their favourite movie moment of all time. 'One guy says: "There's not anything better than the end of *Planet of the Apes*."' A murmur of agreement runs round the room. 'I never told him who I was,' adds the quietly spoken art director, 'but I was really pleased.' Now that is cool. That is -273 degrees of cool on anyone's scale.

# CHAPTER FIFTEEN
# HOMMAGE

Arthur sat in the park in the chilly sunshine of a late spring afternoon and stared off towards the hills, a few miles away, a natural
boundary for the city's northern expansion, still dusted with a late
fall of snow, like icing sugar. His grandchildren Daniel and Marc
were playing on the grass, chasing each other round a tree, with
loud shrieks of horror and delight. Round and round they went.
Daniel somersaulted forward. In doing so, he never lost his stride,
and Marc still could not catch him. Only when they deserted their
tree and raced towards Arthur did their elder's gaze waver from the
hills. He had been far away, with Captain Boulle, dead and buried
almost forty years ago. A little tear formed in the corner of Arthur's
eye at the memory of his friend, but he quickly wiped it away, with
a swift, irritated movement, and he smiled at Daniel and Marc.
They noticed not the fleeting drop of moisture in their grandfa-
ther's eye, nor his smile, nor even his presence. They were too
wrapped up in the business of their game, birling beneath him
once and heading back towards their tree, screaming as they went.
Daniel did another triumphant somersault, landing smack upon
his feet and continuing to run. Daniel liked somersaults and it
seemed he could run and somersault all day without pausing for
rest. These days all Arthur did was rest, and watch, and remember.
A little girl in a bright-red jacket stood some small distance away
pointing Daniel out to the old man and woman who accompanied
her. The woman held her hand. The man smoked a pipe. The little
girl was much the same age as Daniel, and the man and woman
were probably her grandparents. Grandparents, like Arthur.

Arthur was old now, and he never remembered a time when
he somersaulted. Even if he had done so, there would have been
no little girl to appreciate his feats of athleticism with smiles of
encouragement. Things were different these days. Things were
different for Daniel and Marc. They were a part of this. They were
born here and France had always been their home. They grew up
with the chill and the people with their light skins. Daniel and
Marc's faces and hands were hardly darker than those of the little

girl and her guardians … much lighter than those of Captain Boulle, whose hide had been burned by years under a tropical sun. The word skin hardly seemed appropriate for something that had the texture of rhinoceros and was covered by wiry, grey hairs that seemed to stretch from his ankles to the crown of his head. Not that many people ever saw the crown of his head, for Captain Boulle always wore an old sea captain's cap. It must have been white once, but that was before Arthur knew him. Now it was a deep shade of yellow, with a black brim.

Arthur looked from the little girl to his own hands. He stared at the back of them and sighed. They were black, like the night or the brim of Captain Boulle's cap. But they were not cold like the night. Not yet. With quiet deliberation, he stretched ten fingers in the direction of the hills. They were a little stiff these days, but still warm, and through them coursed the same blood that flowed through the veins of Daniel and Marc and the little girl. He became preoccupied by dirt trapped beneath a fingernail and forgot about Captain Boulle. Some days Arthur remembered Captain Boulle and some days he forgot. He was getting old.

Captain Boulle was already in his fifties when he met – or rather saved – Arthur. Of course, Arthur was not called Arthur then. His parents had called him Ham. But Captain Boulle did not know that, and Ham could not tell him – he was only a baby. And Captain Boulle knew nothing about babies. Captain Boulle was born in Marseilles. No relation of the famous writer, he grew up on the dockside and ran away to sea at fourteen, on a cargo ship sailing under a flag of convenience for the Far East. He called the baby Arthur because he once sailed with a man of that name, or so he told Arthur years later. Captain Boulle knew nothing about babies, but he knew all there was to know about the sea, he knew about fighting and drinking and smuggling. He ran guns, in a leaky little cutter, from North Africa to Spain, which was the nearest he had got to returning to France. When Franco won, Captain Boulle turned his back on the sea, just as he had turned his back on the country of his birth. He spent much of the Second World War in Casablanca, before travelling south, overland, and yet always seeming to end up in a port. His journey came to a temporary halt in Bissau, where every morning he would walk to the docks and check out the ships. He would share milky coffee and rum and tales of the sea with men of all nationalities who drifted in and out of the little Portuguese colony. With the passing of the months his tales grew fewer and his intake of rum heavier. He became quite taciturn, content just to listen, or just to sit and sup and not even bother to listen. Latterly he sat alone, without the need for company. It was only when a returning captain remarked on Boulle's absence that they realized no one had seen or heard from him for weeks. Captain Boulle seemed to have disappeared, seemed to have turned his back on humanity.

A wind of change was blowing through Africa when Ham was born, a violent storm that left much devastation in its wake. Ham was born into a country caught in the grip of civil war and famine, the tightening grip of insanity, where men hungered not for food, but for blood. He was born in the forest, with the sound of gunfire in the distance. His family hid from the guns, and were reduced to living on berries and roots. He did not remember much about his family. But he remembered his mother's milky smell enveloping him as he clung to her breast and drifted off into sleep in the clearing. And he remembered being woken by a terrible explosion in his ear. He remembered the screams and remembered men with guns spewing fire and death. Blood splattered the leaves and branches of the trees. Bodies fell lifeless on the ground. His family had no guns. His father grabbed a stick to use as a club and threw himself towards the nearest soldier, knocking him over. As the soldier fell a volley from his rifle cut through the forest canopy. With a horrible yell, another soldier released a burst of gunfire that riddled both Ham's father and the first soldier, and they danced one desperate, bloody *tango macabre* as the falling leaves showered down green upon their black and reddening bodies. With a choked sob that mixed incomprehension, shock and dread, Ham turned to his mother. The breast that had so recently supplied him with milk was torn open and smelled so very different now.

The forest grew suddenly still again. The rest of his family had fled through the trees. The soldiers too were gone. Everyone was gone. Almost everyone. One soldier remained. Ham looked into his eyes as the man levelled his rifle at Ham's head. An eerie, unnatural laugh issued from lips flecked with saliva, and a bloody red finger tightened on the trigger. Instinctively Ham covered his eyes, not wanting to look into the face of his killer. There was a moment when time stood still. The moment seemed to last for ever. Perhaps Ham's life might have flashed before his big, expressive, dark eyes, behind his hand, but he had had no life, there was nothing to remember. He would have cried, but in reality there was no time, for the moment of quiet lasted a mere microsecond before the clearing echoed with one final explosion.

When Ham took his hand away from his eyes he saw the body of the soldier lying dead on the earth some feet away and a dark figure standing over him, in shadow, the figure of a huge white man in a torn cotton shirt with short sleeves that exposed heavily muscled arms, one bearing a tattoo of an anchor, the other the words 'Vive la France'. He also wore a yellowing sea captain's cap.

Captain Boulle lived alone in a one-room shack, with a thatched roof, far up the river. He did not encourage visitors and weeks went by in which he said little to Ham, though he fed him mashed bananas with a little milk from the goats he kept. 'Arthur,' he said, pointing to the little orphan. 'Your name.' And then he repeated it once: 'Arthur', as if to say that even a fool would know it by now. 'Ach,' said the old sea dog when Ham – that is, Arthur – merely smiled in response to his christening. In time Captain Boulle gave Arthur a spoon with his bananas, but Captain Boulle used his fingers, so there was never any incentive for Arthur to use cutlery, though he learned quickly to use other tools and helped Captain Boulle construct a little cot in a corner of the shack in which Arthur slept. Or at least he handed Captain Boulle the hammer when he called for it. But these days Captain Boulle's favourite implement was his pen. He sat at the bare table and wrote in ruled hardback jotters, while Arthur either watched or wandered down to the river to play on the little canoe Captain Boulle kept tied there.

Once every month or so they would set off early in the morning and canoe down the muddy river for many hours to a little town, where Captain Boulle would buy food and provisions. They stayed in a dirty little hotel overnight, sometimes for two or three nights. If it was one of those rare times when the hotel had beer, Captain Boulle would stay on and sit in the garden with half a dozen glasses ranged in front of him. When Arthur was older he would sit with his own glass. And local people would come and

179

talk. Arthur enjoyed listening. His pleasure and affection were reflected in his open, expressive features and in the twinkle in his happy eyes. Arthur felt safe with Captain Boulle and enjoyed his conversation. More and more, with each glass he drained. Captain Boulle looked after him, and he would help him, sometimes even carry him, back to their room. As Captain Boulle laid him on the bed, Arthur puckered his lips and kissed him on the mouth. Captain Boulle laughed.

One day, near the shack, Arthur was playing at the edge of the forest when something dropped suddenly, heavily, from a tree, screamed at him and bared its teeth, challenging him to fight. He did not know the word for it, but it was a chimpanzee. He turned and ran with the chimp in half-hearted pursuit. There were sounds in the night that frightened Arthur – monkeys, cats and things to which he could put neither name nor image. They were merely sounds without shape, the meaning of which could only be guessed. In response to one deep growl, he leapt from his cot, darted across the room and straight under the single grey sheet that covered Captain Boulle. Arthur placed an arm around the captain to check he was there in the darkness, though the moonlight shone through the curtainless window and the sheet rose silver in a huge mound above his bulky form. Always, after that, they slept together, sharing the warmth of each other's bodies in the cool winter nights.

There was nothing Arthur liked more than evenings sitting outside the shack, talking or not talking, mostly not talking, just listening to the sound of the jungle. There was plenty of beer last time they were in town and Captain Boulle loaded so much into the canoe that it sat dangerously low in the water. One night, all of a sudden, Captain Boulle laid down his glass and announced that they would go to France. At dawn he packed a change of underwear and a spare shirt in his old kitbag and gathered his jotters together and wrapped them in oilskin, and they pushed the canoe out from the bank with a sense of adventure. They sat in the shade of the hotel courtyard and told everyone about their plans. They would get the ferry to the city next day. But they missed the ferry next day. So they sat in the courtyard and drank more beer instead. There would be another ferry in a week. Then they would go to France. Oh, the heads would turn to see two such fine, exotic characters as the old sea captain, returned from the sea, and his handsome young companion from Darkest Africa. They would take a house by the sea and watch the ships sail by. They would have croissants for breakfast, for there was nothing Arthur liked better. They might even sail once more, upon the Mediterranean, sail right into Marseilles, go and see the apartment building where Captain Boulle was born.

But it never happened. Next morning Captain Boulle was dead.

Arthur could not go back to the shack by himself. Instead he stayed around the hotel for a while and was popular company with the guests, though hardly his former happy self. The hotel owner gave him Captain Boulle's cap, expecting him to wear it, but he never did. He kept it in the back room he shared with the handyman, and looked at it every day. He missed Captain Boulle, his company and his talk, and he realized he would never see Marseilles. One day a white man came and took Captain Boulle's jotters, and Arthur left with him. The white man took Arthur on aeroplanes, through the skies, to a faraway place, which was much, much colder than Africa. Arthur finally made it to France and they even took him to Marseilles and photographed him there, outside the apartment building where Captain Boulle was born, holding Captain Boulle's book *My Life with Arthur*.

Arthur has lived most of his life in France now, much longer than Captain Boulle spent there. It was hard adjusting to a new country, a new life, new people. There were days when he just sat and thought about Africa and felt homesick, sick for a home that no longer existed, because it was Captain Boulle's home, and Captain Boulle was gone.

Charlotte distracted him, Charlotte interested him, Charlotte shared great times with him. She was equally at home tumbling head over heels in the grass or dining under mean, disapproving eyes at some tea party, where the tea was served in a cup rather than a mug. Arthur had never seen a cup and saucer till he came to France. But like Captain Boulle, Charlotte too is long gone now. They had three children together however, and now there were grandchildren. There were no invitations to tea parties any more. There just did not seem to be tea parties any more, though it was the scent of food that finally brought an end to Daniel and Marc's game of tig and attracted them back towards the house. Arthur took one long last, lingering look at the snowy hills in the distance. He was getting old and he doubted he would see another snowfall. He felt stiff as he rose from his seat, but life returned to his limbs as the scent of croissants wafted into his nostrils. That would be from the cafeteria, it would not be for him. Oh well, never mind. He would go and see what was on the menu tonight. The little girl could just be seen as a distant figure in red as Arthur descended the climbing frame, gripped the rope and swung across the ditch to the house. Isabelle, their young keeper, was dishing out bananas to the other chimpanzees, but she did not mash them like Captain Boulle had done. Before eating, Arthur went to his cage to get Captain Boulle's cap. For some reason, Arthur always liked to have Captain Boulle's cap with him at meal times.

# CHAPTER SIXTEEN

# COULD IT HAPPEN?

*'Let us explore the stars'*
John F. Kennedy, 1961

*'I am an apeman'*
Ray Davies, 1970

One of the most effective moments in the entire *Planet of the Apes* series is the scene at the beginning of *Escape from the Planet of the Apes* in which the astronauts take off their helmets to reveal themselves as chimpanzees. But it should have come as no great surprise to the military top brass. In January 1961, three months before Yuri Gagarin became the first man in space, a US astronaut got there before him, flying at an altitude of more than 100 miles and a speed of 13,000 miles per hour, and successfully returning to base. His name was Ham and he was a chimpanzee. The space race between the Americans and the Soviets was not the only race in town. There was another space race going on between humans and animals, as dramatized in *The Right Stuff*, the 1983 film about America's first astronauts. When John Glenn (Ed Harris) complains that the team's womanizing is endangering the programme, Gus Grissom (Fred Ward) comes out with one of the best lines in the film. 'The issue here ain't pussy,' he says. 'The issue here is monkey.' Philip Kaufman's film presents a montage of training exercises in which a series of identical tasks are completed by humans – the cream of America's pilot corps – and by chimps. And the apes were more cooperative than the big-headed humans. The United States was losing the international space race to the Soviet Union and in a desperate attempt to salvage some pride it launched Ham on *Mercury 2* – though the Soviets had been first to get an animal into space, four years earlier, when Laika the dog flew on *Sputnik 2*. Laika became the first living creature in space (that we know of), and the first dying creature too, for the Soviets, being the Soviets, did not feel it was important to bring her back again. American mice, squirrel monkeys and rhesus monkeys also preceded Ham, Gagarin and Alan Shepard. But when it came to the serious business, the space race bronze medal went to an American, the silver to a Russian and the gold to a chimpanzee.

It is a giant leap from there to flying to a planet dominated by chimps, gorillas and orang-utans, whether that planet is in the solar system of Betelgeuse, as in Boulle's novel, or is really Earth 2,000 years in the future, as the film would have it. Thinking about whether *Planet of the Apes* is possible raises two sets of questions. First there are the questions of space travel and the feasibility of a spaceship travelling so fast that, for its occupants, 'time will almost stand still'. Then there is the question of whether man could really lose his dominant position in the world order and whether apes could develop the power of speech and ride horses, fire guns and organize themselves into an industrial society. Could it happen? Or is it just a load of Boulle?

Everyone knows space is big, but it is sometimes difficult to comprehend the distances involved. It might help illustrate the size of space if we shrink some of the distances and produce an imaginary scale model. If the Earth was represented by a half-inch marble, the distance between it and the sun would be about 160 yards. But the next closest star would be more than 25,000 miles away. At the speed of light it would take four years to reach the nearest star, but man has got nowhere near the speed of light. At the speed of an Apollo spacecraft it would take close on one million years. What is needed is not just a faster rocket, but a whole new approach. The space agency NASA makes the comparison with the quantum leap from sailing ships to steam ships. When sailing ships reached their maximum speed, it was not just a question of rigging them with bigger and better sails to go faster. The solution lay with steam. This sort of quantum leap happens time and again. 'The speed limits of propeller aircraft were exceeded by jet aircraft,' says Marc Millis, project manager for NASA's Breakthrough Propulsion Physics Project. 'The altitude limits of aircraft were exceeded by rockets. The travel limits of rockets will be exceeded by … to be determined.'

But established scientific thinking suggests that, no matter what scientific breakthroughs we make, we may never be able to

travel faster than the speed of light. 'It's a wholly different problem than breaking the sound barrier,' says Millis. 'The sound
barrier was broken by an object that was made of matter, not
sound. The atoms and molecules that make up matter are
connected by electromagnetic fields – the same stuff that light is
made of. In the case of the light-speed barrier, the thing that's
trying to break the barrier is made up of the same stuff as the
barrier itself. How can an object travel faster than that which links
its atoms?' Established thinking is now being challenged,
however. The rules of special relativity prevent anything moving
faster than light ... in space and time as we know it, but we also
now know that space-time itself can theoretically be distorted
under the influence of enormous amounts of matter or energy.
Another analogy: if space were a sheet of newspaper and we were
at the top of the page and our destination was at the bottom we
would never get there. But suppose your teenage son, representing an enormous amount of matter and energy, came along and
folded the paper in two ... the top meets the bottom and, hey
presto, you are there in no time. But all this is actually irrelevant,
because Boulle accepted conventional thinking that man could
never travel faster than the speed of light and Professor Antelle
satisfies himself with travelling at 'the speed of light minus
epsilon' where epsilon is an infinitesimal amount. His theory of
time travel is based on the fact that for the occupants of the spaceship 'at top speed, time will almost stand still,' a point echoed by
Charlton Heston at the beginning of *Planet of the Apes* when he
says: 'According to Dr Hasslein's theory of time in a vehicle travelling nearly the speed of light, the Earth has aged nearly 700
years since we left it, while we have aged hardly at all.'

It may be difficult to believe that time would pass more slowly
on a speeding spaceship than it would in the external universe.
But it is demonstrably true. Experiments with atomic clocks have
shown that a timepiece on an aeroplane 'loses' time compared
with a sister instrument on the ground. An astronaut returning
from the moon is slightly younger than he would have been if he
had not gone. And a person who spends much of their life in
planes will live slightly longer, as measured by clocks on Earth,
than he would if he never left the ground. 'Newton thought he
had everything worked out, but it turned out that if you start

going very fast Newton's laws no longer apply,' says Christopher Welch, principal lecturer in astronautics at Kingston University. It is effectively a whole new ball game, and it does not necessarily last ninety minutes. Welch makes the point that this is not time travel, in the sense that the pilot picks a year and pushes the destination button. 'You are still going forward in time, but at a different rate,' he says ... just as happens in *Planet of the Apes*.

'The physics is fine, whereas lots of other people have written stories about hyperspace, which is still to be given any scientific credibility at all – it's just a vague possibility.' The big question is how much time is involved. In *Planet of the Apes* it was centuries, in our examples it may be no more than a fraction of a single second, but the main point is that the principle is proven beyond all doubt, and as a traveller approaches the speed of light the difference between his time and Earth's time widens enormously. Welch suggests the human body's capacity to withstand acceleration could be significantly improved if, instead of breathing air, astronauts were to breathe oxygenated liquid. Experiments are already well advanced in this area, to the point where it may be a question of fine-tuning rather than establishing principles. Taylor's crew in *Planet of the Apes* spend most of their trip in hibernation. 'Much less work has been done on suspended animation,' says Welch. 'Nobody has succeeded in actually doing it, but it is a theoretical possibility.'

But we are making an assumption here. It is the assumption of continued scientific progress – that, given time, so to speak, we will find a way of travelling faster through space, just as we found a way of travelling faster across the world's seas. But what *Planet of the Apes* suggests is that we might find it difficult to retain the scientific knowledge and expertise we already have. And we would not be the first species to suddenly find it was no longer sitting at the top of the Creation Premier League. 'There are plenty of good examples of "regression" in the animal kingdom,' says D.W. Yalden, senior lecturer in zoology at Manchester University. 'For instance fleas and lice have lost the wings their ancestors had, because being an ectoparasite on warm-blooded hosts with fur or feathers is best furthered by hopping or crawling from one host to another, not flying away and losing contact with hosts. There is a famous mollusc parasite that has even lost its ancestral anus, because it lives on the yolk from eggs of its echinoderm hosts, and they are entirely digestible. But for humans to regress like that would take a long time, and need a positive evolutionary pressure. One could imagine that we would require less food, and less musculature, if we travelled everywhere by vehicle, and allowed, or programmed, computers to do all our thinking for us – brains are expensive to run; and we might even avoid deep vein thrombosis if we had shorter legs with less blood pooling in them.'

Richard Byrne, professor of evolutionary psychology, at St Andrews University, argues that evolution is not 'progressive'. 'Many species have lost their "dominant" positions over the course of evolution: blue-green algae, trilobites, dinosaurs.' 'When Algae Ruled the World' is a concept that many may find difficult to relate to. But dinosaurs are a different matter. Once they were the masters of all they surveyed. Now? The remainder-rack of history. But Darwin's theories about the survival of the fittest are being modified, if not undermined, within modern human civilization. 'Remove the selection pressure,' says Jamie Stevens, a biodiversity research fellow at Hatherly Laboratories, Exeter University, 'and organismal evolution might drift in a previously unknown direction – a direction some might call regression. Replace speech with another form of, say electronic, communication and speech might become redundant, although the actual need to communicate would not.'

*2001: A Space Odyssey* appeared in cinemas within weeks of *Planet of the Apes* and presented astronauts on a similar journey, sleeping, while a computer controlled their spaceship, but in Kubrick's film man's position is threatened by the electronic beast rather than the simian one, and it seems much more likely that if man were to lose his place at the top of the tree it would be the computer that knocked him off his perch. But is there any possibility of apes developing the power of speech, riding horses, firing guns, organizing themselves and ultimately 'taking over' from man? 'Not a chance, in only 2,000 years,' says Yalden, a point echoed by all the other experts to whom I spoke. 'I think film-makers, perhaps the public in general, simply do not grasp the immense periods of time involved. It has taken us something like six million years, minimum, to evolve the differences we have from chimpanzees. To make tools, wield rifles, use computers, would require at least a hand as dexterous as ours. One minor but important difference is that we have a long thumb, which can be opposed to the index finger, and the apes do not. We do not quite know why our brain is three times larger, per body-mass kilogram, than in any of the apes, but this extra size is certainly a factor in our ability to do all the complex thinking that we do, and their smaller brain size surely limits what apes can do. Of course, we could regress, and the apes could evolve, but it would take at least six million years to do either, and I think we are going to exterminate the apes, either deliberately or by removing their forest habitat, long before that. We obviously stand quite a good chance of exterminating ourselves too in that time.'

But others have a different perspective. In the wild chimps not only use branches and stones as tools, but also modify them for specific purposes, stripping leaves from a twig and using it to get at insects or honey. In captivity they have balanced boxes on top of each other to reach bananas and have brandished 'clubs' at predators in adjoining cages. Academics have taught chimps how to add up and circus trainers have taught them to ride and shoot, after a fashion. 'I don't see too much problem with great apes acquiring speech capabilities over a significant period of time,' says Peter Holland, professor of zoology at Reading University. 'They are pretty similar to us.' They are already able to communicate with each other through grunts and gestures. Attempts to teach them human language have so far proven unsuccessful. However a chimp called Washoe, who was raised by two American academics as if she were a deaf human child, learned about 250 words in American sign language and went on to teach other chimps. Could apes develop speech, ride horses, fire guns, organize themselves and take over? Richard Byrne has no doubts whatsoever. 'Apes did do these things,' he insists. 'The apes were called *Homo sapiens*.'

Could *Planet of the Apes* happen?

It already has.

# CHAPTER SEVENTEEN
# A NEW BEGINNING

In November 2000 Richard Zanuck returned to the barren desert lands of the Utah–Arizona border, where Franklin J. Schaffner first called action on *Planet of the Apes* a third of a century earlier. The urbane director was long since dead and gone. Gone too were writers Serling, Wilson, Kelley and Boulle, and Arthur P. Jacobs, the producer whose ambition and tenacity played such a vital role in transforming Boulle's satirical French prose into a blockbuster Hollywood movie. But their vision survived and their legend prospered and grew. Richard Zanuck, who greenlit the film in 1966 as head of Twentieth Century Fox, was still around, still working in the industry. The fresh-faced young executive was now a veteran independent producer. For his new film he returned to Lake Powell, where Charlton Heston's spaceship had crashed so many years before. For Astronaut Taylor Lake Powell represented a trip into the future, for Zanuck a trip into the past. Zanuck was accompanied by the ghosts of many previous collaborators, but he was accompanied too by the very tangible presence of Tim Burton. Burton was a shy little kid in Burbank when *Planet of the Apes* came out, and it helped shape his distinctly offbeat perception of the world. He became one of Hollywood's most visually exciting and imaginative directors with a body of films that included *Batman* – a man who dresses like a bat, *Edward Scissorhands* – a man with scissors for hands, *The Nightmare Before Christmas* – an animated musical horror film that paid tribute to Burton's boyhood hero Vincent Price, *Ed Wood* – a tribute to a man who dressed like a girl and who was responsible for *Plan 9 From Outer Space*, and *Mars Attacks!* – a homage to those awful sci-fi cheapies, with their bug-eyed Martians and ray guns, that had made it so difficult for Arthur Jacobs to convince anyone *Planet of the Apes* was more than just another camp, dressing-up-as-monsters movie. Burton established Weird as a mainstream Hollywood destination. Together he and Zanuck were about to collaborate on a big-budget film that Twentieth Century Fox hoped would be one of the biggest hits of summer 2001. The title used, as a sort of smokescreen, was *The Visitor*, but the film would become better known by another name – *Planet of the Apes*.

It took Arthur P. Jacobs three years to persuade Zanuck to back the original movie, but that was nothing compared with the gestation period for the latest *Apes*. And before Tim Burton assembled his ape armies, the project would go through the hands of numerous different writers and directors, beginning back in the eighties. The A–Z of those who were linked to the film includes: Michael Bay, director of *Pearl Harbor*; James Cameron; Chris Columbus, who wrote *Gremlins* and directed *Home Alone*, *Mrs Doubtfire* and *Harry Potter and the Philosopher's Stone*; Sam Hamm, who wrote Tim Burton's *Batman* movie; Terry Hayes, the Australian writer whose work included the *Mad Max* sequels, which seemed to draw on *Apes* for their dysfunctional, dislocated, post-apocalyptic world; Adam Rifkin, who would later make his mark in Hollywood with the script for another film in which animals played a pivotal role, the hit comedy *Mouse Hunt*; Arnold Schwarzenegger; and Oliver Stone. Stone had successfully melded drama with political and philosophical comment in *JFK* and his Vietnam trilogy *Platoon*, *Born on the Fourth of July* and *Heaven and Earth*. He seemed almost obsessed with re-examining the political and cultural values of the sixties and early seventies, the period in which many of his films, from *JFK* to *The Doors*, are set and in which the original *Apes* films were made. Fox got as far as including his film on their slate of releases for 1995. An Oliver Stone *Planet of the Apes* film is an intriguing proposition, with the opportunities it might have afforded to explore sinister simian conspiracies. Who really blew up the world? But it was not to be.

Recent *Apes* history breaks down into five eras.

Episode one, 1988–89: *Return to the Planet of the Apes* served as an alternative sequel to the original film: civil war has broken out between chimps and gorillas and Cornelius journeys to the Forbidden Zone to find Taylor, hoping Taylor's testimony will convince the apes of the ultimate folly of war.

Episode two, 1993–94: *Return of the Apes* reflected concerns about AIDS and the dangers of new international diseases. The future of mankind is threatened by an epidemic of babies who have apparently died of old age before they are even born. A maverick scientist goes back in time, to the dawn of man, in the hope of sorting out the problems at source and finds the world ruled by apes.

Episode three, 1995–96: *Planet of the Apes*. An alien spaceship crashes on Earth, piloted by an orang-utan, bringing with it the baby-killer virus. A team of astonauts set out for the planet from which the spaceship came. The script draws on elements from previous *Apes* films and the original novel and it manages to mix two preoccupations of contemporary human culture – the fear of international viral infection and the increasing prevalence and seductiveness of electronic voyeurism.

Episode four, 1997–98: Fox were still not happy and a long list of possible writers and directors were linked to the project. It had been rumoured for some time that James Cameron, the director of the *The Terminator* and *Aliens*, might become involved in some capacity, not necessarily as director. In late 1997 the soon-to-be-crowned king of the world announced he would be writing and producing a new *Apes* film, drawing on elements from the original and the first sequel. Given their past history together, it seemed more likely than ever that Schwarzenegger would play the Heston role. Creature specialist Stan Winston, who had worked on *The Terminator*, *Aliens*, *Jurassic Park* and *Congo*, was developing the 'look' of the apes before Cameron's involvement was confirmed. Cameron enthused about his work, but the sticking point remained the script and in the wake of *Titanic*'s success Cameron had other projects vying for his attention, including *True Lies 2*, *Terminator 3* and *Spider-Man*. By the end of 1998 he too had departed.

Episode five, 1999–2001: *Planet of the Apes*. In March 1999, then-Fox studio boss Bill Mechanic and other Fox executives attended an industry event and talked about their plans for the next few years. It was sci-fi all the way, with *The Phantom Menace* set to dominate cinemas in the coming months, *X-Men* lined up for the following summer and *Planet of the Apes* for 2001. William Broyles, whose credits include *Apollo 13*, *Entrapment* and *Cast Away*, was the latest writer to have a shot at reviving the cine-simians. A year later Fox finally had a script they liked, a director and a producer. 'It was a movie that had impact on me as a kid,' said Burton when he visited Hawaii, scouting locations, shortly after his involvement was confirmed. 'It's like a fairy tale, a folk tale, to me.' By that time

Zanuck was also on board. 'When you say *Planet of the Apes* and Tim Burton in the same breath, it spells kind of magic,' he said, 'and I just thought it was a great opportunity with Tim. I couldn't think of anyone that could do it better than Tim and so I eagerly accepted it.' The new *Apes* story would return to the original concept, rather than slot into the established *Planet of the Apes* history as a fifth sequel, but both Burton and Zanuck were keen to avoid the word 'remake', preferring to talk about their film as a 're-imagining' of the original story. 'I had a feeling that there is a way to do it differently,' says Burton, 'exploring thematically similar things but in a different way. I think it can be revisited and re-imagined to a whole new generation.' Zanuck: 'The basic upside-down world – that's very much the same. The story is entirely different, the characters are entirely different. In terms of the logistics, this is much bigger, as befitting the times.' One of the first things Burton and Zanuck did was to bring in yet another two writers, Mark Rosenthal and Lawrence Konner, for further work on the script. Rosenthal and Konner were a long-established team, whose previous films included *Mighty Joe Young* and *The Jewel of the Nile.*

Speculation ran wild on the Internet as the film began casting and neared its start date of November 2000, with suggestions that Mark Wahlberg's astronaut, Leo Davidson, would become involved romantically with a chimpanzee played by Helena Bonham Carter, the dark-haired actress who had had problems shaking off her image as the English rose of period dramas, including *A Room with a View* and *Howards End.* There was sex and full-frontal nudity in *The Wings of the Dove,* but it was still Henry James, and her attempt to go grunge in *Fight Club* was hardly an overwhelming success with the critics.

Davidson lands on a planet, where humans are subservient to apes, though there is considerable division among the apes themselves over the treatment of humans. On the one hand is Thade (Tim Roth – *Pulp Fiction, Rob Roy*), a villainous chimpanzee general, and Attar (Michael Clarke Duncan – the condemned giant in *The Green Mile*), a gorilla warrior, but a much more sympathetic character than Thade, religious and principled, if misguided. On the other hand is Ari, the middle-class liberal chimp played by Bonham Carter. Davidson is captured. And then … Guess what? He escapes, and organizes the human resistance.

Burton considered including baboons in the mix, an idea that at one stage figured in the script for the original film. But make-up designer Rick Baker restricted himself to tried and tested chimps, gorillas and orang-utans. Baker was at the top of his profession, a five-time Oscar winner, and he intended to take a long break after *Nutty Professor II* and *The Grinch*, but a phone call from Burton forced a change in plans. He would have liked a year to perfect the make-up, but had only four months, and, like John Chambers on the original film, he ended up working day and night to meet the deadline. Chambers and his team were pushing back the frontiers of make-up design, whereas Baker was able to use their work as a starting point. 'They had a design for the gorillas and the chimps and the orang-utans, and they pretty much did the same make-up on everybody,' he says. 'The sculptures were basically the same. It's just that the proportions of the face that they put it on made it look different. I really wanted to make them individual characters as much as possible, and give them more mobility. And have them be able to show their teeth.' He designed three levels of make-up. Principals would get individual appliances, Number Ones. Actors in the background would get foam-rubber masks, Number Twos. 'In the first movie, they had one sculpture for the gorilla background mask, duplicated a whole bunch of times. Even as a kid I thought, "It doesn't take that long to knock out a background mask. Why don't you do a couple different ones?" So we made something like 500 background masks. I don't know how many sculptures we did, but there's at least ten of each – chimps, gorillas, orangs.' Extras in the distance got another type of mask, Number Threes. Baker specifically asked Burton and Zanuck to cast actors with small noses, because they were easier to transform into apes. 'When they said Tim Roth was a possibility, I was going: "What part of this big nose thing didn't you understand?"' Nevertheless, Baker did a magnificent job of turning him into a realistic and rather chilling ape, all simian wrinkles, whiskers and animal cunning, capturing the spirit of the cannibalistic chimps of William Boyd's *Brazzaville Beach*. The word 'Oscar' figured prominently in assessments of his work on Roth and Michael Clarke Duncan. One of the biggest challenges, however, was Bonham Carter's character, Ari. The design brief was deceptively simple – Baker had to create a chimpanzee that human men would find attractive. 'I like apes a lot, but never wanted to do it with one,' says Baker, reassuringly. An enormous amount of trial and error went into making Ari look attractive, without making her too human, and the look of the character quickly established itself as the most controversial among fans. The masks varied little from the masks in the original *Apes* films and it still took just as long to put the appliances on the principals. Tim Roth's make-up took about two and a half hours, while Bonham Carter's took up to four. 'Helena Bonham Carter, who plays the main female in the piece, is in the make-up chair at two o'clock every morning, so it's very, very tough on her,' says Zanuck.

Like the other ape actors, Bonham Carter attended ape school before filming began. 'Everyone thinks that you can just monkey around and be an ape,' she says. 'But it requires a strange concentration, a state of mind that still remains sort of elusive to me today ... It was a real bonus to have four weeks of ape training. It makes you much more focused. We did a lot of yoga and breathing. It was taken very seriously. But at the same time it's quite difficult to keep a straight face when you start looking around ... It requires a major suspension of disbelief in this job more than most, because you look around and everyone's got ape heads on.' But it did sometimes have its advantages. 'If you've got a mask, it's a sort of licence to completely misbehave. Because apes are much more tactile, I can get away with feeling people up, and being really naughty.'

The huge Ape City set was built at Sony's lot at Culver City, because there was insufficient space available at Fox, and it was literally shrouded in secrecy, with black curtains across the entranceways to frustrate the prying eyes of those on adjoining sets. Actors were delivered to the set in trams with blackened windows and Burton reportedly shot several different endings in an attempt to keep even the keenest fans and cyber-junkies guessing about how it would all turn out. Rumours about an ape version of the Statue of Liberty refused to go away, and there was also talk of a version of Mount Rushmore with ape faces, an idea that had been used in the cartoon series. The film-makers visited the volcanic tropical landscape of Hawaii and the dry lake beds of Trona (which sounds disconcertingly like Troma, the bargain-basement company that made the Toxic Avenger movies), near Death Valley, as well as Lake Powell. 'It fit the location and the look that we were going for,' says Zanuck. 'But again it's a bit of a tip of the hat, a salute to the old version that was so revered.' It was not the only reference to the original movie. Charlton Heston agreed to a cameo appearance as Thade's father, though it was difficult to pin him to a date. Zanuck provided a role for girl-friend Linda Harrison in the original and he found a small role for ex-wife Linda Harrison in the new film. And Tim Burton paid his respects to the tradition of the series by finding a small ape role for his partner, Lisa Marie. In keeping with the times merchandising was an integral part of the package from the outset. By the start of 2001 more than fifty companies were signed up, including Dark Horse, which had the rights to a new line of comics and graphic novels, and Hasbro, which was producing action figures and toys. The importance of merchandising was reflected in Fox's choice of the New York Toy Fair to launch the teaser trailer and the attendance there of Mark Wahlberg.

'It's hard to imagine now, five pictures later and making a whole new version, but at the time we didn't know whether it would work or not,' says Zanuck. 'And here ... thirty years later, I'm sitting talking to you in the Mojave Desert, where we're shooting with Tim Burton, and hundreds of apes, and a huge caravan of trailers and tents, the likes of which I've never seen in my career and, you know, it's an amazing ...' His sentence trails away, but the sentiment is clear. 'I'm the producer of this, so I'm here every day on the set. I've worked with Tim shoulder to shoulder on the development of the screenplay and all of that, and I'm totally personally involved in this, where I was not – I was making fifteen other pictures at the time of *Planet of the Apes* – as head of the studio. No, it's a whole different involve-ment. It's a whole different kind of thing ... What has happened during the course of the years, this cult that has built up, is quite astonishing to me.'

As he tramped from studio to studio, with his portfolio of sketches of apes in human clothing, Arthur P. Jacobs could never have imagined that a quarter of a century after his death those sceptical executives would still be making films, and making money, from his talking apes. 'You know there's not a day that goes by, in the making of this, that I don't think of Arthur, who was a great friend, and how his enthusiasm for that original idea started all of this,' says Zanuck. 'I'm sitting out here because Arthur came in with his idea, into my office, and he started a franchise for the studio. And here we are starting it all over again …'

# FILMOGRAPHY

*Ratings:* *Bad **OK ***Good ****Very good *****Outstanding
The filmography follows standard practice in giving the year of
release rather than production.

## FEATURE FILMS

*Planet of the Apes* *****
USA, 1968, 112 mins

Three US spacemen travel hundreds of years into the future and crash-
land on a planet where gorillas, chimpanzees and orang-utans rule and
men are a backward species hunted for sport.

*Twentieth Century Fox/Apjac Productions*
Charlton Heston (George Taylor), Roddy McDowall (Cornelius), Kim Hunter
(Zira), Maurice Evans (Zaius), James Whitmore (President of the Assembly),
James Daly (Honorious), Linda Harrison (Nova), Robert Gunner (Landon),
Lou Wagner (Lucius), Woodrow Parfrey (Maximus), Jeff Burton (Dodge), Buck
Kartalian (Julius), Norman Burton (Hunt Leader), Wright King (Galen), Paul
Lambert (Minister)
*Director:* Franklin J. Schaffner
*Screenplay:* Rod Serling, Michael Wilson and John T. Kelley (uncredited), based
   on the novel by Pierre Boulle
*Producer:* Arthur P. Jacobs; *Associate producer:* Mort Abrahams
*Photography:* Leon Shamroy; *Special photographic effects:* L.B. Abbott, Art
   Cruickshank and Emil Kosa Jr
*Creative make-up design:* John Chambers; *Make-up artists:* Ben Nye and Dan
   Striepeke; *Hair stylist:* Edith Lindon
*Costume design:* Morton Haack
*Art direction:* Jack Martin Smith and William Creber; *Production illustrators:* Don
   Peters and Mentor Huebner (both uncredited); *Set decoration:* Walter M. Scott
   and Norman Rockett
*Sound:* Herman Lewis and David Dockendorf
*Unit production manager:* William Eckhardt; *Assistant director:* William Kissel
*Editing:* Hugh S. Fowler
*Music:* Jerry Goldsmith; *Orchestration:* Arthur Morton


*Beneath the Planet of the Apes* **
USA, 1970, 95 mins

Brent follows Taylor's route through space in search of the missing
astronauts and lands on a planet inhabited by talking apes and by
mutant humans, who live underground and worship 'The Bomb'.

*Twentieth Century Fox/Apjac Productions*
James Franciscus (Brent), Kim Hunter (Zira), Maurice Evans (Dr Zaius), Linda
Harrison (Nova), Charlton Heston (Taylor), Paul Richards (Mendez), Victor
Buono (Fat Man), James Gregory (Ursus), Jeff Corey (Caspay), Natalie Trundy

(Albina), Thomas Gomez (Minister), David Watson (Cornelius), Don Pedro Colley (Negro), Tod Andrews (Skipper), Gregory Sierra (Verger), Eldon Burke (Gorilla Sergeant), Lou Wagner (Lucius), Paul Frees (closing narration – uncredited)
*Director:* Ted Post
*Screenplay:* Paul Dehn
*Story:* Paul Dehn and Mort Abrahams, based on characters created by Pierre Boulle
*Producer:* Arthur P. Jacobs; *Associate producer:* Mort Abrahams
*Photography:* Milton Krasner
*Special photographic effects:* L.B. Abbott and Art Cruickshank
*Creative make-up design:* John Chambers; *Make-up supervisor:* Dan Striepeke; *Hair stylist:* Edith Lindon
*Costume design:* Morton Haack
*Art direction:* Jack Martin Smith and William Creber; *Set decoration:* Walter M. Scott and Sven Wickman; *Art illustrator:* Fred Harpman
*Sound:* Stephen Bass and David Dockendorf
*Unit production manager:* Joseph C. Behm; *Assistant director:* Fred Simpson; *Second unit director:* Chuck Roberson
*Editing:* Marion Rothman
*Music:* Leonard Rosenman; *Orchestration:* Ralph Ferraro

*Escape from the Planet of the Apes* \*\*\*\*
USA, 1971, 97 mins
Zira and Cornelius escape the doomed planet in Taylor's spaceship and return to twentieth-century Earth, where they become celebrities, but are also seen as a threat to mankind's future.
*Twentieth Century Fox/Apjac Productions*
Roddy McDowall (Cornelius), Kim Hunter (Zira), Bradford Dillman (Dr Lewis Dixon), Natalie Trundy (Dr Stephanie Branton), Eric Braeden (Dr Otto Hasslein), Ricardo Montalban (Armando), William Windom (President), Sal Mineo (Milo), Albert Salmi (E-1), Jason Evers (E-2), John Randolph (Inquiry chairman), Harry Lauter (General Winthrop), M. Emmet Walsh (Winthrop's aide), Roy Glenn Sr (Lawyer), Peter Forster (Cardinal), Norman Burton (Army officer), William Woodson (Naval officer), Tom Lowell (Orderly), Gene Whittington (Marine captain), Donald Elson (curator), Bill Bonds (TV newscaster), Army Archerd (Boxing referee), James Bacon (General Faulkner)
*Director:* Don Taylor
*Screenplay:* Paul Dehn, based on characters created by Pierre Boulle
*Producer:* Arthur P. Jacobs; Associate producer: Frank Capra Jr
*Photography:* Joseph Biroc
*Special photographic effects:* Howard A. Anderson
*Creative make-up design:* John Chambers; *Make-up supervisor:* Dan Striepeke; *Make-up artist:* Jack Barron; *Hair stylist:* Mary Babcock
*Art direction:* Jack Martin Smith and William Creber; *Set decoration:* Walter M. Scott and Stuart A. Reiss; *Art illustrator:* Bill Sully
*Sound:* Dean Vernon and Theodore Soderberg
*Unit production manager:* Francisco Day; *Assistant director:* Pepi Lenzi
*Editing:* Marion Rothman
*Music:* Jerry Goldsmith; *Orchestration:* Arthur Morton

*Conquest of the Planet of the Apes* \*\*\*
USA, 1972, 88 mins
In the early 1990s apes have been trained to do household chores
and menial labour, but Caesar, son of Zira and Cornelius, grows
up to lead a revolt against their human oppressors.
*Twentieth Century Fox/Apjac Productions*
Roddy McDowall (Caesar), Ricardo Montalban (Armando), Don Murray
(Breck), Natalie Trundy (Lisa), Hari Rhodes (MacDonald), Severn Darden
(Kolp), Lou Wagner (Busboy), John Randolph (Commission chairman), Asa
Maynor (Mrs Riley), H.M. Wynant (Hoskyns), David Chow (Aldo), Buck
Kartalian (Frank), John Dennis (Policeman), Paul Comi (Second policeman),
Gordon Jump (Auctioneer), Dick Spangler (Announcer), Joyce Haber (Zelda),
Hector Soucy (Ape with chain)
*Director:* J. Lee Thompson
*Screenplay:* Paul Dehn, based on characters created by Pierre Boulle
*Producer:* Arthur P. Jacobs; *Associate producer:* Frank Capra Jr
*Photography:* Bruce Surtees
*Creative make-up design:* John Chambers; *Make-up supervisor:* Dan Striepeke; *Make-up artists:* Joe Di Bella and Jack Barron; *Hair stylist:* Carol Pershing
*Art direction:* Philip Jefferies; *Set decoration:* Norman Rockett; *Title design:* Don
Record
*Sound:* Herman Lewis and Don Bassman
*Unit production manager:* William G. Eckhardt; *Assistant director:* David 'Buck' Hall
*Editing:* Marjorie Fowler and Alan Jaggs
*Music:* Tom Scott

*Battle for the Planet of the Apes* \*\*
USA, 1973, 86 mins
Human wars have devastated the great cities and Caesar attempts
to re-establish civilization in the countryside, but his efforts are
threatened by human survivors from the city where he once lived.
*Twentieth Century Fox/Apjac Productions*
Roddy McDowall (Caesar), Claude Akins (Aldo), Natalie Trundy (Lisa), Severn
Darden (Kolp), Lew Ayres (Mandemus), Paul Williams (Virgil), Austin Stoker
(MacDonald), Noah Keen (Teacher), Richard Eastham (Mutant captain),
France Nuyen (Alma), Paul Stevens (Mendez), Heather Lowe (Doctor), Bobby
Porter (Cornelius), Michael Stearns (Jake), Cal Wilson (Soldier), Pat Cardi
(Young chimp), John Landis (Jake's friend), Andy Knight (Mutant on motor-
cycle), John Huston (The Lawgiver).
*Director:* J. Lee Thompson
*Screenplay:* John William Corrington and Joyce Hooper Corrington
*Story:* Paul Dehn, based on characters created by Pierre Boulle
*Producer:* Arthur P. Jacobs; *Associate producer:* Frank Capra Jr
*Photography:* Richard H. Kline
*Creative make-up design:* John Chambers; *Make-up supervisor:* Joe Di Bella; *Make-up artists:* Jack Barron and Werner Keppler; *Hair stylist:* Carol Pershing

*Art direction:* Dale Hennessy; *Set decoration:* Robert deVestel; *Title design:* Don Record
*Special mechanical effects:* Gerald Endler
*Sound:* Herman Lewis and Don Bassman
*Unit production manager:* Michael S. Glick; *Assistant director:* Ric Rondell; *Second assistant director:* Barry Stern
*Editing:* Alan Jaggs and John C. Horger
*Music:* Leonard Rosenman

## Planet of the Apes
## USA, 2001

In the near future an American astronaut lands on a strange planet where talking apes rule and humans are the subservient species.
*Twentieth Century Fox*
Mark Wahlberg (Leo Davidson), Tim Roth (Thade), Helena Bonham Carter (Ari), Michael Clarke Duncan (Attar), Kris Kristofferson (Karubi), Estella Warren (Daena), Paul Giamatti (Limbo), Cary-Hiroyuki Tagawa (Krull), David Warner (Sandar)
*Director:* Tim Burton
*Screenplay:* William Broyles Jr. and Lawrence Konner & Mark D. Rosenthal
*Producer:* Richard D. Zanuck; *Executive producer:* Ralph Winter
*Photography:* Philippe Rousselot; *Make-up design and creation:* Rick Baker; *Costume design:* Colleen Atwood; *Production design:* Rick Heinrichs; *Special animation and visual effects:* ILM; *Editing:* Chris Lebenzon; *Music:* Danny Elfman

## TELEVISION
Planet of the Apes
USA, 1974, 14 x 55 mins

Two astronauts travel through time to the thirty-first century, when Earth is ruled by apes.
*Twentieth Century Fox Television*
Roddy McDowall (Galen), Ron Harper (Alan Virdon), James Naughton (Pete Burke), Mark Lenard (Urko), Booth Colman (Zaius), Eldon Burke and Ron Stein (gorilla regulars)
*Producer:* Stan Hough; *Executive producer:* Herbert Hirschman; *Developed by* Anthony Wilson
*Executive story consultant:* Howard Dimsdale; *Story consultants:* Joe Ruby and Ken Spears
*Photography:* Gerald Perry Finnerman; *Make-up:* Dan Striepeke; *Art director:* Arch Bacon; *Music:* Lalo Schifrin, Richard Lasalle, Earle Hagen.

### 1 *Escape from Tomorrow* **
Virdon and Burke are captured, but chimp Galen helps them escape, and all three become fugitives.
*Guest stars:* Royal Dano (Farrow), Woodrow Parfrey (Veska), Biff Elliot (Ullman), Bobby Porter (Arno), Jerome Thor (Proto)
*Director:* Don Weis; *Writer:* Art Wallace

## 2 *The Gladiators* **

Virdon and Burke are captured (again), in an outlying village and forced to fight as gladiators.
*Guest stars:* William Smith (Tolar), John Hoyt (Barlow), Marc Singer (Dalton), Pat Renella (Jason)
*Director:* Don McDougall; *Writer:* Art Wallace

## 3 *The Trap* ***

Urko and Burke are trapped in the ruins of the San Francisco area subway and must work together to survive.
*Guest stars:* Norm Alden (Zako), John Milford (Miller), Cindy Eilbacher (Lisa Miller), Wallace Earl (Mary Miller), Mickey LeClair (Jick Miller)
*Director:* Arnold Laven; *Writer:* Edward J. Lakso

## 4 *The Good Seeds* ***

Virdon's knowledge of farming helps win the trust of superstitious ape peasants.
*Guest stars:* Geoffrey Deuel (Anto), Lonny Chapman (Polar), Jacqueline Scott (Zantes), Bobby Porter (Remus) Eileen Ditz (Jillia)
*Director:* Don Weis; *Writer:* Robert W. Lenski

## 5 *The Legacy* **

The fugitives visit the ruins of Oakland and discover a long-forgotten computer databank.
Zina Bethune (Arn), Jackie Earle Haley (Kraik), Robert Phillips (Gorilla captain), Jon Lormer (Scientist)
*Director:* Bernard McEveety; *Writer:* Robert Hamner

## 6 *Tomorrow's Tide* *

Virdon and Burke do for fishing what they did for farming in *The Good Seeds.*
Roscoe Lee Browne (Hurton), Jay Robinson (Bandor), John McLiam (Gahto), Jim Storm (Romar), Kathleen Bracken (Soma).
*Director:* Don McDougall; *Writer:* Robert W. Lenski

## 7 *The Surgeon* **

Ape *ER* with Virdon on the table and chimp doctors.
Jacqueline Scott (Kira), Michael Strong (Travin), Martin Brooks (Leander), Jamie Smith Jackson (Girl)
*Director:* Arnold Laven; *Writer:* Barry Oringer

## 8 *The Deception* ****

A blind ape falls in love with Burke, while Galen infiltrates the ape version of the Ku Klux Klan.
Jane Actman (Fauna), Pat Renella (Zon), John Milford (Sestus), Hal Baylor (Jasko), Baynes Barron (Perdix)

*Director:* Don McDougall; *Story:* Anthony Lawrence, *Writers:* Anthony Lawrence, Ken Spears and Joe Ruby

### 9 *The Horse Race* \*\*

Virdon shows he is not just a great farmer and fisherman, but a champion jockey too.

Morgan Woodward (Martin), John Hoyt (Barlow), Richard Devon (Zandar), Henry Levin (Prefect), Meegan King (Gregor)
*Director:* Jack Starrett; *Writers:* David P. Lewis and Booker Bradshaw

### 10 *The Interrogation* \*\*

Sinister, bespectacled chimp scientist Wanda brainwashes Burke by sticking him on a roundabout and refusing to let him off.

Beverly Garland (Wanda), Anne Seymour (Ann), Norman Burton (Yalu), Harry Townes (Malthus)
*Director:* Alf Kjellin; *Writer:* Richard Collins

### 11 *The Tyrant* \*\*

Galen exposes a corrupt local official by enticing him into a plot against Urko.

Percy Rodrigues (Aboro), Michael Conrad (Janor), James Daughton (Mikal), Joseph Ruskin (Daku)
*Director:* Ralph Senensky; *Writer:* Walter Black

### 12 *The Cure* \*\*

Virdon and Burke's areas of expertise include medicine and they clear up an outbreak of malaria.

David Sheiner (Zoran), Sondra Locke (Amy), Ron Soble (Kava), George Wallace (Talbert)
*Director:* Bernard McEveety; *Writer:* Edward J. Lakso

### 13 *The Liberator* \*\*\*

Galen, Virdon and Burke come across a strange and deadly local cult.

John Ireland (Brun), Ben Andrews (Miro), Jennifer Ashley (Talia), Peter G. Skinner (Clim)
*Director:* Arnold Laven; *Writer* Howard Dimsdale

### 14 *Up Above the World So High* \*

One small step for a chimp, one giant leap for apekind when Galen goes hang-gliding.

Joanna Barnes (Carsia), Frank Aletter (Leuric), Martin Brooks (Konag)
*Director:* John Meredyth Lucas; *Story:* S. Bar-David; *Writers:* S. Bar-David and Arthur Browne Jr

## TV Movies

Several of the above episodes were subsequently stitched together and presented as television 'movies': *Back to the Planet of the Apes* (*Escape from Tomorrow* and *The Trap*); *Forgotten City of the Planet of the Apes* (*The Gladiators* and *The Legacy*); *Life, Liberty and Pursuit on the Planet of the Apes* (*The Surgeon* and *The Interrogation*); *Treachery and Greed on the Planet of the Apes* (*The Horse Race* and *The Tyrant*); *Farewell to the Planet of the Apes* (*Tomorrow's Tide* and *Up Above the World So High*).

## Return to the Planet of the Apes
USA, 1975, 13 x 24 mins
Cartoon series drawing on the characters and storyline of the first two films, with extra monsters.
*Twentieth Century Fox Television/DFE Films*
*Voice cast:* Tom Williams, Austin Stoker, Claudette Nevins, Henry Corden, Phillippa Harris, Edwin Mills, Richard Blackburn
*Developed for television and produced by* David H. DePatie and Fritz Freleng
*Supervising director/associate producer:* Doug Wildey
*Animation director:* Cullen Houghtaling; *Storyboard directors:* Morris Gollub, Doug Wildey, Jan Green; *Graphic design:* Moe Gollub, Leo Swenson, Tony Sgroi, George Wheeler, Zygamond Jablecki, Hak Ficq, Norley Paat, Earl Martin, John Dorman, John Messina; *Animation:* Reuben Timmins, Ed Aardal, Lee Halpern, Bob Kirk, Jim Brummett, Joe Roman Jr, Jack Foster, Janice Stocks; *Music:* Dean Elliott

1 *Flames of Doom* \*\*\*
Astronauts Bill, Jeff and Judy land on a planet ruled by apes. Bill is captured, Judy disappears.
*Writer:* Larry Spiegel

2 *Escape from Ape City* \*\*
Chimp scientists Cornelius and Zira help Bill escape.
*Writer:* Larry Spiegel

3 *The Unearthly Prophecy* \*\*\*
Bill and Jeff are reunited with Judy and meet the cloaked Underdwellers in the ruins of New York.
*Writers:* Jack Kaplan and John Barrett

4 *Tunnel of Fear* **
Bill and Jeff return to Ape City to see Cornelius and Zira and are caught in a giant spider's web.
*Writer:* Larry Spiegel

5 *Lagoon of Peril* **
Bill and Jeff determine to destroy the space capsule before its existence is confirmed and used as an excuse to wipe out humanoids.
*Writer:* J.C. Strong

6 *Terror on Ice Mountain* ***
Cornelius finds a book about a zoo and plans for a hot-air balloon, and he and Bill fly to a mystical mountain ape community.
*Writer:* Bruce Shelly

7 *River of Flames* **
Bill and Jeff help the Underdwellers when they are threatened by rising lava.
*Writers:* John Barrett and Jack Kaplan

8 *Screaming Wings* ***
Urko finds a Second World War fighter plane and intends to use it against the humanoids.
*Writers:* John Barrett and Jack Kaplan

9 *Trail to the Unknown* **
Bill, Jeff and Judy lead the humanoids in search of a new home, and meet another stranded astronaut, Brent.
*Writer:* Larry Spiegel

10 *Attack from the Clouds* **
Apes and humans are both terrorized by a giant flying lizard.
*Writer:* Larry Spiegel

11 *Mission of Mercy* **
Judy flies to Ape City to get medicine from Cornelius and Zira after Nova falls ill.
*Writer:* Larry Spiegel

12 *Invasion of the Underdwellers* \*\*\*
Urko's men dress in cloaks and steal precious works of ape art to provoke war with the Underdwellers.
*Writer:* J.C. Strong

13 *Battle of the Titans* \*\*
Cornelius and Bill return to the mountain ape community, while Urko plans a new attack.
*Writer:* Bruce Shelly

*Behind the Planet of the Apes* \*\*\*\*
USA, 1998, 54 mins
Roddy McDowall presents a documentary history of the Planet of the Apes series, including make-up tests with Edward G. Robinson as the orang-utan Zaius.
*Van Ness Films, in association with Foxstar Productions, Twentieth Century Fox Home Entertainment and American Movie Classics*
*Director/executive producer:* Kevin Burns; *Producer:* Shelley Lyons
*Writers:* Brian Anthony, David Comtois and Kevin Burns.
Extracts from this documentary appear on Planet of the Apes video boxed sets.

# SELECT
# BIBLIOGRAPHY

**Books**

Adami, Luiz Saulo: *O Unico Humano Bom é Aquele que Está Morto!* (The Only Good Human is a Dead Human!), Editora Aleph, São Paulo, Brazil, 1996

Becker, Lucille Frackman: *Pierre Boulle*, Twayne, New York, 1996

Boulle, Pierre: *The Bridge Over the River Kwai* (translated by Xan Fielding), Gramercy, New York, 2000

—: *Planet of the Apes* (translated by Xan Fielding), Gramercy, New York, 2000

Brassey, Richard: *How to Speak Chimpanzee*, Dolphin, London, 1996

Brosnan, John: *The Primal Screen – A History of Science Fiction Film*, Orbit, London, 1991

Brownlow, Kevin: *David Lean*, Richard Cohen Books, London, 1996

Charity, Tom: *The Right Stuff*, British Film Institute, London, 1997

Defoe, Daniel: *Robinson Crusoe*, Minster Classics, London

Dunne, John Gregory: *The Studio*, W.H. Allen, London, 1970

Engel, Joel: *Rod Serling – The Dreams and Nightmares of Life in the Twilight Zone*, Contemporary Books, Chicago, 1989

Finler, Joel W: *The Hollywood Story*, Mandarin, London, 1992

French, Sean: *The Terminator*, British Film Institute, London, 1996

Gansberg, Alan L: *Little Caesar – A Biography of Edward G. Robinson*, New English Library, Sevenoaks, Kent, 1983

Greene, Eric: *Planet of the Apes as American Myth – Race, Politics, and Popular Culture*, Wesleyan University Press/University Press of New England, Hanover, New Hampshire, 1998

Heston, Charlton: *The Actor's Life – Journals 1956–1976*, Pocket Books, New York, 1978

—: *In the Arena – The Autobiography*, HarperCollins, London, 1995

Holden, Anthony: *The Oscars – The Secret History of Hollywood's Academy Awards*, Little, Brown, London, 1993

Iaccino, James F: *Jungian Reflections Within the Cinema – A Psychological Analysis of Sci-Fi and Fantasy Archetypes*, Praeger, Westport, Connecticut, 1998

Kim, Erwin: *Franklin J. Schaffner*, Scarecrow Press, Metuchen, New Jersey, 1985
Mitchell, Adrian: *Man Friday*, Futura, London, 1975
Morris, Desmond: *The Naked Ape*, Corgi, London, 1968
Pendreigh, Brian: *On Location – The Film Fan's Guide to Britain and Ireland*, Mainstream, Edinburgh, 1995
Silverman, Stephen M.: *The Fox that Got Away – The Last Days of the Zanuck Dynasty at Twentieth Century-Fox*, Lyle Stuart, Secaucus, New Jersey, 1988
Solomon, Aubrey: *Twentieth Century-Fox – A Corporate and Financial History*, Scarecrow Press, Metuchen, New Jersey, 1988
Swift, Jonathan: *Gulliver's Travels*, Minster Classics, London

**Articles**

Freer, Ian: It Came from the Bargain Basement, *Empire* (sci-fi supplement), London, February 1998
Goodwin, Richard: They Made Monkeys Out of Us, *Hotdog*, London, December 2000
Kael, Pauline: Apes Must Be Remembered, Charlie, *New Yorker*, 17 February 1968
Kennedy, Colin: Instant Cool, *Empire*, London, April 2001
Morgenstern, Joseph: Monkey Lands, *Newsweek*, 26 February, 1968
Mortimer, Penelope: *Planet of the Apes* review, *Observer*, London, 24 March 1968
Murf: *Planet of the Apes* review, *Variety*, 1 February 1968
McCabe, Bob: Planet of the Apes, *Empire* (sci-fi supplement), London, February 1998
Pendreigh, Brian: Lock, Stock and TV channels, *Sunday Times*, London, 19 March 2000
Robinson, David: *Planet of the Apes* review, *Financial Times*, London, 22 March 1968
Russo, Joe, and Landsman, Larry; with Gross, Edward: Planet of the Apes Revisited, *Starlog*, April 1986
Schickel, Richard: Second Thoughts on Ape-Men, *Life*, 10 May 1968
Sidhu, Suni: Helena Bonham Carter, *Total Film*, London, April 2001
Winogura, Dale: Dialogues on Apes, Apes and More Apes, *Cinefantastique*, Elmwood Park, Illinois, Summer 1972

**Internet sites**

Ain't It Cool News: More from Rachel on Tim Burton's Planet of the Apes: aintitcoolnews.com/display.cgi?id=6155

CNN.com: The Web Goes Ape over John Glenn by Neal Weinberg: www.cnn.com/TECH/computing/9812/08/glen-nape.idg/index.html

Apes of the Imagination: A Bibliography, compiled by Marion W. Copeland: www2.h-net.msu.edu/~nilas/bibs/ape.html

Cinescape: Planet of the Apes: www.cinescape.com/links/mvplanetapesreturnnr.html

Coming Attractions: Planet of the Apes: www.corona.bc.ca/films/details/apes.html

The History Place: The Dred Scott Decision: www.historyplace.com/specials/calendar/docs-pix/mar-dred-scott.htm

From Book to Script to Screen: Visualising Planet of the Apes, thesis by John L. Flynn: www.towson.edu/~flynn/apes.html

Internet Movie Database: www.imdb.com

John Glenn/Planet of the Apes Jokes: www.cs.berkeley.edu/~danyelf/Apes/

NASA: Warp drive, when?: www.lerc.nasa.gov/WWW/PAO/warp.htm

Official Linda Harrison Website: www.lindaharrison.com/indexn.html

Official Lou Wagner Website: www.louwagner.com/

Official Natalie Trundy Website: www.natalietrundy.com/

PBS: Scientific American Frontiers: Animal Einsteins: www.pbs.org/saf/transcripts/transcript903.htm

Planet of the Apes: The Forbidden Zone: members.xoom.com/planetofapes/index.html

Planet of the Apes: Rule the Planet (Twentieth Century Fox): www.planetoftheapes.com/pota_site.html

Planet of the Apes International Fan Club: www.dlcwest.com/~comicsape/ape.htm

Rod Serling Memorial Foundation: 30 Years Later – Rod Serling's Planet of the Apes by Gordon C. Webb: www.rodserling.com/POTA.htm (first published in *Creative Screenwriting*, Los Angeles, July–August 1998)

Tim Burton's Planet of the Apes: planetoapes.terrashare.com

Time Machine Collectibles: www.timem.com.

# SELECT BIBLIOGRAPHY

TNMC Movies: Monkey Business: www.tnmc.org/dp/0301011.shtml
Central Washington University: Chimpanzee and Human
  Communication Institute: www.cwu.edu/~cwuchci/quanda/html


## General film reference books

Cook, Samantha (ed.): *International Dictionary of Films and Filmmakers 4 – Writers and Production Artists*, St James Press, Detroit, 1993

Katz, Ephraim: *The Macmillan International Film Encyclopedia*, Macmillan, London, 1998

Law, Jonathan (ed.): *Cassell Companion to Cinema*, Cassell, London, 1997

Lewis, Jon E., and Stempel, Penny: *The Ultimate TV Guide*, Orion, London, 1999

Maltin, Leonard (ed.): *Movie and Video Guide*, Penguin, London, 1999

*The Movie*, Bloomsbury, London, 1984

Pallot, James, and Levich, Jacob: *The Virgin Film Guide*, Virgin, London, 1996

Pym, John (ed.): *Time Out Film Guide*, Penguin, London, 2000

Rees, Dafydd, and Lazell, Barry: *The Illustrated Book of Film Lists*, Virgin, London, 1982

Thomson, David: *A Biographical Dictionary of Film*, André Deutsch, London, 1994

Walker, John (ed.): *Halliwell's Film and Video Guide*, HarperCollins, London, 1999

Walker, John (ed.): *Halliwell's Who's Who in the Movies*, HarperCollins, London, 1999

# INDEX

# INDEX